REAL CHOICE
REAL FREEDOM

In American Education

Kerry L. Morgan

**The Legal and Constitutional Case
For Parental Rights and Against Governmental
Control of American Education**

University Press of America,® Inc.
Lanham • New York • Oxford

Copyright © 1997 by
University Press of America,® Inc.
4720 Boston Way
Lanham, Maryland 20706

12 Hid's Copse Rd.
Cummor Hill, Oxford OX2 9JJ

Library of Congress Cataloging-in-Publication Data

Morgan, Kerry L.
Real choice, real freedom in American education : the legal and
constitutional case for parental rights and against governmental
control of American education / Kerry L. Morgan.
p. cm.
Includes bibliographical references and indexes.
1. Education law and legislation--United States. 2. Parent and child
(Law)--United States. 3. Academic freedom--United States. I.
Title.
KF4119.M67 1997 344.73'07--dc21 97-28253 CIP

ISBN 0-7618-0854-X (cloth: alk. ppr.)
ISBN 0-7618-0855-8 (pbk: alk. ppr.)

♾™ The paper used in this publication meets the minimum
requirements of American National Standard for information
Sciences—Permanence of Paper for Printed Library Materials,
ANSI Z39.48—1984

To Lisa

Acknowledgements

No book can be written except with the patience and assistance of many helpful and dedicated, colleagues, friends and family members. Several people deserve specific acknowledgment for their contribution to this book. I do not mean to suggest that they concur or dissent from its particular themes, but only that they have alerted me to true ideas and for that valuable contribution, I am thankful.

It is fitting, therefore, that professional colleagues such as Gerald R. Thompson, Esq., Herbert W. Titus, Esq., Neil F. Markva, Esq., and Gary T. Amos, Esq., should be mentioned and complimented for their dedication to true legal ideas. With no less fanfare, Dr. Walter W. Davis and Paul S. McConnell, Esq., also deserve special mention for their editorial assistance, encouragement and furnishing of materials and reference books. Many of the ideas pertaining to federal jurisdiction and parental rights were fleshed out during conversations with Richard K. Jefferson, Virginia M. McInerney, Alan P. Reed, Esq., William C. Wood, Jr., Esq., Richard A. Huenefeld, Esq., Scott M. Robe, Esq., and Daniel K. Blackford.

Thanks to Robert K. Skolrood, Esq. who introduced me to the fine world of the Legal Classics Library. Encouragement and assistance were also provided by P. George and Laurie Tryfiates, Robert P. Schuerman, Ellen Smith Rogers, Dr. Daniel Palm, and the late Calvin Bertolette. Eminent appreciation goes to Wanda Tarkenton Remington for her faithful typing and computer work on crucial parts of the manuscript.

Of course, my mother Carroll H. Morgan has always been a superb editor and proved to be a great help in manuscript preparation. My father, William C. Morgan has always supported and encouraged me to charge ahead into new and uncharted territory, doing what is right without regard to the nay-sayers or petty opinions of critics. To my parents, I am immeasurably indebted and grateful.

William Greenman of American *Speedy* Printing Centers, Livonia, Michigan was truly generous in the use of his print shop facilities for production

Acknowledgments

of page proofs. University Press of America was more than patient as the manuscript was revised and improved.

The adage that the "last shall be first" is not without application. I wish to thank my wife, Elizabeth (Lisa) A. Morgan, Ph.D., for her inspiration, encouragement and daily conversation about the ideas and themes in this book. To her this book is dedicated.

Finally, the reader should note that the contents of this book are intended for educational and informational purposes only. They are not to be considered as the rendering of legal advice for specific cases or jurisdictions. Readers are responsible for obtaining such advice from their own legal counsel.

Table of Contents

Part I

1. The Laws Of Nature And Of Nature's God 5

Man, considered as a creature, must necessarily be subject to the laws of his creator, for he is entirely a dependent being.

2. A Declaration to Free Mankind 9

We hold these truths to be self-evident, that all men are created equal, that they are endowed by their Creator with certain unalienable Rights, that among these are Life, Liberty and the pursuit of Happiness. That to secure these rights, Governments are instituted among Men.

Part II
Secondary Principles of Choice and Freedom

12. The Bureau Of Education - 1867 179

Then what is this bureau to do? Simply to collect information: nothing more than that. It will be but an extension of the census of the people . . . . Therefore the [Bureau of education] bill in that regard is not amenable to the objection of centralization: if it were I would not press it.

13. The Department Of Education - 1979 197

[T]he United States will help ensure that education issues receive proper treatment at the Federal level, and will enable the Federal Government to coordinate its education activities more effectively.

14. Standardizing the American Mind 209

[E]very school in America will ensure that all students learn to use their minds well, so they may be prepared for responsible citizenship, further learning, and productive employment in our Nation's modern economy.
The German youth, besides being reared within the family and school, shall be educated physically, intellectually, and morally in the spirit of National Socialism to serve the people and the community, through the Hitler Youth.

Part III
Choosing Freedom in American Education

15. Real Freedom

The duties of parents to their children, as being their natural guardians, consist in maintaining and educating them during the season of infancy and youth, and in making reasonable provision for their future usefulness and happiness in life, by a situation suited to their habits, and a competent provision for the exigencies of that situation.

Introduction

American education suffers from three underlying infirmities. First, American education has rejected the legal principle of parental rights. Second, American education has been dominated by enforcement of state laws that undermine and contravene parental rights. Third, American education has suffered the ravages of an unconstitutional expansion of federal power.

The solution to these disorders is straightforward. First, state governments must recognize that parents have the unalienable right to direct the education and upbringing of their own children. The Declaration of Independence recognizes pre-existing rights of this kind and establishes that civil governments are subsequently created to respect and guarantee them, not regulate or abridge their exercise. Second, state governments must therefore enact laws which are designed to secure the unalienable rights of parents and repeal those laws which regulate, alienate, or deny parental rights. Third, the federal government must disentangle itself from education altogether. The exercise of federal jurisdiction over education is contrary to the Constitution, the opinion of numerous Presidential Administrations and Congresses, and is contrary to the natural and unalienable rights of parents.

✓ Key Idea:

☞ REAL CHOICE AND FREEDOM IN EDUCATION HAVE ONE CENTRAL ELEMENT: BREAKING IT FREE OF CIVIL GOVERNMENT'S POWER.

This book is not primarily about modern notions of educational reform. It is not written to revitalize the failing public school monopoly or to debate whether the American mind is "closed" or in need of "opening." Perhaps the American mind is not even awake. This book is not especially concerned with charter schools, tuition tax credits, or vouchers. It is not focused on curriculums, outcome based education, or whether equalization in financing education is warranted. This book raises more cardinal and rudimentary questions: "How can parents enjoy real legal choice and freedom in education?" "Who has the right to direct a child's mind?" "Can our Republic maintain real freedom when the civil government controls the education of its youngest citizens?"

The astute reader will recognize that we cannot long ignore the rights of parents. We dare not further compromise intellectual freedom. Nor can we enjoy real choice or freedom in the education of our own children, without also recognizing that real choice and freedom are grounded in the disestablishment of civil government's interference, regulation, and control of education.

Disestablishment, however, is not yet the goal of political parties, educational institutions, or civil governments. From the standpoint of money and prestige, those in charge of practically all our academic, professional and religious educational institutions have benefitted from governmental control and/or some degree of governmental subsidy or support for many years. These institutions, therefore, are not going to willingly surrender either their lucre or monopoly. Virtually all of our schools are government schools. It is vain to ask them to stop spending our money or disestablish their monopoly.

If it is not the powerful educational institutions of our day who will lead us from the miry pit of governmental control, who then will? Thinking parents and persons of goodwill, who also vote *for principles*, will change the face of American education. Emancipation of education from the control of local, state and the federal government is the natural task of parents who desire to make real choices about the education of their own children.

This is not just a book about education or parental rights. This is a book about a way of life and a way of governing. It is a book on freeing that which is now controlled--freeing American education from governmental control and pompous academic collusion. This book is about breaking the government educational mold by making real choice and real freedom in education a reality for parents and students alike.

To achieve this goal the book is divided into three parts. Part I concentrates on the foundational legal principles necessary for freedom in American education. It examines these principles and discusses their importance in a local and state setting. Part II adds other principles found in the federal Constitution. It examines these principles and draws conclusions about their meaning in light of federal control of education. Part III considers arguments and objections to these principles and proposes a strategy and approach to state and federal disestablishment of control over American education.

REAL CHOICE
REAL FREEDOM

in American Education

THE LEGAL AND CONSTITUTIONAL CASE
FOR PARENTAL RIGHTS AND AGAINST GOVERNMENTAL
CONTROL OF AMERICAN EDUCATION

Part I

First Principles of Choice and Freedom

Part I

First Principles of Choice and Freedom

To break the educational mold and revive education, we must first break free of the ideas that perpetuate that mold. We must break free of the ideas that we have accepted which undermine real choice and freedom. Part I focuses on four ideas that will break the educational mold by first helping our minds to see and acknowledge that we are not now free in the way we think about reviving American education. The mold-busting ideas are not complex. They may be stated plainly as follows:

1) American law is based on the laws of nature and of nature's God;
2) The principles of the American Declaration of Independence are expressly based on the laws of nature and of nature's God;
3) In principle, the Declaration recognizes that the Creator endows parents with the unalienable right to direct the education and upbringing of their children free from governmental interference, regulation or control;
4) In principle, the Declaration recognizes that the Creator endows every person with the right to intellectual liberty--that is to say, it acknowledges that every person has a right to be free from governmental compulsion or coercion in things that pertain to the mind.

These four ideas reflect principles of both choice and freedom which are exercised within the constraints of law. While other principles or ideas are important, these four are critical to reviving American education. These four principles have the power to free our minds--minds which are now encased in the mold of government approved education.

Part I is written to articulate the key educational ideas found in the laws of nature and of nature's God. It is written in order to explain the impact of those key ideas on education and to educate parents and other persons interested in education, about the historical, legal and Constitutional context of American education. It is written with the recognition that the Constitution's framers knew what they were talking about when they appealed to the laws of nature and of nature's God as the foundation of this country's existence. Part I is not written in order to prove the truth of the laws of nature. It is not written to defend every nuance of that law or present a unified discourse on the differing interpretations about what constitutes the length, depth and breadth of the law.

Those who want to understand the educational ideas found in the laws of nature and of nature's God, and how that law is defined as far as the present context demands, will find this Part helpful. It will refresh those persons who are weary of an endless parade of secular, religious and non-profit solicitations seeking significant financial contributions for insignificant and counterproductive "educational reforms." It is written for the activist who is tired of being deceived by special interest groups who, in polite and private conversation with legislators, barter away choice and freedom so that the special interest can maintain their "political viability" and, of course, raise money. It is especially written for those who can think beyond a piecemeal agenda of political action which simply rearranges the deck chairs on the *Titanic* of public educational reform.

Those seeking to understand the principles of reform and the Declaration's relevance to education, and who want to enjoy freedom--*real* freedom--will want to read this Part carefully. Part I in particular, will equip parents and other persons of good will to understand, articulate and then secure parental rights. They in turn, will be able to free the minds of their children from a system of compulsory exposure to government approved ideas by government certified teachers in government regulated institutions financed by government taxation on private incomes and property.

Chapter 1

The Laws Of Nature And Of Nature's God

Man, considered as a creature, must necessarily be subject to the laws of his creator, for he is entirely a dependent being.[1]

First Things First

Most people think that the first place to begin thinking about education is with *what* should be taught. The issue of what should be taught is certainly important, but it is not the first and foremost consideration. Still others think that the initial focus should be on *who* has the right to teach our children. The list of contenders includes individuals and organizations as diverse as parents, philanthropists, charter schools, corporate America, religious leaders, teachers and their unions, school boards, university administrators and various local, state and federal officials. The question of who has the right to teach, while important, however, is also not the place to begin an examination of American education.

The place to begin thinking about education is to make a decision about the following question: "What law governs America?" This may seem like a peculiar place to start, but it is actually quite logical. The question seems peculiar because our minds deem it peculiar. And our minds deem it so because we have been taught to regard it in no other way. No one has really asked why we think this way. We simply accept it and begin to argue our position of education without ever looking back to the foundations. But an examination of what law governs America will lead to an understanding of the foundations of the law which governs American education. And an understanding of that inquiry will, in turn, lead to recognition of *who* has the right to control American education and eventually, *what* should be taught. To begin thinking about American education any place else is to invite folly and encourages confusion itself to rule the legal temple of the law of education.

The Laws of Our Creator and Our Laws

The basic answer to the question, "What law governs America?" was asked and answered by the framers of the American order. We do not have to reinvent their inquiry. As will be discussed in the next Chapter, the framers characterized this law in the Declaration of Independence as a totality--they called it "the Laws of Nature and of Nature's God." They asserted that this law entitled the colonies to "assume among the Powers of the earth, the separate and equal station" of nationhood. Since the laws of nature directly impacted the creation of America, they must certainly impact the law of American education.

Neither this Chapter, nor those that follow, attempt to defend or justify this law. Such a measure is not necessary. The Declaration asserts this law as true and binding. The People and their various civil governments bound themselves to this law. We need not carry the burden of reproving it all over again. Those who ignore, deny or reject this law, however, bear the burden that every revolutionary must bear--to establish a better foundation for law and then successfully conduct a revolution reestablishing this country on that new legal foundation. In the meantime, America is anchored to the Declaration's reliance on the laws of nature and of nature's God. This law is the legal basis upon which depend all our rights, as well as the purpose and power of any legitimate civil government we have created.

Examination of the impact of the laws of nature and of nature's God on the subject of education and its reform, will follow in due course and Chapters. For now, it is enough that Chapter 1 has offered a key idea:

✓ Key Idea:

☞ AMERICAN LAW IS BASED ON THE LAWS OF NATURE AND OF NATURE'S GOD.

Before we examine the relationship between this law and the *education laws* of the United States, it is important to consider in the next Chapter, the extent to which the laws of nature and of nature's God have been recognized in American legal documents. The assertion that American law is based on the laws of nature and of nature's God is a rather substantial one and well deserves an extensive discussion prior to consideration of its implications for American education.

★ **HYPOTHETICALLY SPEAKING . . . .**

Problem: The people living in the land decided to establish a Nation. They claimed the right to become a nation because of "self-determination." They wrote up a Constitution and began to govern, but they didn't

acknowledge the laws of nature or nature's God. Do the laws of nature still apply to this Nation?

Answer: The laws of nature and of nature's God are not dependent upon recognition of that fact by the people or documents of that Nation. The law is fixed, uniform and universal, binding all nations. Failure of the Nation to acknowledge this law does not diminish the law of nature, it only codifies the fact that the Nation desires to be governed by men alone, and not law. To the degree any Nation ignores this law, it does so to its own national peril. The degree to which any Nation attempts to determine the laws of nature and follow them, then to that degree a nation will be benefitted and prosper.

Notes

1. WILLIAM BLACKSTONE, COMMENTARIES ON THE LAW OF ENGLAND, (Oxford: Clarendon Press, 1765; reprint ed., Birmingham: The Legal Classics Library, 1983) 1:39.

Chapter 2

A Declaration to Free Mankind

We hold these truths to be self-evident, that all men are created equal, that they are endowed by their Creator with certain unalienable Rights, that among these are Life, Liberty and the pursuit of Happiness. That to secure these rights, Governments are instituted among Men.

Self-Evident Truths and The Creation of Civil Government

It would be easier to read (and to write) a book which simply provided a detailed description of what is wrong with American education. That approach, however, is not going to empower parents or help them fight the local school board. It will not help the lawyer trying to write a legally defensible brief in order to keep his client out of jail for violating a state compulsory attendance statute. Such a superficial approach will not help the minister, priest or rabbi trying to form a view of education inspired by Revelation. It will not help the conscientious politician who wants to do what is right and lawful but has to face political repercussions.

By learning something new about America's founding principles, however, the parent, lawyer, religious leader and politician can better engage their entrenched and subsidized opponents. This Book is intended to empower them to carry the debate with solid ideas and principles. Therefore, an examination of the Declaration of Independence with this understanding in mind is the first order of business.

Of course, a treatise on how the principles of the Declaration apply to every possible legal problem is beyond the present undertaking.[1] Such a treatise certainly needs to be written, but the immediate concern (in the next few Chapters) is with the specific inquiry of whether the principles of the Declaration permit American education to be *government-controlled*, or whether those principles define and protect the *right of parents* to direct the education of their own children free from the interference, regulation or control of civil government.

The Laws of Nature and of Nature's God

Chapter 1 asserted that America adopted the laws of nature and nature's God as the basis of its legal system. While various individuals, peoples, and governments have interpreted this law differently at different times,[2] the framers of the American system of government were in one legal accord in "presuppos[ing] the existence of a God, the moral ruler of the universe, and a rule of right and wrong, of just and unjust, binding upon man, preceding all institutions of human society and government."[3] In other words, the framers recognized that God laid down rules or laws which governed the universe and that these laws could be sufficiently understood because they are communicated by a God who wants mankind to know them.[4] They presupposed a God who is not silent.[5] Though the supremacy of the laws of nature and of nature's God was widely recognized from antiquity and prior to the revolution,[6] this view has now fallen into executive and legislative disuse because of the federal judiciary's unprecedented disdain of constitutional recognition of legal principles necessarily grounded in nature or "nature's God".[7]

Respect for both law and precedent, however, requires that the Declaration of Independence be recognized as the law of the land. Many people are familiar with the Declaration's second paragraph and its recognition of equality and unalienable rights, but it is the first paragraph that sets the important legal stage for the indispensable relevance of the laws of our Creator. It declares:

> When in the Course of human events, it becomes necessary for one people to dissolve the political bands which have connected them with another, and to assume among the Powers of the earth, the separate and equal station to which the Laws of Nature and of Nature's God entitle them, a decent respect to the opinions of mankind requires that they should declare the causes which impel them to the separation.

By invoking the "Laws of Nature and of Nature's God," the signers of the Declaration intended to incorporate a legal standard of freedom into the forms of civil government which would follow. The theory of freedom they adopted was simply that the laws of nature and of nature's God were supreme and gave freedom. The phrase "Laws of Nature and of Nature's God" referred to the laws that God, in his capacity as the Creator of the universe and all therein, had established for the governance of mankind, nations and nature.[8] These laws are variously described as the laws of creation, sometimes as natural law, or as the framers elected to refer to them, as the laws of nature and of nature's God. This body of law, whatever its particular designation, can be ascertained by mankind through collective examination of God's creation and revelation, *i.e.*, nature, instinct, reason and the Bible.

The decision to expressly rely upon this law was not a superficial one, but ably debated for many years before and after the Declaration was drafted. Thomas Jefferson, for instance, reflecting on the Declaration of Independence, wrote in 1825 that its essential point was "[n]ot to find out new principles, or new arguments, never before thought of, not merely to say things which had never been said before; but to place before mankind the common sense of the subject, in terms so plain and firm as to command their assent . . . [It was] intended to be an expression of the American mind."[9]

Former President John Quincy Adams, writing in 1839, looked back at the founding period and recognized the meaning of the Declaration's true reliance on the "Laws of Nature and of Nature's God." He observed that the American people's "charter was the Declaration of Independence. Their rights, the natural rights of mankind. Their government, such as should be instituted by themselves, *under the solemn mutual pledges of perpetual union*, founded on the self-evident truths proclaimed in the Declaration."[10] His perspective accurately defines our legal heritage.[11] But can the American mind still grasp this perspective today?

The Declaration of Independence as a Finite Articulation of the Law of Nature and of Nature's God

Whenever *God* or the notion of *His law* is discussed, however, the usual response is to whine that religion is being "forced" upon the public, that religion and politics or church and state do not mix, or that nobody can know the substance of the law of nature and nature's God, so it is a useless legal concept. There is always the rallying cry that such talk violates the Establishment clause of the Constitution's First Amendment. While these views are interesting and predictable, they are essentially irrelevant. They are irrelevant because the substance of the laws of nature and nature's God was not first established by the Declaration only to be subsequently disestablished by the Constitution's First Amendment. Neither is the substance of the laws of nature a function of some religion or rendered useless by a lack of knowledge.

✓ Key Idea:

☞ THE DECLARATION OF INDEPENDENCE IS A FINITE ARTICULATION OF THE LAW OF NATURE AS IT RELATES TO THE RIGHTS OF THE PEOPLE AND THE CREATION AND PURPOSE OF CIVIL GOVERNMENT.

We can know the substance of the laws of nature and of nature's God, as far as it is relevant to the American system of government, by recourse to the Declaration of Independence itself. We may look to other evidence if that is helpful, but we need not consult with mystics or petition the judiciary for a dispensation of knowledge. The evidence is plainly written before us. The substance of the law was written down in the Declaration. It can be read, discussed and applied. The law's basic principles are not left to endless whining, speculation, or demagoguery. An understanding of the specific implications of the laws of nature is basically a function of the Declaration's text, and not of mistaken Constitutional adjudication, religious doctrine, or political wrangling.

So what does the Declaration say about the laws of nature and of nature's God? By its own terms the Declaration of Independence reflects a focused and finite articulation of that law. The Declaration outlines and explains a few of the most important principles that are embodied in the laws of nature and of nature's God: equality, unalienable rights and government by consent.[12]

Dedicating a Government to Secure Unalienable Rights

The framers understood that the principles of the Declaration not only empowered them to define the purpose of civil government, but also to create or establish civil governments. They understood that the civil governments they would establish, had a definite purpose--the equal security of God-given unalienable rights. It seems fairly clear, therefore, that they accepted the idea that God gave rights to human beings and that human beings could know these rights with some degree of sophistication. After all, the framers and founders would have looked particularly irrational had they gone to the trouble of creating a new government dedicated to securing the unalienable rights of the people, if they really believed that it was impossible for the people to know what those rights were or could not understand the origin of those rights. Nor did the framers say that the people needed a court to tell the people what rights they actually possessed.

The framers were practical theoreticians. They did not hide their legal theoretical principles under the carpet of political expediency as is so common today among modern elected officials, judges, and political operatives who would have Americans wrongly believe it is impossible to know that some rights are in fact unalienable or that such rights come from God. The modern legal mind seems to prefer the conceptualization of rights as a function of something other than law.

The framers, however, recognized that legal equality and unalienable rights came from God and they said so with clarity. They proclaimed, "we hold these truths to be self-evident, that all men are created equal . . . ." The idea of legal equality is tied to the creation of man--that men and women are created in God's image, that they are equally human beings before God.[13] The framers also declared that all human beings are "endowed by their creator with certain unalienable Rights, that among these are Life, Liberty and the pursuit of Happiness . . . ." In figuring out how the framers applied this understanding of the purpose of civil government, consider the Declaration's assertion:

We hold these truths to be self-evident, that all men are created equal, that they are endowed by their creator with certain unalienable Rights, that among these are Life, Liberty and the pursuit of Happiness. That to secure these rights, Governments are instituted among Men.

One is immediately struck with the framers' interest in the purpose of civil government. What is it supposed to do? The Declaration says that civil governments are instituted to secure our unalienable God-given rights. So, the Declaration made positive that which was formerly abstract. It made specific and clear that which was general. It sufficiently articulated the basic purpose of civil government under the laws of nature and of nature's God. The Declaration did not establish a theocracy. It did not establish religion. The Declaration established the principles of government under law. The Declaration acknowledged that God was not a subset of or created by law, government or religion, but rather that law, government and religion were all created by the Creator. Consequently, the subsequent Constitutional "no religious establishment" principle is also a subset of the Creator's universe, not His master.

Unalienable Rights From God
The Declaration recognizes that unalienable rights are defined *a priori* by God. In this sense, the law governing the exercise of unalienable rights is from eternity. *Lex est ab æterno.*[14] Neither the Declaration nor the Constitution could enumerate all the rights which were to be protected. They could, however, point to the source of rights--our Creator--for reference by future generations. Each succeeding generation could then look to the Creator and petition the legislature (or proceed with a Constitutional amendment) to codify the particular rights God granted to all human beings which that generation considered were most suitable to assuring its own safety and happiness.

Unfortunately, the present generation looks to courts, not the Creator, for the definition of the particular rights that it considers are most suitable to assuring safety and happiness. While courts have authority to secure legislatively identified rights, courts do not have authority to define, proclaim or codify unalienable rights.[15]

If our minds are to fully capture the idea of unalienable rights, we must first understand the legal definition of "unalienable" and "rights." Consider the word "unalienable." Unalienable means undeniable or inherent. By definition, unalienable means incapable of alienation. In other words an unalienable right cannot be *given* away or *taken* away. Nor can unalienable rights be *balanced* away against some actual or pretended state interest by the courts.[16] The idea that certain rights are unalienable, inalienable, indefeasible, indubitable, inherent or natural, was part and parcel of the framers' worldview and proceeds mathematically from the laws of nature and of nature's God. Though these different words may not have precisely the same meaning, they all carry the same essence--that every human being has certain duties to God which are free from interference by other men.[17]

The idea of unalienability is easier to grasp than the idea of rights. This condition is owing to modern deterioration of the definition of rights through impure construction. Unalienability on the other hand, has just been ignored. To the modern jurist, a right is considered a right simply because it is asserted as a right. Black's Law Dictionary reflects this approach well, declaring that "the primal rights pertaining to men are undoubtedly enjoyed by human beings purely as such, being grounded in personality, and existing antecedently to their recognition by positive law."[18]   The source of rights identified here is the "primal" aspect of man *qua* man.   This approach reflects a humanistic jurisprudence and is an absolute *non sequitur* from the laws of nature.

A humanistic jurisprudence is directly descended from the evolutionary framework of law made popular by individual jurists such as Oliver Wendell Holmes, Jr., and his book *The Common Law*.[19]   This humanistic approach, however, is the antithesis of the Declaration's observation that human beings are "endowed" with unalienable rights by their Creator. There is no middle ground. "Primal" rights cannot be "endowed" and "endowed" rights cannot be grounded in mere "human personality."

✓ Key Idea:

☞   GOD GIVES EVERY HUMAN BEING CERTAIN
       ABSOLUTE RIGHTS AND CIVIL GOVERNMENT
       MUST RESPECT AND PROTECT THOSE PARTICULAR
       RIGHTS ABSOLUTELY.

Compare the humanist definition of rights with Noah Webster's 1828 dictionary definition. Webster did not declare that rights were primal or grounded in personality. He declared that a right is:

> [c]onformity to the will of God, or to his law, the perfect standard of truth
> and justice. In the literal sense, right is a straight line of conduct, and
> wrong a crooked one. Right therefore is rectitude or straightness, and
> perfect rectitude is found only in an infinite Being and his will.

Webster defines a right as conformity to the law of God--to rectitude. Humanistic jurisprudence founded upon evolution, mere positivism or blind faith in judicial utterances, however, discards the need for rectitude. It envisions a system of law and justice animated by a jurisprudence in which rights may be wrongs.[20]   This system, however, is contrary to the rule that *jus ex injuria non oritur*.[21]   Civil governments are bound to respect these rights because they are granted by the Creator, not by the family, church, society or civil government.[22]

Government by Consent

The Declaration goes on to describe a specific unalienable right by announcing that "Governments are instituted among Men, deriving their just powers from the consent of the governed." President George Washington declared: "The basis of our political systems is the right of the people to make and to alter their constitutions of government."[23] He did not say that the basis and security of our system lies in the right of the government to alter our constitutions at will.

The principle that governments are instituted by the consent of the people is not the same as the principle that representatives ought to be elected or chosen by the people. The idea that the people should choose their own representatives is actually the principle of Republican government which has been a continually discussed theme.[24] And while it is an important theme, it is not the central focus of the Declaration's assertion that "Governments are instituted among Men, deriving their just powers from the consent of the governed."

The Declaration focused on the formation and power of the civil government, and not principally who serves in public office, how they got there and how long they ought to stay. The idea of government by consent essentially means that the state and federal forms of civil government, may not be altered by the civil government itself. The courts cannot add to their power, or take power from another branch or take from the people that power which is not given to the courts by a constitution. The same rule applies to the executive and legislative branches as well.[25]

The principle of government by consent is not only concerned with the formation of civil government, but also its dissolution:

> that whenever any Form of Government becomes destructive of these ends, it is the Right of the People to alter or to abolish it, and to institute new Government, laying its foundation on such principles, and organizing its powers in such form, as to them shall seem most likely to effect their Safety and Happiness.

The phrase "destructive of these ends" refers to the unalienable rights which civil government is instituted to preserve. It was the right to alter or abolish the form of government which the people exercised when Independence was declared. The nature of this right presumes that it is not to be exercised lightly.

In his 1644 best seller *Lex, Rex*,[26] Samuel Rutherford wrote that the character of men makes it "natural that they join in a civil society, though the manner of union in a politic body . . . be voluntary."[27] Rutherford asserted that men were at liberty, according to the law of God, to choose and alter the form of their civil government. Rutherford also noted the steps involved in exercising such a right.[28] First, the people are required to petition the government for a redress of their grievances. If this fails to secure their liberty or is a nullity and their petitions are extinguished or exhausted, fleeing to another state or jurisdiction is the next option when the oppression becomes substantial. If tyranny is so widespread that fleeing is not possible or practicable, then resisting the tyranny of unlawful power is appropriate.

The Declaration of Independence reflects this progression quite closely.

> Prudence, indeed, will dictate that Governments long established should not be changed for light and transient causes; and accordingly all experience hath shown, that mankind are more disposed to suffer, while evils are sufferable, than to right themselves by abolishing the forms to which they are accustomed.

The framers recognized that "[s]uch has been the patient sufferance of these Colonies." They noted that in "every stage of these Oppressions we have Petitioned for Redress in the most humble terms." Petitioning, however, was not a sufficient remedy for the people, for "when a long train of abuses and usurpations, pursuing invariably the same Object, evinces a design to reduce them under absolute Despotism, it is their right, it is their duty, to throw off such Government, and to provide new Guards for their future security."[29]

In other words, the people will revise their civil governments themselves, but not for frivolous or short term reasons. Experience has shown that people are more willing to suffer under a mediocre government, than to go to the trouble of altering or abolishing it, as long as they can still be relatively free to live as they want and exercise their rights freely. The time invariably comes, however, when suffering is no longer an option. In such an instance the form of government may be altered or even abolished, and a new form or government instituted in its place by the people (not as individuals or a mob). A new form is necessary since the old form failed to secure rights.

A prudent citizenry prepares for this eventuality and acquires the proper means of self-defense, including weaponry, necessary to make the security of their unalienable rights a reality. When the civil government interferes with the civilian acquisition, possession or otherwise lawful use of hand or shoulder held military firearms, it not only impairs the ability of the People to protect themselves from a tyrannical government, but also preempts the exercise of the unalienable right of the People to alter or abolish their form of government by lawful force of arms if necessary. Such preemption is the ultimate treason.[30]

Organizing a Government to Secure Unalienable Rights

The framers of the Constitution took the foregoing principles--equality, unalienable rights and government by consent--and from them established certain legal rules and standards. These rules related to the relationship between the state governments they proposed to create (or were already created) and the rights they proposed such governments would protect. The principles also dictated the type of national/federal government they would create in the 1770s and then recreate (more perfectly) in the 1780s.

The framers, however, did not quit with just defining a theoretical relationship. They also applied their mind to the practical work of *organizing* a government in a way that would best secure their unalienable rights. They knew the Declaration asserted that the people were responsible for instituting a new government "laying its foundation on such principles, and organizing its powers in such form as to them shall seem most likely to effect their Safety and Happiness."

It is important to review how they figured out what this meant in practice with respect to the formation of a national government. In 1774 the representatives in the First Continental Congress initially organized the powers of a new national government under the Articles of Association. In 1777 this organization took on a different character. John Dickinson, then a delegate from Pennsylvania (who voted against the Declaration of Independence) put forward "the Articles of Confederation and Perpetual Union." The brief history of the national government under these Articles, however, demonstrated that there was "no congeniality of principle between the Declaration of Independence and the Articles of Confederation."[31] The Confederation's powers were organized in such a way as to undermine rather than "to provide new Guards for their future Security," their safety and happiness.

President John Quincy Adams would later observe that the "fabric of the Declaration and that of the Confederation . . . were the productions of different minds and adverse passions."[32] In an effort to revise the Articles of Confederation, a convention was called. Within four months the framers had written a partly national and partly federal Constitution which was more consistent with the principles of the Declaration of Independence. That government was therefore better able than the existing Articles to secure the safety and the unalienable rights of the people.

✓ Key Idea:

☞ THE AMERICAN SYSTEM OF STATE AND FEDERAL GOVERNMENT WAS INSTITUTED AND ORGANIZED IN ORDER TO SECURE GOD-GIVEN RIGHTS.

The Constitution ultimately achieved this compatibility by first altering the form of government from a monarchal to a republican one. James Madison, writing in *Federalist No. 39* stated: "It is evident that no other form would be reconcilable with the genius of the People of America; with the fundamental principles of the Revolution; or with that honorable determination which animates every votary of freedom, to rest all our political experiments on the capacity of mankind for self-government."[33]

Beyond this, the framers set about to organize the national government's power by separating it in two ways. First, they separated the power of the national government into executive, legislative and judicial branches. The framers did this because they believed it would secure their unalienable rights better than their old form of government. Without these divisions, the accumulation of power in a central government or in one man would quickly lead to tyranny. Because the framers knew men to be finite and fallen, a division of powers seemed one reliable way to partially check the tyranny which historically resulted from concentration of power in one man or a group of men.[34]

Noting that "[t]he accumulation of all powers legislative, executive, and judiciary in the same hands . . . may justly be pronounced the very definition of tyranny,"[35] the framers made each branch separate and distinct, with only a few exceptions. For instance, the President's veto power noted in Article I, section 7 extends to the Executive a measure of legislative authority. The Senate, as a check on the other branches, is granted a measure of judicial authority to try impeachments according to Article I, section 3.

Generally, however, the three branches of the national government exercise different types of power as defined for each branch by the written Constitution. As separate branches, they are also independent from each other. This keeps one from asserting power over an unwilling other. Madison said: "If it be a fundamental principle of free Government that the Legislative, Executive & Judiciary powers should be *separately* exercised, it is equally so that they be *independently* exercised."[36] Thus, the framers not only separated power, but they separated different types of power as between the branches of government.[37] If one branch did exercise another's power, it would not be according to the Constitution, but by usurpation.

Second, the framers divided civil power between the states and the national government. This federal structure was also premised on the imperfect or fallen condition of men. According to *Federalist No. 39*, the jurisdiction of the national component of the federal system "extends to certain enumerated objects only, and leaves to the several States a residuary and inviolable sovereignty over all other objects."[38] The states do not exercise national power, and the national government does not exercise state power. Each government exercises only those powers granted in its respective federal or state constitution.

The Tenth Amendment affirms this division of powers between the state and national government by declaring: "[t]he powers not delegated to the United States by the Constitution, nor prohibited by it to the States, are reserved to the States respectively, or to the people."[39] This division of power reflects an underlying commitment to self-government as well as reaffirms that the national government has only a few powers best handled by the people as one nation. The vast bulk of civil power was intended to rest Constitutionally with the people acting through state and local governments according to state constitutions, and in their capacity as individual citizens.[40]

In summary, this Chapter has reviewed the basic elements of the laws of nature as articulated in the Declaration and as conceptually defined and embedded in the constitutions of this country. It has noted that equality, unalienable rights and government by consent lie at the heart of America's laws, legal system and civil governments. The purpose of all our civil governments is to secure unalienable rights to the extent that a particular government, either state or federal, or a particular branch, either legislative, executive or judicial, is so empowered constitutionally. This legal foundation is essential for an understanding of parental rights and intellectual freedom discussed in Chapters to come. It is also critical to the realization that the Declaration's foundations have been assaulted with malice by the civil governments of our land.

Those who would hold to the Declaration, however, have the hope that freedom can be first grounded in law and that educational freedom can then be revived under that law. Those who do not hold to the Declaration, have only the comfort of the hollow political falsehood, that criminal and contemptible usurpation of power will somehow make us more free.[41] Perhaps such persons, particularly in education, who maintain this great faith in government by usurpation, and who continue to believe in unlimited government against all reason and evidence, do so because they, their livelihood and security depend upon it. Servitude, not freedom is their lot.

★ HYPOTHETICALLY SPEAKING . . . .

Problem: **The Nation of Nuvo has undergone many changes in technology and information systems since the Nation was instituted about 200 years ago. Nation Nuvo has hired many lawyers in its Department of Just-Us who argue that these tremendous changes mean that God no longer gives the citizens of the nation any specific rights which the government must respect. They argue that Nation Nuvo doesn't need to protect those rights because the idea of God-given rights is too old, not scientific, not cost-effective and interferes with all known partisan political objectives. Do advances in technology and information systems nullify or diminish the God-given rights of human beings or the obligations of Nation Nuvo to protect those rights?**

Answer: **No. God-given rights do not change over time. If the Nation of Nuvo fails to protect the God-given rights of its citizens, then the leaders of the Nation have forfeited their right to govern. Nation Nuvo is bound to conform its law to secure unalienable rights as best as it can collectively or legislatively discern them. If the leaders of Nation Nuvo desire to continue to govern, they must at least determine what rights God has given to the people and then establish a system of justice to secure them. Otherwise the People of Nuvo have the right to alter or abolish their government and institute a new one that will secure their rights.**

Notes

1. *See John Quincy Adams, The Jubilee of the Constitution, a Discourse delivered at the request of the New York Historical Society, on Tuesday, the 30th of April, 1839,* in J. OF CHRISTIAN JURIS. 1 (1986). In his speech, Adams charts the relationship between the laws of nature and of nature's God, the Declaration and the Constitution.

2. For a discussion of Virginia's early adaptation of the laws of nature and nature's God, *see For the Colony in Virginea-Britannia: Lawes Divine, Morall and Martiall, &c.* (1612) reprinted in TRACTS AND OTHER PAPERS RELATING PRINCIPALLY TO THE ORIGIN, SETTLEMENT, AND PROGRESS OF THE COLONIES IN NORTH AMERICA, 4 vols. (Compiled by Peter Force, Washington, D.C., 1844; reprint ed., Gloucester, MA: Peter Smith, 1963) 3:9-19. For a discussion of the later Puritan adaptation of same, *see generally* COTTON MATHER, MAGNALIA CHRISTI AMERICANA [THE GREAT WORKS OF CHRIST IN AMERICA] (Carlisle, PA: Banner of Truth Trust, 1979). One of their first codified statute books, entitled "The Laws and Liberties of Massachusetts of 1648," cited capital offenses next to their corresponding Biblical chapter and verse. THE LAWS AND LIBERTIES OF MASSACHUSETTS OF 1648 (Reprint ed., Birmingham, AL: The Legal Classics Library, 1982) 5-6.

3. ADAMS, DISCOURSE *supra* note 1 at 6.

4. Not every law of God, however, has been made known to man or is knowable by man. This condition is inherent in the fact that God is infinite and mankind, his creation, is finite.

5. The full title of the Declaration is "The Unanimous Declaration of the thirteen united States of America." For an in-depth historical analysis of the Declaration that discusses these affirmations, *see* GARY T. AMOS, DEFENDING THE DECLARATION (Brentwood, Tennessee: Wolgemuth & Hyatt, Publishers Inc., 1989). The Supreme Court has also acknowledged that "the Declaration of Independence recognizes the presence of the Divine in human affairs." Church of the Holy Trinity v. United States, 143 U.S. 457, 467, (1892).

6. *See generally,* ST. THOMAS AQUINAS, SUMMA THEOLOGICA 5 vols. (circa 1254-71, reprint ed., Westminster, Maryland: Christian Classics, 1981) 2:1008-13 [Question 94: Of the Natural Law]; J.T. MCNEILL, ED., JOHN CALVIN, INSTITUTES OF THE CHRISTIAN RELIGION 2 vols. (1536; reprint ed. Philadelphia: Westminster Press, 1977) 2:367-79, [Chapter VIII, Explanation of the Moral Law] 2:1504-05 [Chapter 20, pt. 15, Moral, ceremonial, and judicial law distinguished, et seq.]; STEPHEN JUNIUS BRUTUS [PHILIPPE DU PLESSIS-MORNAY], VINDICIAE CONTRA TYRANNOS [A DEFENSE OF LIBERTY AGAINST TYRANTS] (1579) in W. EBENSTEIN, ED., GREAT POLITICAL THINKERS, (Hinsdale, Illinois: Dryden Press, 4th ed., 1969) 331-48; HUGO GROTIUS, DE JURE BELLI AC PACIS LIBRI TRES, [THE LAW OF WAR AND PEACE] (Amsterdam, John Blaeu, 1646; reprint ed., Oxford: Clarendon Press, 1925) 9-30 [Prolegomena]; BARON DE MONTESQUIEU, THE SPIRIT OF LAWS (Dublin, 1751; reprint ed., Birmingham, AL: Legal Classics Library, 1984) 1-7, 165-67 [Bk. I, Chaps. I & II; Bk. XXVI, Chaps. I & II); JEAN JACQUES BURLAMAQUI, THE PRINCIPLES OF NATURAL AND POLITIC LAW (1748; reprint ed., New York: Legal Classics Library, 1995) 1-5; EMERICH DE VATTEL, THE LAW OF NATIONS OR THE PRINCIPLES OF NATURAL LAW (1758; reprint ed., New York: The Legal Classics Library, 1993) 3-9; REV. SAMUEL RUTHERFORD, LEX, REX (London: John Field, 1644; reprint ed., Harrisonburg, Virginia: Sprinkle Publications 1980) 1-2 [Question 2, Whether or Not Government be Warranted by the Law of Nature]; W. VON LEYDEN, ED., JOHN LOCKE, ESSAYS ON THE LAW OF NATURE (1676; reprint ed., Oxford: Clarendon Press,

1965) 185-89; H. DE. BRACTON, A TREATISE ON THE LAWS AND CUSTOMS OF ENGLAND 2 vols. (reprint ed., Cambridge, MA: Belknap Press, 1968) 2:22-28, 33, 110, 302-06; SIR WILLIAM BLACKSTONE, COMMENTARIES ON THE LAWS OF ENGLAND 4 vols. (Oxford: Clarendon Press, 1765; reprint ed., Birmingham, AL: The Legal Classics Library, 1983) 1:38-43; *Roger Williams, The Bloudy Tenet, Of Persecution, for the Cause of Conscience* (1644), in M. JENSEN, ED., ENGLISH HISTORICAL DOCUMENTS, AMERICAN COLONIAL DOCUMENTS TO 1776 (New York: Oxford University Press, 1969) 172-77; JOHN WINTHROP, THE HISTORY OF NEW ENGLAND FROM 1630 TO 1649 2 vols. (Boston: Little Brown and Company, 1853) 2:279-82; *Jonathan Mayhew, Concerning Unlimited Submission and Non-Resistance to the Higher Powers* (1750), in B. BAILYN, ED., PAMPHLETS OF THE AMERICAN REVOLUTION 1750-1776 (Cambridge, MA: The Belknap Press, 1965) 203-47; *Samuel Adams, The Rights of the Colonists* (1772), in MORTIMER J. ADLER. ED., THE ANNALS OF AMERICA. 18 vols. (Chicago: Encyclopedia Britannica, 1968) 2:217-20; JOHN ADAMS, NOVANGLUS AND MASSACHUSETTENSIS (New York: Russell and Russell, 1968); CHARLES S. HYNEMAN & DONALD S. LUTZ, AMERICAN POLITICAL WRITING DURING THE FOUNDING ERA, 1760-1805 (Indianapolis: Liberty Press, 1983) 1:163-64; JOHN WINGATE THORNTON, THE PULPIT AND THE AMERICAN REVOLUTION (Boston: Gould & Lincoln, 1860; reprint ed., New York: Da Capo Press, 1970); and ELLIS SANDOZ, POLITICAL SERMONS OF THE AMERICAN FOUNDING ERA, 1730-1805 (Indianapolis: Liberty Press, 1991).

For discussion of the educational views of the founding fathers *see* JAMES J. WALSH, EDUCATION OF THE FOUNDING FATHERS OF THE REPUBLIC: SCHOLASTICISM IN THE COLONIAL COLLEGES (New York: Fordham University Press, 1935); LORRAINE S. PANGLE AND THOMAS L. PANGLE, THE LEARNING OF LIBERTY: THE EDUCATIONAL IDEAS OF THE AMERICAN FOUNDERS (University of Kansas Press, 1993); and John C. Eastman, *On the Perpetuation of Our Institutions: Thoughts on Public Education at the American Founding,* (Ph.D. diss., The Claremont Graduate School, 1993).

7.   Contrary to contemporary perception, nothing in our form of government or the text of the Constitution indicates that it is either necessary or practical to conduct the affairs of civil government on a legal basis devoid of recognition of the law of God. Moreover, the assumption that God is irrelevant to the institution and operation of civil government was expressly rejected by the signers of the Declaration and is at odds with the meaning and terms of the Constitution.   While the religion clauses of the Constitution's First Amendment expressly limit the exercise of Congressional power, they do not limit the recognition, implementation or administration of principles that gave rise to the formation of state governments, the creation of a national government, or the ultimate legal rules which bind every civilized society.   For discussion on the religion clauses *see generally*, CHARLES F. JAMES, DOCUMENTARY HISTORY OF THE STRUGGLE FOR RELIGIOUS LIBERTY IN VIRGINIA (Lynchburg: J. P. Bell Co., 1900; reprint ed., New York: Da Capo Press, 1971) and ISAAC A. CORNELISON, THE RELATION OF RELIGION TO CIVIL GOVERNMENT IN THE UNITED STATES OF AMERICA (New York: G. P. Putnam's Sons, 1895; reprint ed., New York: Da Capo Press, 1970).

8.   The term "Creator" appears in the second paragraph of the Declaration. The terms "Supreme Judge" and "Divine Providence" which appear in the last paragraph, refer to God in the first paragraph, *i.e.*, the "Laws of Nature and of Nature's God."   *See* AMOS, *supra* note 5 at 40-41 and 50-59.

9.   THOMAS JEFFERSON, THOMAS JEFFERSON, WRITINGS (New York: The Library of America, 1984) 1501.   A letter to Henry Lee dated May 8, 1825.

10. ADAMS, DISCOURSE *supra* note 1 at 4 (emphasis in original).

11. This heritage is not a peculiarly American concept by any means. In 1751 the French Baron de Montesquieu, whose legal treatise *The Spirit of Laws* was known to the framers and founders, also acknowledged that God was the lawgiver and Creator of the universe. "God is related to the universe as creator and preserver; the laws by which he has created all things, are those by which he preserves them." BARON DE MONTESQUIEU, THE SPIRIT OF LAWS (Dublin: G. & A. Ewing, 1751; reprint ed., Birmingham: The Legal Classics Library, 1984) 2.

12. These principles were subsequently incorporated into the federal and many state constitutions. The framers of the federal Constitution, however, deliberately left to the states the business of fleshing out additional particulars of the law of nature and of nature's God in their respective state constitutions. (*See* Chapter 3 for a discussion of the applicability of the Declaration in a state context.) It is disquieting that this obligation of state officials and citizens has remained largely unrecognized and unfulfilled. This crisis is owing in no insignificant measure to the decline of serious reflection about the origins and nature of law among lawyers and the clergy, as well as federal usurpation of state legislative power.

13. Genesis 1:26-27 indicates that "God created man in his own image, in the image of God He created him; male and female He created them." Thomas Jefferson realized the political and legal implications of this condition in terms of equality (though he attributed its recognition to advances in science) when he declared in the context of slavery that "the mass of mankind has not been born with saddles on their backs, nor a favored few booted and spurred, ready to ride them . . . ." THOMAS JEFFERSON, THOMAS JEFFERSON'S WRITINGS (New York: The Library of America, 1984) 1517. A letter to Roger C. Weightman dated June 24, 1826. Abraham Lincoln was more cognizant of the Creator than Jefferson when, commenting on the Declaration's equality principle, he remarked that it reflected a "lofty, and wise, and nobel understanding of the justice of the Creator to His creatures." PAUL M. ANGLE, ED., CREATED EQUAL? THE COMPLETE LINCOLN-DOUGLAS DEBATES OF 1858 (Chicago: The University of Chicago Press, 1958) 100.

14. Law is from everlasting.

15. Federal courts in particular have not been given any general jurisdiction to construe the "Laws of Nature and of Nature's God." Federal courts only enjoy jurisdiction to construe those unalienable rights that are constitutionally enumerated and are properly before the court in an Article III case or controversy, or come within the court's jurisdiction as a result of being enumerated in a treaty. Federal courts do not have jurisdiction to, *sua sponte*, discover and declare any other rights that are derived from the "Laws of Nature and of Nature's God." That power is rather, reserved to the state legislature or the people under the Ninth and Tenth Amendments. It is the legislatures or the people *qua* citizens which are empowered to further discover and declare their many God-given inalienable rights. *See generally* ROBERT H. BORK, THE TEMPTING OF AMERICA: THE POLITICAL SEDUCTION OF THE LAW (New York: The Free Press) 1990.

This view was articulated with clarity in the context of a federal court presuming to void state laws it considered contrary to natural justice. In the case of Loan Association v. Topeka, 87 U.S. (20 Wall.) 655 (1874), dissenting Justice Nathan Clifford properly observed that:

> where the Constitution of the State contains no prohibition upon the subject, express or implied, neither the State nor Federal courts can declare a statute of the State void as unwise, unjust, or inexpedient, nor for any other cause, unless it be repugnant to the Federal Constitution. Except where the Constitution has imposed

limits upon the legislative power the rule of law appears to be that the power of legislation must be considered as practically absolute, whether the law operates according to natural justice or not in any particular case, for the reason that courts are not the guardians of the rights of the people of the State, save where those rights are secured by some constitutional provision which comes within judicial cognizance.

Id. at 668. Several commentators understand that the people retain rights not enumerated in the Constitution's Bill of Rights, but many are uncertain about turning to the laws of nature and of nature's God in order to determine the definitive substance of those rights. Consequently, their conception of unalienable rights is limited to the historical record alone. *See generally,* Berger, *The Ninth Amendment,* 66 CORNELL L. REV. 1 (1981); Caplan, *The History and Meaning of The Ninth Amendment,* 69 VA. L. REV. 223 (1983) and R. BARNETT, ED., THE RIGHTS RETAINED BY THE PEOPLE (George Mason University Press, 1989). *See also* Note, *On Reading and Using the Tenth Amendment,* 93 YALE L. J. 723 (1984). *But see,* Scott Lumsden, *The Ninth Amendment in Light of The Declaration of Independence,* (Masters Thesis, Regent University, 1990).

16. Noah Webster's 1828 Dictionary defines unalienable as that which "cannot be legally or justly alienated or transferred to another." The concept of unalienability (assuming due process), however, does not preclude civil government from alienating human life in punishment for murder, from alienating a man's liberty through imprisonment upon conviction of crimes, or alienating a man's property through levy and execution for payment of legal judgments. The concept of unalienable rights does preclude civil government from balancing rights against governmental interests, whether such interests are compelling, rational or otherwise.

17. Virginia's 1776 Constitution declared that "all men are by nature equally free and independent, and have certain inherent rights . . . ." RICHARD L. PERRY, ED., SOURCES OF OUR LIBERTIES (Chicago: American Bar Foundation, 1978), 311. Pennsylvania's 1776 Constitution stated that "all men are born equally free and independent, and have certain natural, inherent and inalienable rights . . . ." *Id.* at 329.

18. Henry Campbell Black, BLACK'S LAW DICTIONARY: DEFINITIONS OF THE TERMS AND PHRASES OF AMERICAN AND ENGLISH JURISPRUDENCE, ANCIENT AND MODERN. Rev. 4th. ed. (St. Paul, MN: West Publishing Co., 1968) 1486.

19. OLIVER W. HOLMES, JR., THE COMMON LAW & OTHER WRITINGS (Boston: Little, Brown, and Company, 1881; reprint ed., Birmingham, AL: The Legal Classics Library, 1982).

20. The right of "privacy," for instance, has been stretched beyond its valid fourth amendment meaning to permit abortion, an act which was regarded at the common law as subject to criminal sanction. The right of "privacy" is invoked to excuse common law crimes such as adultery, fornication, and prostitution. Conduct such as sodomy and bestiality, which are crimes "against nature," have also been advocated as rights. The underlying legal paradigm which drives these legal aberrations is the idea that mutual consent supersedes the rule of law or that law is noncompulsory and may be nullified by mutual consent. At common law, anytime mutual consent was present in opposition to the law, the result was not an abrogation of the law, but rather a charge of "conspiracy to commit," as well as a charge on the underlying offense.

21. A right does (or can) not rise out of a wrong.

22. The United States Constitution does not expressly refer to "unalienable rights" because the Constitution was not primarily designed to enumerate rights. Its principal purpose was to create a national government, granting it only limited and enumerated power. An examination of the powers granted to Congress by the Constitution, chiefly

found in Article I, section 8, reveals that the framers respected the unalienable rights of the people. The powers they granted to Congress in this section are consistent with and not antagonistic to their unalienable rights.

Men such as George Mason, however, argued extensively for a Bill of Rights to explicitly prohibit the national government from interfering with the unalienable rights held by each person. Several of these rights are now expressly contained in the Bill of Rights. Some of these enumerated rights are unalienable, while others are merely civil, or alienable. For those rights not listed, the Ninth Amendment makes clear that "[t]he enumeration in the Constitution of certain rights shall not be construed to deny or disparage others retained by the people."

As to unalienable rights, all civil governments must refrain from interference with their exercise. As to other rights acknowledged in the Constitution or reserved by the Ninth Amendment which are not God-given, civil government may regulate according to the Constitutional consent of the people. For a discussion on the unalienable right of property, *see* Richard A. Huenefeld, *The Challenge to Secure Unalienable Property Rights in the United States*, (Masters Thesis, Regent University, 1989).

23. JAMES D. RICHARDSON, ED., COMPILATION OF THE MESSAGES AND PAPERS OF THE PRESIDENTS, 1789-1897 (Washington, D.C.: Government Printing Office, 1896) 1:217. Farewell Address of George Washington, September 17, 1796.

24. For example, John Winthrop stated in 1645:
> The great questions that have troubled the country are about the authority of the magistrates and the liberty of the people. It is yourselves who have called us to this office, and being called by you, we have our authority from God, in way of an ordinance, such as hath the image of God eminently stamped upon it, the contempt and violation whereof hath been vindicated with examples of divine vengeance. I entreat you to consider that when you choose magistrates you take them from among yourselves, men subject to like passions as you are. Therefore when you see infirmities in us, you should reflect upon your own, and that would make you bear the more with us, and not be severe censures of the failings of your magistrates, when you have continual experience of the like infirmities in yourself and others.

JOHN WINTHROP, THE HISTORY OF NEW ENGLAND FROM 1630-1649, 2 vols. (Boston: Little Brown, 1853) 2:280.

25. In societies governed by written constitutions, the principle of government by consent requires that civil government exercise only those powers which are granted according to the terms of the constitution. If a power is not granted, the civil government does not posses it. Hence, if the People request or demand that their representatives or civil government act beyond the scope of their written Constitutional power, but the People themselves have not properly extended that power to their government, or the People demand that their civil government act contrary to the laws of nature, then the representative has a duty to refuse. For in either case the People act as a mob outside of the law and not as citizens.

Thus, if the People desire the federal government to engage in an activity or pass legislation which would require the exercise of a power not Constitutionally enumerated or extended to the Congress, then the People need to proceed through the proper channels and extend that power to the federal government through an amendment to the Constitution. This process will ensure that there is no mistake as to the nature, extent and type of power given, the proper scope, limits and conditions of its exercise, and the branch and level of government to which it has been entrusted. It will also prevent the federal government from self-expansion of its own powers--which is by definition, tyranny.

President James Monroe affirmed the principle of government by consent when he acknowledged that "it comports with the nature and origin of our institutions, and will contribute much to preserve them, to apply to our constituents for an explicit grant of power. We may confidently rely that if it appears to their satisfaction that the power is necessary, it will always be granted." RICHARDSON, PRESIDENTS, *supra* note 23 at 2:18, First Annual Message of James Monroe, December 2, 1817.

26. SAMUEL RUTHERFORD, LEX, REX (London: John Field, 1644; reprint ed. Harrisonburg: Sprinkle Publications, 1980).

27. *Id.* at 2.

28. *Id.* at 152-66.

29. John Winthrop observed a similar concept to "suffering while evils are sufferable" in 1645 when he discussed the distinction between a public official's poor skill and ill will. He declared:

> We account him a good servant, who breaks not his covenant. The covenant between you [the people] and us [your public servants] is the oath you have taken of us, which is to this purpose, that we shall govern you and judge your causes by the rules of God's laws and our own, according to our best skill. When you agree with a workman to build you a ship or house, etc., he undertakes as well for his skill as for his faithfulness, for it is his profession, and you pay him for both. But when you call one to be a magistrate, he doth not profess nor undertake to have sufficient skill for that office, nor can you furnish him with gifts, etc., therefore you must run the hazard of his skill and ability. But if he fails in his faithfulness, which by his oath he is bound unto, that he must answer for. If it fall out that the case be clear to common apprehension and the rule clear also, if he transgress here, the error is not in the skill, but in the evil of the will: it must be required of him. But if the case be doubtful, or the rule doubtful, to men of such understanding and parts as your magistrates are, if your magistrates should err here, yourselves must bear it.

WINTHROP *supra* note 24 at 2:280.

30. Sir William Shakespeare put it directly in *Henry V*, when he wrote of the rule of law for the lawless, whether prince or subject:

> Wherein you would have sold your king to slaughter,
> His princes and his peers to servitude,
> His subjects to oppression and contempt,
> And his whole kingdom into desolation.
> Touching our person we seek no revenge,
> But we our kingdom's safety must so tender,
> Whose ruin you have sought, that to her laws
> We do deliver you.

HENRY V, PART 2, SCENE 2, LINES 170-177.

Under the laws of nature and the Constitution, it is no part of the civil government's power to disarm individuals seeking the lawful defense of themselves, their family or their community. Civil government may not substitute its judgment for that of the people as to the means necessary to exercise their unalienable rights. The Second Amendment of the United States Constitution was designed to prevent the federal government from disarming the people or substituting in the place of the individual, its own official view of weaponry suitable for defense. The amendment was adopted to give effect to the unalienable right of individual self-defense *and* the right of the community to resist civil tyranny through the militia.

The militia function provides an additional safeguard that recognizes the right of protecting one's local community from foreign and domestic tyranny. Even though the Constitution provides for a limited shared jurisdiction between the states and Congress with respect to the militia function, and Congress has the power to provide for organizing, *arming* and disciplining the militia, neither a state or Congress has power to *dis*arm the people or the militia.

The federal ban on civilian purchase and possession of machine guns made after 1986 and the September 1994 Congressional ban on "semi-automatic assault weapons" and over ten round magazines, are beyond the power of Congress under Article I, section 8, contrary to the security of unalienable rights, violate the second amendment and are precluded by implication under Article I, section 8 as constituting an unlawful means of *dis*arming the people. These types of interference are not only unconstitutional, but they strike at the heart of the unalienable right of the community to alter or abolish its civil government according to the steps prescribed in the Declaration (as a community, and never as individuals or a mob).

Those who contemplate such steps, however, would be well advised to first recall the distinction noted by John Winthrop, between holding a public official accountable for poor skill in governing which the people must bear, and holding him accountable for ill will which he alone must bear. But where the ill will of public officials becomes institutionalized and produces a long train of abuses and usurpations, invariably tending toward alienation of the people's unalienable rights, then holding this or that public official accountable to his oath is not the sole remedy; it is proper to also alter, and then if requisite, to abolish that form of government which has codified such deprivations. But if the People have no concept of unalienable rights, talk of revolution is lawless blind anarchy. See WINTHROP *supra* notes 24 and 29 at 2:280.

31. ADAMS, DISCOURSE *supra* note 1 at 7.

32. ADAMS, DISCOURSE *supra* note 1 at 7-8. The United States Army Center of Military History has noted that "Congress tried to establish a basic governmental framework with the Articles of Confederation, ratified by the states in 1781. But the central government remained little more than a loose wartime alliance of independent states, and Congress, under the Articles experienced serious difficulty in restoring a war-torn economy, regulating foreign trade, and protecting and developing the frontier . . . ." *The Annapolis Convention, The U.S. Army Bicentennial Series*, 1986.

33. THE FEDERALIST NO. 39 (J. Madison).

34. *Id.*

35. THE FEDERALIST NO. 47 (J. Madison).

36. *See* JAMES MADISON, NOTES OF DEBATES IN THE FEDERAL CONVENTION OF 1787 (Athens: Ohio University Press, 1966) 326 (emphasis in original).

37. Alexander Hamilton noted these differences in *Federalist No. 78* when he wrote:
The executive not only dispenses the honors, but holds the sword of the community. The legislature not only commands the purse, but prescribes the rules by which the duties and rights of every citizen are to be regulated. The Judiciary, on the contrary, has no influence over either the sword or the purse, no direction either of the strength or of the wealth of the society, and can take no active resolution whatever. It may truly be said to have neither FORCE nor WILL, but merely judgment; and must ultimately depend upon the aid of the executive arm even for the efficacy of its judgments.
THE FEDERALIST NO. 78 (A. Hamilton).

38. THE FEDERALIST NO. 39 (J. Madison).

39. U.S. CONST. amend. X.

40. The President, for instance, may not exercise the power of the state governor, nor exercise legislative or judicial power. The national judiciary may not exercise either state judicial power or national legislative power. The national Congress may not exercise state legislative power or national executive power. The doctrine also presupposes that each branch of government confine its actions to those powers the people previously delegated in writing--through their constitutions.

41. RICHARDSON, PRESIDENTS *supra* note 23 at 2:311, First Annual Message of John Quincy Adams, December 6, 1825.

Chapter 3

A Declaration to Rule the Rulers

If the declaration of independence is not obligatory, our intire political fabrick has lost its magna charta, and is without any solid foundation. But if it is the basis of our form of government, it is the true expositor of the principles and terms we have adopted.[1]

Introduction

Chapter 1 introduced the term "laws of nature and of nature's God." Chapter 2 explored the principles of that body of law in greater detail. Those Chapters established that civil governments are created and organized for at least one central purpose: to defend and secure the unalienable rights of the people. The obvious questions which follow are "Who has unalienable rights with respect to education?" and "Do our civil governments, especially our various state governments, actually defend unalienable rights with respect to the education of children?" Chapter 3 and those that follow, logically address these questions.

But first one more part of the legal foundation needs examination. It must be determined whether or not our various civil governments (local, state and federal) are *legally* bound by the Declaration's principles. Most of those who pay any serious attention to the Declaration only regard its principles as historical and thus not obligatory as a matter of law. Chapter 3 will address this issue first. If the Declaration's principles are not legally binding, then civil governments are not obliged to respect or defend unalienable rights. But if the Declaration's principles form the legal foundation of our various levels of government, then it is the true legal foundation upon which the reform of education must rest. So this is an important issue.

We are examining this issue in order to determine if the civil government, including local and state school boards, are in fact legally restrained from trampling upon unalienable rights. Such restraint is obviously mandatory as a matter of law if unalienable rights are stated or enumerated in state constitutional or statutory provisions.[2] But what about states that have not expressly codified the principles of the Declaration in their laws? Are they under a legal obligation to do so?

Once the nature of the Declaration is explored, then the question of who is actually endowed with an unalienable right that relates to education, will be discussed. Everybody is claiming some kind of right to teach children, but who actually has an unalienable right to do so? Without the Declaration's principles, civil government has no standard to say with certainty which rights it will defend and which it will abridge. Chapter 4 will tackle this political and legal leviathan as well as consider whether or not the various civil governments in America defend such unalienable rights. Chapters 5 and 6 will then examine the favorite arguments used by civil governments to abridge a parent's unalienable rights.

Principles that Bind the Federal Government

What therefore, is the legal effect of the Declaration's legal principles on the government of the United States? Consider first, the force and effect of the Declaration's adoption and approval. After the Declaration was adopted, it defined the non-negotiable principles essential to the lawful formation *and conduct* of any subsequent state or federal government.[3] Americans relied upon the Declaration's adoption to legitimate, in the eyes of the community of nations, their revolution against Great Britain.[4]

✓ Key Idea:

    ☞   THE U.S. CONSTITUTION REFLECTS AND ESTABLISHES THE PRINCIPLES ARTICULATED IN THE DECLARATION OF INDEPENDENCE.

The Declaration announced to the world that the colonists were "one people."[5] This collective legal entity so created was referred to as the "united States" of America.[6] In law, the "united States" was created by the Declaration of Independence in 1776. The "united states" existed before the current Constitution was ever written. We must understand that the Preamble of the 1787 Constitution simply reaffirmed what the Declaration had already made clear. The Preamble affirmed that Americans were the "people of the United States" and went on to add that the people were forming "a more perfect union"--a union more perfect than that created by the Articles of Confederation and Perpetual Union in 1777.[7]

Far from demonstrating that the Declaration's principles were superseded by adoption of the Constitution, internal evidence from the Constitution itself shows that the Constitution relies upon and puts into effect the principles of the

Declaration. The Constitution's provisions establishing qualifications for federal office are examples. For instance, Article I, section 2, stipulates that representatives must have been "seven years a citizen of the United States" prior to holding federal office. It would not have been possible for the first House of Representatives to convene in 1789 if the Constitution were construed so that persons born in the United States became citizens only after the Constitution was ratified. The Constitution relied upon the Declaration to establish when American citizenship was inaugurated.[8]

This same proposition holds true for Senators. Article I, section 3 establishes the qualification of "nine years a citizen of the United States." This means that any person serving in the senate in 1789 must have been a United States citizen by at least 1780.

Likewise, Article II, section 1 of the Constitution places a similar requirement upon the office of President but with an added twist. To be eligible for the office of President a person must have been "a natural born citizen, or a citizen of the United States, at the time of the adoption of this Constitution." The requirement of "a natural born citizen" indicates that United States citizenship existed before the Constitution. Moreover, the person must also be "fourteen years a resident within the United States" meaning that an association of "United States" *i.e.,* states united together with no form of central government, existed around 1775.[9]

Article VII of the Constitution also reaffirms the Constitution's reliance upon the Declaration, particularly the principle of government by consent. That Article recognizes that the unanimous consent of those in the Constitutional convention was recorded in the year of "the independence of the United States of America the twelfth." This recognition reaffirms that the "United States" as a legal entity, began no later than 1776, and that the Constitution and the Declaration are legally inseparable.[10]

New States Governed by Legal Principles

The Declaration's principles not only bind the United States, but the same pattern holds true for the various states as well, whether the original thirteen states or states admitted into the Union thereafter. One precedent for this pattern is evidenced by Congressional adoption of the Northwest Ordinance.[11] After the Continental Congress came into possession of the land situated north and west of the Ohio river, the Congress eventually passed an ordinance relating to that land. Adopted on May 20, 1785 and again on July 13, 1787, Congress sought to induce sale, settlement and government of the territory of the United States northwest of the Ohio river. This ordinance also contained an internal compact or agreement in which Congress promised not to keep the land for the United States itself, but instead promised to form states out of the territory and admit them into the union on equal footing with the original states.

Congress had already promised as early as 1780 that states formed within that territory would be distinct republican States, and admitted members of the federal Union, having the same rights of sovereignty, freedom and independence as the other States. The compact contained in the Northwest Ordinance proceeded to crystallize this promise into an enforceable agreement between all of the states, future states and the United States government.[12] Specifically, the Articles of Compact in the Northwest Ordinance declared that all such states "shall be republican, and in conformity to the principles contained in these articles," and shall stand on "equal footing" with the original states.[13] As a matter of fact, subsequent Congressional statutes for admitting Louisiana, Mississippi, Alabama, and Tennessee into the Union refer to the Articles of the Northwest Ordinance as authoritative even though those states are clearly *south* of the Ohio river. In fact, all admission statutes passed by Congress contain the words "equal footing" or, to identical effect "same footing," with the "original States."

So what is the point that all states have equal footing with the original states? By affirming "equal footing" with the original states in the Articles of Compact and in subsequent state admission statutes, Congress intended to bind new states to the legal principles adopted by the original states--namely, the principles of the Declaration of Independence.[14] Congress made this mandate abundantly clear when it expressly provided that the respective state constitutions of various newly admitted states shall be both republican in form and "not repugnant to the principles of the Declaration of Independence."[15] Because every state is admitted "on equal footing with the original States,"[16] they are each admitted equally in all respects whatsoever.[17]

✓ Key Idea:

☞   NO STATE GOVERNMENT MAY ACT CONTRARY TO THE PRINCIPLES OF THE DECLARATION OF INDEPENDENCE.

Consequently, the legal principles of the Declaration of Independence are not merely nice ideas, or simply ideas that have interesting historical or moral dimensions. *The controlling rule of law is that a state government may not act in any way that is repugnant to the principles of the Declaration of Independence.* Those principles are legally binding on every state in the Union and are binding on an equal basis in all respects whatsoever.[18]

The fact that the 13 original states signed the Declaration, the fact that Congress affirmed "equal footing with the original States" in the Northwest Ordinance, and the fact that Congress mandated in various state admission statutes that state constitutions not be "repugnant to the principles of the Declaration," *brought all states under the principles of the Declaration* in the same manner and on the same footing as the original states which were bound to the Declaration.

The Declaration Today

In reviving the American republic of the 1860s, President Abraham Lincoln grasped hold of the Declaration of Independence. He affirmed its legal principle that the United States was "conceived in Liberty, and dedicated to the proposition that all men are created equal."[19] Like the framers, Lincoln realized that certain ideas applied to all men and nations without regard to the age in which they lived, their location on the globe, or the circumstances of history which surrounded them.

He spoke of one such idea in a speech at Springfield in 1857. He said that through the Declaration, the framers "meant to set up a standard maxim for free society, which should be familiar to all, and revered by all; constantly looked to, constantly labored for, and even though never perfectly attained, constantly approximated, and thereby constantly spreading and deepening its influence and augmenting the happiness and value of life to all people of all colors everywhere."[20]

But is this standard maxim of freedom familiar to the modern mind? Do we recognize that the principles of the Declaration are America's legal foundations? The framers understood how those principles applied to the creation and organization of a civil government. They also figured out how government could best secure our God-given rights. Those who are now concerned with figuring out the implications of such principles as they apply to the American mind and education may follow the framers' example. It is the challenge of each generation of Americans to rediscover the content of the laws of nature and of nature's God and to give those laws legally binding effect through their state and federal constitutions or laws.

There are always those who will ignore, degrade, or ridicule the Declaration--lawyers, Justices and elected officials, chief among them. They have been taught that the Declaration is just historical and of no legal effect. They have been taught that unalienable rights and the laws of nature are irrelevant. They have been taught these things in government accredited law schools and believe them still. Though Lincoln pleads with them, yet perhaps they are greater? For those who will listen, Lincoln says:

> Now, my countrymen if you have been taught doctrines conflicting with the great landmarks of the Declaration of Independence; if you have listened to suggestions which would take away from its grandeur, and mutilate the fair symmetry of its proportions; if you have been inclined to believe that all men are *not* created equal in those inalienable rights enumerated by our chart[er] of liberty, let me entreat you to come back. Return to the fountain whose waters spring close by the blood of the Revolution. Think nothing of me--take no thought for the political fate of any man whomsoever--but come back to the truths that are in the Declaration of Independence.[21]

★ HYPOTHETICALLY SPEAKING . . . .

Problem: The people living in the land of Greenacre, decided to establish the Nation of Greenville. They wrote down their rationale for nationhood in a "Letter of Agreement" and signed it. They also carefully wrote down the limited power that their government was to exercise. They made their government officials take an oath not to use any power not given in writing to the government. The people made it perfectly clear that the government was to use its limited power to secure their God-given rights.

About two hundred years later most of the people in the Nation thought the original rationale for Greenville was out-dated and irrelevant. (Wrinkled copies of the "letter of agreement," however, did make nice graduation gifts.) About this time, the Greenzees (as the people were called) were faced with an economic crisis of great proportion. Some of the people who had the most to gain financially went to the government and asked it to ignore the original "Letter." They asked the government to say that the old letter really allowed it to exercise power not contained in the original letter.

Should the government of Greenville exercise power not given to it if it will really help the people through this time of crisis?

Answer: No. The government doesn't have the right to change its own powers. Only the people have that right. In this situation, if the government redefined its own power, it would have violated the God-given right of the people to change the government according to their consent. The government of Greenville may not violate the Greenzees' right to government by consent just because a poll shows many people think it is a good idea or even if it is a good idea.

If the people of Greenville, rather than a special financial interest group really wanted to give the government more power to solve the crisis, the people can amend the original "Letter." To the extent their amendment reorganized the government of Greenville so as to better secure their rights, then to that extent the people would be more like free men. To the extent that the people's amendment organized the government of Greenville so as to render their God-given rights insecure, then to that extent the people would be more like slaves.

Notes

1. JOHN TAYLOR [OF CAROLINE], NEW VIEWS OF THE CONSTITUTION OF THE UNITED STATES (Washington City: Way and Gideon, 1823; reprint ed., New York: Da Capo Press, 1971) 2. For an overview of the Declaration of Independence and its relationship to the Constitution and unalienable rights, *see generally* THE JOURNAL OF CHRISTIAN JURISPRUDENCE, 3 vols., *Reviving The American Republic* (1986, 1987 and 1990 ed).

2. This is not to say that a court can order the legislature to adopt this or that principle of the Declaration. It is to simply say that state governments are under a legal obligation to adhere to the principles of the Declaration. To the extent that this obligation is fulfilled through adoption of state constitutional provisions or state statutes, then to that extent courts have jurisdiction to enforce those provisions. To the extent that state legislatures renege on their obligation, however, then to that extent the people have a right to alter that state government or institute a new one laying its foundations on such principles and organizing its powers in such a way as to them shall seem most likely to secure their unalienable rights on an equal basis.

3. To employ a concept from the law of Corporations (first explained to me by John Brabner Smith, Esq.), the Declaration is this country's original and only "Articles of Incorporation." The Constitution, which followed several years later, constitutes its "By-Laws."

4. Richard Henry Lee's resolution, adopted July 2, 1776, constituted the actual legal act and basis of Independence. The Continental Congress resolved, "That these United Colonies are, and, of right, ought to be, Free and Independent States; that they are absolved from all allegiance to the British crown, and that all political connection between them, and the state of Great-Britain, is, and ought to be, totally dissolved." RICHARD PERRY, ED., SOURCES OF OUR LIBERTIES (American Bar Foundation: Chicago, Ill., 1978) 317. The Declaration which followed two days later established its legitimacy in the eyes of the international community by appealing to the "Laws of Nature and of Nature's God" as an internationally recognized body of law.

5. "The Statesmen who drew the law of citizenship in 1776 made no distinction of nationalities, or tribes, or ranks, or occupations, or faiths, or wealth, and knew only inhabitants bearing allegiance to the governments of the several states in union." GEORGE BANCROFT, HISTORY OF THE FORMATION OF THE CONSTITUTION OF THE UNITED STATES OF AMERICA (New York: Appleton & Co. 1885) 443.

6. The people of the "united States" maintained that their unalienable rights came to them from their "Creator" and that "in order to secure these rights, governments are instituted among men." As Americans, they contended for the rights common to all human beings according to the "immutable laws of nature." *See The Declaration and Resolves of the First Continental Congress* in PERRY, SOURCES *supra* note 4 at 286-89.

7. The Articles of Confederation, however, which preceded the Constitution, were inconsistent with the Declaration's premise that the *people* establish the form of government. The Articles were erroneously premised upon the notion that the *states alone* could establish a general government.

8. The framers and founders would have looked comical in establishing a government in which no one was eligible to serve in the House of Representatives until seven years had expired. The question of who is a citizen of the United States was factually clarified and made legally explicit by the Fourteenth Amendment which declares in part: "All persons born or naturalized in the United States and subject to the jurisdiction thereof, are citizens of the United States and of the State wherein they reside." The Declaration, however, tells us when the United States began, and implies that those persons born therein were citizens.

9. The residency requirement dates to 1773 or 1775 depending on whether time is counted from 1787 when the Constitution was adopted or 1789 when it was ratified. The residency requirement refers to the United States not so much as a particular government, but more as a geographical place. Thus, the requirement is that the President be "fourteen years a resident *within* the United States." This is contrasted with the seven and nine year "citizen *of* the United States" requirement for representatives and senators. In his First

Inaugural Address, President Abraham Lincoln observed that the *republic* was, at least in fact, older than the Constitution. Lincoln found that the republic dated from 1774, when the first Congress met on the American Continent. He said: "The Union is much older than the Constitution. It was formed, in fact, by the Articles of Association in 1774. It was matured and continued by the Declaration of Independence in 1776. It was further matured, and the faith of all the then thirteen States expressly plighted and engaged that it should be perpetual, by the Articles of Confederation in 1778. And finally, in 1787, one of the declared objects for ordering and establishing the Constitution was *to form a more perfect Union.*" JAMES D. RICHARDSON, ED., COMPILATION OF THE MESSAGES AND PAPERS OF THE PRESIDENTS, 1789-1897 (Washington, D.C.: Government Printing Office, 1896) 6:7. First Inaugural Address of Abraham Lincoln, March 4, 1861 (italics in original).

10. The Supreme Court in Monongahela Navigation Co. v. United States, 148 U.S. 312, 324 (1893) also observed that the Bill of Rights to the Constitution was adopted to protect "those rights of persons and property which by the Declaration of Independence were affirmed to be unalienable rights." The Great Seal of the United States also affirms the inseparability of the Declaration and the Constitution by its pictorial representation that a "New Order of the Ages" was instituted in 1776.

11. Ten years before the Constitutional Convention had even convened, Congress was busy trying to reduce the Revolutionary War deficit. Unto this end Congress requested Virginia in particular to surrender its claims over certain lands (now west and north of Virginia's present boundary). Virginia claimed its title to these lands were derived from the King, but Congress now asked that these lands be given to itself. The government hoped to dispose of these lands by sale. The money it obtained from the sale would help pay the war debt.

There was a problem, however, with Maryland. It refused to endorse the Articles of Confederation thereby denying the national government legitimacy, until all the other states and especially Virginia, conveyed to the national government its claims on these lands. Maryland recognized that a large land state would dominate a smaller land state economically and politically. Thus Maryland being small, objected to Virginia which was large. Maryland's objections effectively blocked the formation of the Confederation until roughly 1784. As soon as the Confederation Congress became effective, it began to adopt plans to sell off the tracts of the newly acquired land. In fact, by 1802 "all of the large land-owning States had ceded to the General Government the tracts of territory out of which were later formed the States of Kentucky, Tennessee, Ohio, Indiana, Mississippi, Illinois, Alabama, Michigan, and Wisconsin." GEORGE B. GERMANN, NATIONAL LEGISLATION CONCERNING EDUCATION (New York: Columbia University, 1899, Library of American Civilization 15623) 13-14.

12. Its terms also provided other conditions that would apply to the formation of future states out of federally held territory. For instance, the states of Michigan, Ohio, Indiana, Illinois and Wisconsin were required to acknowledge: "The fundamental principles of civil and religious liberty, which form the basis whereon these republics, their laws and constitutions, are erected; to fix and establish those principles as the basis of all laws, constitutions, and governments, which forever hereafter shall be formed . . . and for their admission . . . on equal footing with the original States." PERRY, SOURCES *supra* note 4 at 395, quoting An Ordinance for the Government of the Territory of the United States Northwest of the River Ohio, Sec. 13.

13. A primary concern of the states was equality with existing sister states. Equality was defined in terms of representation in the "federal councils" of Congress. Provisions of the Articles of Confederation gave each state one vote. Thus, each state was on equal footing with the other states when represented in the confederation congress. Much of

the Constitutional Convention was centered upon the debate over equal representation. The larger states contended that by allowing each state one vote, the smaller states became proportionally more powerful than the larger states. The smaller states, however, argued that if representation were to be based upon population, the citizens of larger states would be proportionally more powerful than the less populated smaller states.

Roger Sherman's Great Compromise proposal recommended that each state legislature appoint two Senators to represent the state. Representation in the Senate would always be equal regardless of population. The people would then be apportioned representation in the House according to population and popular vote.

The seventeenth amendment to the Constitution undermined this arrangement. For an analysis of this amendment, *see* Virginia M. McInerney, *Repeal of the Seventeenth Amendment: A Step toward the Restoration of Federalism in America*, (Masters Thesis, Regent University, 1987).

14. By precluding the national government from holding land for itself and requiring it to make future states out of land it held in trust for both the present states and all future states (in accordance with the Articles of Compact in the Northwest Ordinance), the parties intended that the people moving into a federal territory would eventually enjoy the right to be governed by their own consent via a state legislature, and in Congress in their own right as the people of a state in the House of Representatives, and as a state itself in the Senate. If this scheme was not honored, the people in the territories would be governed in perpetuity by a federal Congress elected by others.

Nevertheless, the federal government continues to hold vast amounts of real estate contrary to their obligation to all the states (irrespective of their physical location) under the Articles of Compact in the northwest ordinance. Including Alaska and sections of many western states, the federal government owns about 740 million acres--nearly a third of the United States! These lands are within states, not a territory. Federal retention of property in these states violates the Compact in the Northwest Ordinance. That Compact affirmed that Congress should admit the territory into the Union on equal footing with all the other states when those areas became sufficiently populated. Equal footing applies to all states, past present and future. PERRY, SOURCES *supra* note 4 at 395.

15. These States include Nevada (1864), Nebraska (1867), Colorado (1876), Washington (1889), Montana (1889), Utah (1896), North and South Dakota (1899), Arizona, New Mexico (1912), Alaska (1958) and Hawaii (1959). *See generally*, EDWARD DUMBAULD, THE DECLARATION OF INDEPENDENCE AND WHAT IT MEANS TODAY (Norman, OK: University of Oklahoma Press, 1950) 63.

16. *See* Coyle v. Smith, 221 U.S. 559 (1911). The States of New Hampshire, Massachusetts, Rhode-Island and Providence Plantations, Connecticut, New York, New Jersey, Pennsylvania, Delaware, Maryland, Virginia, North Carolina, South Carolina and Georgia were not "admitted" to the Union since these States ratified and established the Constitution of the Union in the first instance. Virginia, North Carolina, South Carolina, Georgia are listed below as "restored" to the Union. This point of view was taken by the Supreme Court when it declared that "by reference to the formula used in the several reconstruction acts, as compared with those for the original admission of new States into the Union, that in regard to the States in rebellion there was a simple recognition of their restored right to representation in Congress, and no readmission into the Union." Keith v. Clark 97 U.S. (7 Otto) 454, 462 (1878). It should be noted, however, that President Lincoln and Congress bitterly disagreed over the precise legal basis of secession and each assumed a position which empowered them to act consistent with the Constitution the way they understood their respective powers.

17. Federal enabling legislation including state restoration legislation is as follows: Alabama, Mar. 2, 1819, c. 47, 3 Stat. 489, Dec. 14, 1819, 3 Stat. 608, June 25, 1868, c. 70, 15 Stat. 73; Alaska, July 7, 1958, P.L. 85-508, 72 Stat. 339; Arizona, June 20, 1910, c. 310, 36 Stat. 557, Aug. 21, 1911, No. 8, 37 Stat. 39, Feb. 14, 1912, 37 Stat. 1728; Arkansas, June 15, 1836, c. 100, 5 Stat. 50, June 22, 1868, c. 69, 15 Stat. 72; California, Sept. 9, 1850, c. 50, 9 Stat. 452; Colorado, Mar. 21, 1864, c. 37, 13 Stat. 32, Mar. 3, 1875, c. 139, 18 Stat. 474, Aug. 1, 1876, 19 Stat. 665; Florida, Mar. 3, 1845, c. 48, 5 Stat. 742, Mar. 3, 1845, c. 75, 5 Stat. 788, June 25, 1868, c. 70, 15 Stat. 73; Georgia, July 15, 1870, c. 299, 16 Stat. 363; Hawaii, Mar. 18, 1959, P.L. 86-3, 73 Stat. 4; Idaho, July 3, 1890, c. 656, 26 Stat. 215; Illinois, Apr. 18, 1818, c. 67, 3 Stat. 428, Dec. 3, 1818, 3 Stat. 536; Indiana, Apr. 19, 1816, c. 57, 3 Stat. 289, Dec. 11, 1816, 3 Stat. 399; Iowa, Mar. 3, 1845, c. 48, 5 Stat. 742, Mar. 3, 1845, c. 76, 5 Stat. 789, Dec. 28, 1846, c. 1, 9 Stat. 117; Kansas, May 4, 1858, c. 26, 11 Stat. 269, Jan. 29, 1861, c. 20, 12 Stat. 126; Kentucky, Feb. 4, 1791, c. 4, 1 Stat. 189; Louisiana, Feb. 20 1811, c. 21, 2 Stat. 641, Apr. 8, 1812, c. 50, 2 Stat. 701, June 25, 1868, c. 70, 15 Stat. 73; Maine, Mar. 3, 1820, c. 19, 3 Stat. 544; Michigan, June 15, 1836, c. 99, 5 Stat. 49, Jan. 26, 1837, c. 6, 5 Stat. 144; Minnesota, Feb. 26, 1857, c. 60, 11 Stat. 166, May 11, 1858, c. 31, 11 Stat. 285; Mississippi, Mar. 1, 1817, c. 23, 3 Stat. 348, Dec. 10, 1817, Res. 1, 3 Stat. 472, Feb. 23, 1870, c. 19, 16 Stat. 67; Missouri, Mar. 6, 1820, c. 22, 3 Stat. 545, Mar. 2, 1821, Res. No. 1, 3 Stat. 645; Montana, Feb. 22, 1889, c. 180, 25 Stat. 676, Nov. 8, 1889, No. 7, 26 Stat. 1551; Nebraska, Apr. 19, 1864, c. 59, 13 Stat. 47, Feb. 9, 1867, c. 36, 14 Stat. 391, Mar. 1, 1867, No. 9, 14 Stat. 820; Nevada, March 21, 1864, c. 36, 13 Stat. 30, Oct. 31, 1864, No. 22, 13 Stat. 749; New Mexico, June 20, 1910, c. 310, 36 Stat. 557, §§1 to 18, Aug. 21, 1911, No. 8, 37 Stat. 39, Jan. 6, 1912, 37 Stat. 1723; North Carolina, June 25, 1868, c. 70, 15 Stat. 73; North Dakota, Feb. 22, 1889, c. 180, 25 Stat. 676, Nov. 2, 1889, No. 5, 26 Stat. 1548; Ohio, Apr. 30, 1802, c. 40, 2 Stat. 173; Oklahoma, June 16, 1906, c. 3335, 34 Stat. 267, Nov. 16, 1907, 35 Stat. 2160; Oregon, Feb. 14, 1859, c. 33, 11 Stat. 383; South Carolina, June 25, 1868, c. 70, 15 Stat. 73; South Dakota, Feb. 22, 1889, c. 180, 25 Stat. 676, Nov. 2, 1889, No. 6, 26 Stat. 1549; Tennessee, June 1, 1796, c. 47, 1 Stat. 491, July 24, 1866, No. 73, 14 Stat. 364, Texas, Mar. 1, 1845, No. 8, 5 Stat. 797, Dec. 29, 1845, No. 1, 9 Stat. 108, Mar. 30, 1870, c. 39, 16 Stat. 80; Utah, July 16, 1894, c. 138, 28 Stat. 107, Jan. 4, 1896, No. 9, 29 Stat. 876; Vermont, Feb. 18, 1791, c. 7, 1 Stat. 191; Virginia, Jan. 26, 1870, c. 10, 16 Stat. 62; Washington, Feb. 22, 1889, c. 180, 25 Stat. 676; West Virginia, Dec. 31, 1862, c. 6, 12 Stat. 633, Apr. 20, 1863, No. 3, 13 Stat. 731; Wisconsin, Aug. 6, 1846, c. 89, 9 Stat. 56, May 29, 1848, c. 50, 9 Stat. 233; Wyoming, July 10, 1890, c. 664, 26 Stat. 222.

18.   It is essential that state officials (and federal officials to the extent Constitutionally authorized) recognize they are bound to observe the principles of the Declaration as well as those of the Constitution.   State legislators have a weighty responsibility to draft and enact only those laws which conform to the principles contained in the Declaration. Federal representatives in Congress also have this responsibility as far as their power is Constitutionally grounded or enumerated. Such laws must reflect the fact that unalienable rights are not derived from civil government, nor subject to alienation.   Of course, the people have the duty and right to turn out of office those officials who refuse to abide by these principles; the people also have the right and duty to lawfully alter or abolish a government that fails systematically to secure their God-given rights.

19.   Abraham Lincoln, "Gettysburg Address," quoted in A. CRAVEN, W. JOHNSON AND F. R. DUNN, ED., A DOCUMENTARY HISTORY OF THE AMERICAN PEOPLE (Boston: Ginn & Co., 1951) 409.

20. Abraham Lincoln, Speech at Springfield, 1857, quoted in LIVING IDEAS IN AMERICA, HENRY S. COMMANGER, ED., (New York: Harper and Row, 1964) 234.

21. PAUL M. ANGLE, ED., CREATED EQUAL? THE COMPLETE LINCOLN-DOUGLAS DEBATES OF 1858 (Chicago: The University of Chicago Press, 1958) 101.

Chapter 4

The Unalienable Rights Of Parents

[T]he law of nature and nature's God, which ordains that it is both the right and duty of parents to educate their children "in such manner as they believe will be most for their future happiness" is utterly disregarded and set at naught by the State, which ordains that it is neither the right nor the duty of parents, but of the State, to say when, where, by whom, and in what manner our children shall be educated.[1]

Parental Rights: Are They Really Unalienable?

It has been suggested in prior Chapters that America's civil governments are legally and morally required to observe and implement the principles articulated in the Declaration of Independence. One such principle stated in the Declaration and established in "the laws of nature and of nature's God," is that "all men are created equal and endowed by their Creator with certain unalienable rights." Another principle is that civil governments are legally commanded to guard and defend those unalienable rights.

Given these principles, we therefore might properly inquire: "What are the rights of parents according to the laws of nature and of nature's God with respect to the education of their children?" and "Are those rights unalienable?" In order to examine these questions, we must first look at the nature of the parent-child relationship, how it is formed and for what end.

To begin with, nature itself teaches that children are born to their parents and not to the church, state or a public school board. In fact, no comparable relationship exists between a child and any other person, governmental entity or organization. Nature--the physical act of conception and birth--not only establishes the relationship between a parent and child, but also creates the basic

41

responsibility or duty of a parent with respect to his or her own child. Nature universally impresses upon parents the responsibility to care for, to feed and clothe, and to generally provide for the education of their own flesh and blood. This universal obligation of parents is inherent in the parent-child relationship, a relationship which is *created* according to the laws of nature and of nature's God.

Because the duty of parents with respect to their own children springs from conception and birth, it is axiomatic that parents do not enjoy authority over their children because of their beliefs, religious or otherwise. Parents who do not believe in God enjoy parental authority in equal measure with those who worship God. Neither does parental authority, including the authority to educate their children, spring from parental knowledge, possession of an academic degree, or any other state educational qualification.

✓ Key Idea:

> ☞ THE RIGHT OF A PARENT TO EDUCATE SPRINGS NEITHER FROM THEIR RELIGIOUS BELIEF NOR FROM THEIR DEGREE OF LEARNING, BUT RATHER FROM THEIR NATURAL STATUS AS A PARENT.

But does such parental authority translate into an unalienable right? Certain actions are deemed *rights* to the extent they conform to the will of the Creator or his law. When parents conceive and bear children, they act in accordance with the will of the Creator and his laws of reproduction. Rights in turn, are deemed *unalienable* to the extent they are given or endowed by the Creator. Other rights which are merely civil are given by the state. In the case of parents, their rights are unalienable because they are given by the Creator through the act of conceiving and bearing children.

The authority to care for, instruct and educate the child is inseparably tied to the authority of parents to conceive the child. Care, upbringing and education may not be divorced from conception. The unalienable right in a parent to care for and educate their child continues until their children become adults. Conversely, neither creation nor nature establishes any "right" in a church or civil government (including the local school board) in and of their own authority or legitimate power, to conceive, bear, care for or educate any child whose parents are alive and not under a legal disability.

Biblical Norms and the Parent-Child Relationship

The law of nature is thus self-evident: children are born to their parents. Nature teaches that parents are to care for, feed and educate their children for useful service and future labor. What other evidence, however, may be considered that will supplement this understanding of the law of nature? Does the Bible say anything about this parental obligation or right? Is the Bible even relevant to a discussion of law or rights? It is certainly appropriate to consider the Bible for religious ideas, but what about the parental context? Some may argue: "The Bible is religious and I don't care about religion or God or a Creator or that such things are not relevant." Some may even contend that the law of nature analysis is itself suspect because it necessarily means the Creator or a creator must be discussed.

These are fair suspicions. For the sake of scholarship we must set aside what has been taught in our government approved schools or our tax-exempt churches about the Bible and the Creator and the place of religion in general, and focus on law. We are discussing the *legal* basis of a parent's unalienable right. We have looked to one document--the Declaration of Independence for some legal guidance in understanding that right and the Declaration refers to the legally cognizable fact that our "Creator" gives us certain rights. We may, therefore, also look to the Biblical record to see what it might contribute to the discussion. The Bible is a book of law, even more so than the Declaration.

The Bible recognizes that God is the source of truth.[2] In order to teach children truth, God entrusts them to their parents."[3] Parents are essentially responsible "to teach their children" the truth about all things, especially the laws of right and wrong.[4] Parents, "[i]mpress [these laws] upon your children. Talk about them when you sit at home and when you walk along the road, when you lie down and when you get up."[5] Moreover, to facilitate this responsibility the sixth commandment exhorts children to honor their father and mother.[6]

While both parents are responsible to teach their children the truth, a father is specifically instructed to bring children up in the nurture and admonition of the Lord.[7] This instruction is not limited to knowledge about religion since God is not limited to religious knowledge. God is the Creator of all things. He has given mankind law. Consequently, parental instruction of children carries the real freedom to instruct a child in any and all subjects.[8] God gives all parents, whether religious or not, this real freedom. Corresponding to this freedom is the unalienable right to be free from others (including federal, state, and local officials) who seek to interfere with, regulate or control its exercise.

✓ Key Idea:

☞ THE BIBLICAL RECORD ESTABLISHES THAT PARENTS ARE ACCOUNTABLE TO GOD FOR THE EDUCATION OF THEIR OWN CHILDREN.

Historically, Israelite parents were obliged to educate their children in like manner. They were specifically required to diligently teach the words of the law of God to their children.[9] They were admonished to hold systematic classes.[10] Children were to be warned of the dangers of ignoring the law of God.[11] Fathers were particularly accountable to God for teaching the laws and history of their nation and communicating the obligations of citizenship.[12]   This paternal responsibility stands in stark contrast to the modern view that the state must control education in order to produce good citizens and workers.

The foregoing examination indicates that the parent and child are bound together as a matter of nature and Biblical rule. Both establish and sustain the idea that parents are responsible to direct the care, education and upbringing of their own children. Parents and not the civil government, are endowed with the authority, power and right to educate children. A different rule may apply, however, where the parent-child relationship is legally dissolved or forfeited under certain common law doctrines discussed in subsequent Chapters, but this is not the general or controlling rule.

What do the Standard Writers on the Subject Say?

In examining various periods of our history, celebrated writers have argued that the laws of nature as well as the Bible support parental rights. In fact, it has been observed that, "[e]very standard writer on the subject of either law or morals proclaims with one voice that parents are bound by the natural law to feed, clothe, and educate their children."[13] In his famous *Commentaries on American Law*, James Kent observed that:

> The duties of parents to their children, as being their natural guardians, consist in maintaining and educating them during the season of infancy and youth, and in making reasonable provision for their future usefulness and happiness in life, by a situation suited to their habits, and a competent provision for the exigencies of that situation.[14]

In other words, Kent recognized that parents were required by Providence and the laws of nature, to provide for the *individualized* education and instruction of their children until such time as their children were old enough to make their way in life. The instruction that Kent refers to is not standardized in any way. It is not a uniform or universal program of education that he commends--not at all. The education that is required by the laws of nature is an education relative to the individual capacity of each child. It is also an education relative to the parent's own situation and station in life.   This is not a call for state standardization of our children's minds or a call to adopt national standards or mandatory testing. It is quite the opposite position. Kent is calling for the highly individualized and *diverse* education of children.[15]

Kent also acknowledged that "[t]he rights of parents result from their duties."[16] In a clear exposition of these rights, he concluded that as parents "are bound to maintain and educate their children, the law has given them a right to such authority; and in the support of that authority, a right to the exercise of such discipline, as may be requisite for the discharge of their sacred trust."[17] Kent understood the proper function of the civil government and the law when it came to education. The law should defend parents in the discharge of *their parental rights* to educate their own children. The law should not interfere with or restrain the full enjoyment of that right.

Parents should not be regulated or interfered with by anyone while they provide their child with training or instruction. The wisdom and judgment of the parent alone, as to what content, approach or language is suitable for that child at any given time is not to be disturbed by anyone or any government. This legal rule also provides that the duration and extent of such instruction are wholly within the discretion and direction of parents to regulate and control.

As far as the eminent jurist James Kent was concerned, the laws of nature vested parents with the legal right to direct the education of their own child or children. Like the framers, Kent, based his thinking upon the broad principles of creation and the laws of nature, and then applied those principles to the specific area of education. Kent concluded that the civil law's function was to protect the natural right of parents. The civil law was not to be used to regulate the unalienable right of parents to direct the education of their own children. The civil law was not to be used to subvert that right or permit the civil government to substitute its judgment in the place of parents as to what shall constitute "necessary attendance" or "an appropriate education."

The understanding that parents have certain unalienable rights was also accepted by prominent writers in the Academy. For instance, Francis Wayland, President of Brown University, authored *The Elements of Moral Science*.[18] The book immediately became a standard university textbook. In multiple editions Wayland wrote about the several duties of a parent. He remarked that parents were responsible to provide their children with a physical, intellectual and moral education. Reiterating the authority or jurisdiction of parents in general (and a father in particular) Wayland affirmed that:

> The right of the parent over his child is, of course, commensurate with his duties. If he be under obligation to educate his child in such manner as he supposes will most conduce to the child's happiness and the welfare of society, he has, from necessity, the right to control the child in everything necessary to the fulfillment of this obligation. The only limits imposed are, that he exert this control no further than is necessary to the fulfillment of his obligation, and that he exert it with the intention for which it was conferred. While he discharges his parental duties within these limits, he is, by the law of God, exempt from interference both from the individual and from society.[19]

The key point of the preceding passage is that "While he [the father] discharges his parental duties within these limits, he is, by the law of God, exempt from interference both from the individual and from society." Wayland is saying that parents have a right according to the law of God. As parents have such a right from God, it is unalienable. Note also that the extent and content of the instruction are not questioned or limited. The only limits imposed are, that the parent exert control no further than he supposes will be most conducive to secure the child's happiness and not be shown to be contrary to the welfare of society.

Sometimes lawyers, judges and public officials see the phrase "welfare of society" and wrongfully conclude that this concept gives the civil government *carte blanche*, or unlimited power, to do what it wants. They conclude that the scope of civil power should not be limited to the security of unalienable rights or the provision of a civil remedy for those who interfere with another's unalienable rights. They misuse the "welfare of society" as a pretext to regulate the exercise of rights, to balance those rights into mere state certified privileges, and eventually to substitute their own ideas of what is proper in lieu of a parent's ideas.[20]

The term "welfare of society" and its companion phrase "social welfare," however, do not have unlimited meaning. Invoking the "welfare of society" does not authorize the state to usurp parental rights, for the usurpation or interference with God-given rights is never consistent with the general welfare of any society. When civil government usurps unalienable rights, it is contrary to the welfare of *any* society, especially one grounded in a system of limited constitutional government derived from the laws of nature and of nature's God. But a civil government which promotes "social welfare" by abridging unalienable rights, promotes slavery to its own will.

What about the "Best Interest of the Child?"

The danger of enslavement through usurpation also arises when the civil government asserts that abridgement of unalienable parental rights is warranted because of the "best interest of the child." The "best interest of the child," however, is secured when the state protects a parent's unalienable right from civil regulation and unwanted private interference, whether philanthropic or otherwise. The "best interest of the child" must serve the Declaration's purpose for civil government. It is not a convenient trump card to be played against parental rights by the state.[21]

✓ Key Idea:
> ☞ PARENTS OUGHT TO BE EXEMPT FROM GOVERNMENTAL INTERFERENCE WHEN EXERCISING THEIR PARENTAL RIGHT TO EDUCATE.

Nor may the civil government substitute its judgment for that of parents (under the pretext of the child's best interest) as to what is a proper or approved education. Parents enjoy a wide berth in the exercise of their rights and the state ought not second guess the exercise of those rights by maintaining that a child could be better educated, educated in a different setting, or educated by more knowledgeable persons.

Absent the legal destruction of the marital relationship or a lawful adjudication of unfitness based on physical abuse, the civil government is not authorized to act in the "best interest of the child." Absent the existence of such legal disabilities, the "best interest of the child" is always protected by security of the rights of parents to care for and educate their own children. Governmental interference, however, with the child's education abuses the unalienable right of a parent and is contrary to the child's best interest. If the rule were otherwise, civil officials would simply approve or condemn the educational practices of parents only as those practices square with or differ from their own. This is not a legal standard, but is wholly unlimited and arbitrary.[22]

The Supreme Court and State Education Laws

The real lesson to be learned is that individuals, society, civil governments and its officials, are by the laws of nature and of nature's God, prohibited from interfering with parental control of their children's education. That means teachers and their unions are prohibited from interfering with parental rights. It also means that the state legislature and the school board are forbidden from regulating a parent in the exercise of their right.

The crux of the present problem, however, is that *state governments* are the single largest abuser of the unalienable rights of parents. Maintenance of state established or regulated elementary and secondary schools through, 1) compulsory or state approved curriculums, textbooks and tests, 2) compulsory certification or licensing of schools and teachers, 3) compulsory funding through taxation or state subsidies, and 4) compulsory attendance at a state established or regulated school or schools is unquestionably, the major force denying and disparaging the unalienable rights of parents when it comes to the education of their own children.[23]

When analyzing the power of state governments over education, several Supreme Court decisions are significant. For instance, in *Meyer v. Nebraska,*[24] the Court considered the conviction of a *parochial* school teacher for teaching German where a state law forbade the teaching of German until the eighth grade. The Court struck down the law on the grounds that it interfered with the liberty of the teacher under the Fourteenth Amendment. Justice McReynolds carefully constructed an argument that would limit the state's power to punish the teaching of German, but preserve the state's power to compel attendance. In other words, the Court embarked upon a balancing of the relative interests of the state, the teacher and the parent. Whether or not one agrees with the outcome is not the issue. The issue is whether the Court has the constitutional power to find or create natural rights, or balance rights against alleged state interests.

Looking a bit more closely at the case, the Court rightly observed that "[t]he American people have always regarded education and acquisition of knowledge as matters of supreme importance which should be diligently promoted."[25] To this it added that "[c]orresponding to the right of control, it is the natural duty of the parent to give his children education suitable to their station in life . . . ." So far, so good.

The Court understood that parents have a natural duty and corresponding right to control the education of their children *suitable to their station in life*. The flow of the Court's language should sound familiar. Remember what James Kent wrote? "The duties of parents to their children, as being their natural guardians, consist in maintaining and educating them . . . by a situation suited to their habits." Recall what Francis Wayland observed: "[The parent] is bound to inform himself of the peculiar habits and reflect upon the probable future situation of his child, and deliberately to consider what sort of education will most conduce to his future happiness and usefulness."

But instead of following its premise that "it is the natural duty of the parent to give his children education suitable to their station in life" the Court wrongfully concluded that, "nearly all the States, including Nebraska, enforce this obligation by compulsory laws"[26] and that "[p]ractically, education of the young is only possible in schools conducted by especially qualified persons who devote themselves thereto."[27] In other words, on the one hand, the Court is saying that parents enjoy the natural duty to direct the education of their own children. On the other hand, the Court is saying that "qualified persons" have the real power to educate by the force of state compulsory attendance laws.

Both assertions, however, cannot be true. Either parents enjoy the right to educate their children from which it follows that they are free to require attendance, select their teachers and determine the curriculum (including whether or not German will be taught); or a parent does not enjoy such a right, in which case the state (and not a parent) may compel attendance, select its teachers and determine its own curriculum (including whether or not German will be taught).

Over thirty years later in *Brown v. Board of Education*,[28] the Supreme Court eventually recognized that it could not logically defend compulsory education as a function of a parent's natural right. The Court, therefore, abandoned its historical pretext. The Court first reiterated the importance of education in "awakening the child," but noted that education should awaken the child to "cultural values" rather than the values of his or her parents. Least understood by the general public and bar, however, and most harmful to those parties the Court professed to favor, is the fact that the justification of compulsory attendance laws as an extension of natural parental rights was abandoned. Compulsory attendance laws were now judicially reincarnated as an expression "of our recognition of the importance of education to our democratic society." The Court did not mention that in *Meyer* it had pretended that such laws were first put into effect to aid the "natural duty of the parent to give his children education suitable to their station in life." That pretext is now gone. The Court's jurisprudential pendulum has swung away from parental rights and toward governmental power. Instead of supporting the natural rights of parents, the Court glorified civil government's usurpation of parental rights by declaring in nationalistic tones, that "education is perhaps the most important function of State and local governments."[29]

Fundamental Rights or Unalienable Rights?

Has there been any legal or political resistance, however, to counter such a radical usurpation of parental rights by "State and local governments"? Have parental rights groups recognized this usurpation and dedicated themselves to its reversal? Regrettably, many activists are not disciples of law but children of politics. They accept local and state usurpation of parental rights through compulsory attendance laws as completely normal and even principled! The government educated mind is a terrible thing to waste.

Recent attempts to amend state constitutions through inclusion of parental rights amendments are an interesting case in point. The effort represents a combination of personal goodwill and the government educated mind in action. Its advocates are concerned with the "fundamental rights of parents." They do not discuss the critical distinction between unalienable or natural parental rights, and fundamental rights. State constitutional recognition of a *fundamental* parental right means that the courts are free to weigh competing claims to the mind and education of a child. Courts may freely balance the state's purported interest in an educated citizenry on the one hand against a fundamental parental right on the other. Parents will invariably lose against the power of the state.

Such a limited right will never result, however, in real choice or real freedom in American education. Its embodiment in a state constitution will never result in a parent's choice and freedom to direct the education and upbringing of his or her own child, free from state interference, regulation, control, or taxation. Nor can such a limited right ever be equated with the discharge of a parental duty in which a parent "is, by the law of God, exempt from interference both from the individual and from society."[30] Where the civil government interferes with a parent's unalienable right to educate his or her own child, it does so only by usurpation. Proponents of the limited idea of fundamental parental right will not, and indeed can not, muster the legal firepower necessary to question, let alone strike down state usurpation of parental rights.

The doctrine of unalienable rights on the other hand, admits of no such balancing whatsoever. Courts may only inquire whether the right being exercised is in fact an unalienable right. Courts may certainly consider whether or not the parental conduct at issue merely invokes the right as a pretext to conceal wrongful conduct. If, after review, however, the Court finds that the parental conduct at issue constitutes the exercise of an unalienable right, then no state interest, compelling, rational or otherwise may encumber it whatsoever.

Unalienable Rights--The Better Argument

Consider the legal precision that Zach Montgomery employed to defend the unalienable right of parents to direct the education and upbringing of their children. Montgomery was a United States Assistant Attorney General with the Justice Department in the 1880s. He published a treatise entitled *The School Question from a Parental and Non-Sectarian Stand Point.* He wrote:

> [T]he law of nature and nature's God, which ordains that it is both the right and duty of parents to educate their children "in such manner as they believe will be most for their future happiness" is utterly disregarded and set at naught by the State, which ordains that it is neither the right nor the duty of parents, but of the State, to say when, where, by whom, and in what manner our children shall be educated.[31]

Montgomery was an attorney. He understood the laws of nature and of nature's God. He quotes Wayland's view, which we have previously examined, as an authoritative construction and interpretation of parental rights. But more significantly, he shows us that his thinking followed that of the framers. He began with the laws of creation, and proceeded to figure out what that law required of parents. He also took the next step and figured out what that law means for parents with respect to the education of their own children.

He said that a parent's right is utterly disregarded by the state when the state passes any law indicating that it is not the right or the duty of parents, but of the state, to say when, where, by whom, and in what manner children shall be educated. In other words, compulsory attendance laws among others, are contrary to the laws of nature, *even if they were originally instituted in order to enforce the duty of parents.* Not even "a desirable end can be promoted by prohibited means."[32] The desirable end of civil government in encouraging education cannot be accomplished by the prohibited means of force or coercion. *Nil Consensui Tam Contrarium Est Quam Vis Atque Metus.*[33]

Parents have an unalienable right to educate their own children free from state and private interference, regulation and control.[34] Parental *rights* must be secured first; then parental *choice* will follow.

★ HYPOTHETICALLY SPEAKING . . . .

Problem: **A farmer rented out his farm to some trusted friends for six years. After a few years, however, the renters began to think of themselves as the owners because they had become experts in farming. After six years the farmer decided against renewing the lease and farm his land himself.**

When the time came, however, for the renters to leave the farm, they refused to leave. The farmer reminded them that it was his farm all along, but they mocked him saying, "We are experts in farming. How dare you

lecture us. We know what is best!" and they threw the farmer off his own land. If the renters were actually better farmers than the owner, would that give them a right to farm his land?

Answer: No. The renters have no right to farm another's land even if they are the best farmers in the world. They certainly have no greater right than that which the owner has given them. The land is the farmer's land. He owns it and it is his to till. The renters only have a right to till once they first obtain the permission of the farmer.

So also parents are not to be interfered with by "expert" educators when exercising their parental right to educate. Teachers must likewise first obtain the permission of the child's parents before beginning to teach that child.

Notes

1. ZACH MONTGOMERY, COMP., THE SCHOOL QUESTION FROM A PARENTAL AND NON-SECTARIAN STAND POINT, 4th ed. (Washington: Gibson Bros., 1889; reprint ed.; New York: Arno Press, 1972) 52 *quoting* FRANCIS WAYLAND, THE ELEMENTS OF MORAL SCIENCE, 4th ed. (Boston: Gould, Kendall and Lincoln, 1841) 316.

2. *See* Exodus 20:1-17; Isaiah 38:19; Psalm 25:4-5 & 8-9; Psalm 36:9; Psalm 40:11; Psalm 86:11; Psalm 100:5; Psalm 119:142 & 151; John 1:14 & 17; John 8:31-32; John 14:6; John 15:26; John 16:13; John 17:17; 1 John 5:20.

3. *See* Genesis 1:28a; Genesis 4:1; Genesis 33:5; Genesis 48:8-9; 1 Samuel 1:20; Psalm 78:5; Psalm 113:9; Psalm 127:3-4; Isaiah 29:23; Malachi 2:15.

4. *See* Genesis 18:18-19; Exodus 10:2; Deuteronomy 4:5-10; Deuteronomy 11:18-21; Deuteronomy 32:45-46; Psalms 34:11; Proverbs 2:1-5; Proverbs 3:12; Proverbs 4:20-27; Proverbs 6:20-23; Proverbs 13:1; Isaiah 38:19; Joel 1:3; 1 Thessalonians 2:11.

5. Deuteronomy 6:7.

6. Exodus 20:12. *See also* Proverbs 1:8; Proverbs 4:1; Ephesians 6:1-2; Colossians 3:20.

7. Ephesians 6:4. To bring a child up in the *nurture* of the Lord means to train, foster and encourage a child to become familiar with God and knowledgeable about all of God's creation.

To instruct in the *admonition* of the Lord means to remind, warn and reprove. When a father instructs his children in the admonition of the Lord, he reminds them of the knowledge of God and creation. He also counsels his children to heed the responsibility of their knowledge including knowledge of God's rules of right and wrong thought and conduct. Parents have the authority from God to instruct their child's mind in what is morally right and wrong, an authority the civil government lacks.

Admonition also includes reproof of instruction. Reproof requires that children must learn to test their knowledge to see if it is true or if it has been wrongly represented to them by their parents or others. The object of admonition is not to ensure that the child thinks like his parents, though that may result, but that the child sees the world from God's point of view as much as is humanly possible. Of course the civil government is not qualified to judge if a child achieves that perspective.

8. Language -- Genesis 1:3,27, Romans 10:13,17, II Timothy 3:16, Genesis 2:7,19,23, I Corinthians 10:31, Titus 2:8, Genesis 11:9, Colossians 4:6, Hebrews 1:1,2, Deuteronomy 17:19, I Thes. 5:17, I Peter 1:19-21, Psalms 119:11, I Timothy 4:13, I Peter 3:15, Matthew 12:36,37, II Timothy 2:15, Revelation 1:3, Matthew 28:18-20. Mathematics -- Genesis 1:5, Psalms 90:12, Luke 14:28, Genesis 2:10-14, Malachi 3:6, Romans 14:12, Genesis 6, Malachi 3:10, I Corinthians 14:40, Exodus 25-28, Matthew 18:22, I Corinthians 16:1,2, II Chronicles 1-6, Matthew 25:14-30, Revelation 21:12-17, Job 38:18,32,33,37. Science -- Genesis 1, II Chronicles 2:1-18, John 1:3, Genesis 2:7, Job 22-38, John 17:17, Genesis 10:1-30, Psalms 107:23,24, Colossians 1:16,17, Genesis 14-16, Ecclesiastes 1:6,7, Colossians 2:8, Genesis 15:5, Isaiah 40:22, I Timothy 6:20, Numbers 22:28, Jeremiah 8:22, Hebrews 1:3, Joshua 10:12, Ezekiel 40:5,6, II Peter 3:3-9, I Kings 4:33, Mark 5:41. History -- Genesis 1:1,27, Ezekiel 22:25-29, Romans 10:9,10,13, Genesis 2:7, John 3:16, I Corinthians 1:19-25, Genesis 3, Acts 16:6-10, II Peter 2:13, Genesis 6-9, Romans 2:1-6, Revelation 10:6, Joshua 4:20-24, Romans 3:10,23, Revelation 21:1, Psalms 76:6-12, Romans 5:8. Economics -- Genesis 2:8-14, Proverbs 22:7, Matthew 22:21, Genesis 3:17-19, Proverbs 31:10-31, Luke 12:33,34, Leviticus 27:30-34, Ecclesiastes 5:18-20, Luke 16:10,11, Deuteronomy 28, Isaiah 48:17, II Corinthians 9:6-11, Proverbs 3:9,10, Matthew 6:19-34, I Thes. 4:10-12, Proverbs 14:23, Matthew 18:23-35. Sociology -- Genesis 2:20-25,29, Leviticus 18:22,23, Matthew 19:6, Genesis 9:6, Leviticus 19:20, Ephesians 5:3-33, Exodus 20:3,4,7, Deuteronomy 6:4-8, Ephesians 6:1-4, Exodus 20:14-16, Psalms 139:14-16, II Thes. 3:16, Exodus 21:24, Proverbs 6:16,17. Law -- Exodus 20, Psalms 19:7, Romans 3:19, Psalms 1:2, Psalms 37:31, Romans 6:23, Psalms 2:10,11, Psalms 119:1-8, James 1:25. The Arts -- Genesis 1:1, Psalms 104, Romans 1:22,23, Exodus 20:4,5, Ecclesiastes 3:11, I Corinthians 10:31, Psalms 19:1-6, John 1:3, Ephesians 2:10, Psalms 90:17. Music -- Genesis 4:21, Psalms 40:3, Isaiah 44:23, I Kings 4:29-32, Psalms 100:1, I Cor. 10:31, II Chron. 5:12,13, Psalms 104:33, Ephesians 5:18,19, Job 35:10, Psalms 137:4, Colossians 3:16, Psalms 28:7, Proverbs 29:6, James 5:13. Physical Education -- II Samuel 1:23, I Corinthians 6:19,20, I Timothy 4:8, I Chronicles 12:1-7, I Corinthians 9:25,27, II Timothy 2:3, Isaiah 40:28-31, I Corinthians 15:51-55. Health -- Exodus 15:6, Proverbs 3:23, Jeremiah 17:14, Leviticus 15, Proverbs 4:20-22, John 4:46-53, Leviticus 25:18, Proverbs 28:7, Acts 27:34, Psalms 41:4, Isaiah 6:10, I Corinthians 6:19,20, Psalms 119:117, Jeremiah 3:22, James 5:14,15, Proverbs 2:11, Jeremiah 8:22. Career Education -- Matthew 6:24-34, Ephesians 4:1, I Timothy 6:1-3, I Cor. 3:11-23, Ephesians 6:5-9, Hebrews 11:13,14, I Cor. 10:31, II Thes. 3:4-13, James 4:12, II Cor. 5:14-20. Psychology -- Genesis 1:27, John 10:10, Galatians 5:22,23, Genesis 2:7, Romans 5:8,9,12, Ephesians 2:8,9, Ecclesiastes 12:7, Romans 6:23, Ephesians 5:18, Matthew 5:3-12, Romans 7:14-25, I Thes. 5:23, John 4:14, Romans 10:13.

9. Deuteronomy 6:1-7.

10. Deuteronomy 6:7.

11. Deuteronomy 6:15.

12. Deuteronomy 6:21-25; Exodus 19:5-6; Deuteronomy 17:18-20 & 31:10-11.

13. MONTGOMERY *supra* note 1 at 50 (emphasis omitted).

14. JAMES KENT, COMMENTARIES ON AMERICAN LAW, 4 volumes (New York: O. Halsted, 1826; reprint ed., New York: Da Capo Press, 1971) 2:159.

> The next domestic relation which we are to consider, is that of parent and child. The duties that reciprocally result from this connection, are prescribed, as well as those feelings of parental love and filial reverence which Providence has implanted in the human breast, as by the positive precepts of religion, and of our municipal law.

The wants and weaknesses of children render it necessary that some person maintain them, and the voice of nature has pointed out the parent as the most fit and proper person. The laws and customs of all nations have enforced this plain precept of universal law. *Id.*

This domestic relationship was by definition, an essential ingredient of education. In Noah Webster's 1828 dictionary, "education" is defined as:

The bringing up, as of a child; instruction; formation of manners. Education comprehends all that series of instruction and discipline which is intended to enlighten the understanding, correct the temper, and form the manners and habits of youth, and fit them for usefulness in their future station. To give children a good education in manners, arts and science, is important; to give them a religious education is indispensable; and an immense responsibility rests on parents and guardians who neglect these duties.

Webster thus reiterates the key aspects of Kent's discussion on parental rights and education.

15. It should be evident to even the most detached observer that parents who simply wish to transmit their religious or their cultural values to their children, or perhaps desire to teach their children in their native tongue, would benefit from such an approach. These parents would not have to spend their valuable time arguing with the local government or its school board over curriculums adverse to their religion, cultural values or language.

16. KENT *supra* note 14 at 2:169.

17. KENT *supra* note 14 at 2:169.

18. FRANCIS WAYLAND, THE ELEMENTS OF MORAL SCIENCE, 4th ed. (Boston: Gould, Kendall and Lincoln, 1841).

19. *Id.* at 324.

20. A parent may not hide behind the pretended exercise of their unalienable right and utilize their children in criminal enterprises while claiming that it is an unalienable right which they are exercising. Such activity would be a pretext since parents would not be exercising a right, but engaging in a criminal wrong. But by the same force of reasoning, government incantation of "general welfare" or "the child's best interests" does not itself establish a legal basis for usurpation of parental rights. The abuse of power through pretext is certainly not beyond the civil government's capacity either.

21. The rule has been stated, that "[a] natural parent should not be deprived of its child's custody by a non-parent except upon a finding of unfitness for the exercise of parental responsibility, of parental neglect, or of abandonment." In re Ernst, 373 Mich 337, 129 NW2D 430 (1964). The parent has and should have a superior right to the custody of his child and his poverty or lack of financial means should not be given any great weight to deprive him of this natural right.

Three different types of "best interest" cases exist which depend on the relationship of the parties to the child. The parties are usually the state versus parents, parent versus parents, and parents versus non-parent third parties.

First, there are cases in which the state seeks to deprive the natural parent of his or her child for statutory neglect or abandonment. These proceedings neither require nor permit any judicial consideration of "the child's best interests" unless and until an initial finding of parental neglect or abandonment has been made. Second, there are cases in which one parent is pitted against the other parent for their child's custody, or in proceedings ancillary to divorce actions which present the opportunity for a judicial custodial disposition of a child. In these second types of cases, the Court will first consider the child's best interest without any prior need to establish unfitness, abandonment or terminate parental rights.

Third, there are cases that equate the child's best interest with the natural parents' right to their child. These are the cases in which a natural parent seeks to recover custody of his child from a third party (who is not the other parent). In such instances, a Court will generally equate the child's best interests with custodial care by its natural parent, rather than a third party stranger. This is so because,

> 'In all civilized countries, in which the family is regarded as the unit of social organization, its minor members must and ought to be subject to the custody and control of those who are immediately responsible for their being, for the reason that by nature there has been implanted in the human heart those seeds of parental and filial affection that will assure to the infant care and protection in the years of its helplessness, to be returned to the parents again when they in their turn may need protection, in their years of helplessness and of their child's strength and maturity. The law, at the birth of an infant, imposes upon the parents the duty of such care and protection, to the performance of which the instincts of nature so readily prompts, and clothes him with the right of custody, that he may perform it effectually, upon the presumption that such custody, being in harmony with nature, is best for the interest, not only of the parent and child, but also of society; conceding, however, that the primary object is the interest of the child, the presumption of the law is that its interest is to be in the custody of its parent.'

In re Ernst, 373 Mich at 364-65 citing Weir v. Marley, 99 Mo 484, 494, 495 (12 SW 798, 6 LRA 672).

22. Someone will no doubt create a factual hypothetical to test the outer boundaries of this rule. They will cast parents in the worst possible light as ignorant or to be pitied. The civil government, however, (as these arguments generally go) is presented as the incarnation of virtue and compassion. No valid presumption, however, can be drawn against all parents generally and in favor of all levels of government irrespective of whatever a specific fact pattern may indicate. The correct rule should be that absent the legal destruction of the marital relationship or a lawful adjudication of unfitness based on physical abuse, the civil government simply has no jurisdiction and is not authorized to act in the "best interest of the child."

Both Kent and Wayland recognized parental rights and understood that its exceptions do not generally empower the state to trample the unalienable rights of all parents or implement its vision of a good society in which the civil power ultimately makes all of the educational decisions *for all parents*. Government abuse of parental rights will certainly not be pointed out by the government. Parents will, therefore, have to assert that a good society is not one identified by the systematic obstruction of unalienable rights.

23. The shortcomings and wrongfulness of governmental control of education and schools is discussed in ROCKNE M. MCCARTHY, JAMES W. SKILLEN, & WILLIAM A. HARPER, EDS., DISESTABLISHMENT A SECOND TIME: GENUINE PLURALISM FOR AMERICAN SCHOOLS (Grand Rapids, MI: Christian University Press, 1982); JOHN T. GATTO, DUMBING US DOWN: THE HIDDEN CURRICULUM OF COMPULSORY SCHOOLING (Philadelphia: New Society Publishers, 1992); DAVID HARMER, SCHOOL CHOICE: WHY YOU NEED IT-HOW YOU GET IT (Washington, D.C.: CATO Institute, 1994); SHELDON RICHMAN, SEPARATING SCHOOL AND STATE: HOW TO LIBERATE AMERICA'S FAMILIES, (Fairfax, Virginia: The Future of Freedom Foundation, 1994); MARSHALL FRITZ, NO MORE "PUBLIC SCHOOL REFORM" (Fresno, CA: Separation of School and State Alliance, 1996).

24. 262 U.S. 390 (1923).

25. *Id.* at 400 citing the Northwest Ordinance of 1787 which declares: "Religion, morality, and knowledge being necessary to good government and the happiness of mankind, schools and the means of education shall forever be encouraged."

26. 262 U.S. at 400. The holding in *Meyer* has been severely distorted by various lower courts. For instance in Clonlara Inc. v. Runkel, 722 F.Supp. 1442 (E.D. Mich, 1989) the Magistrate's opinion cited *Meyer* for the proposition that parental rights are not fundamental, meaning that state regulation of parental rights need not be strictly scrutinized by the courts. *Id.* at 1456. The court therefore concluded that reasonable regulations on the rights of parents are permissible.

What portion of the *Meyer* opinion led the lower court to this interpretation? The lower court quoted the Supreme Court: "The power of the state to compel attendance at some school and to make reasonable regulations for all schools, including a requirement that they shall give instructions in English, is not questioned." *Id.* citing 262 U.S. at 402. Examination of the context in which the *Meyer* court made this statement, however, indicates that the Supreme Court was declaring that pervasive regulation was *not at issue* before the Court. The Supreme Court was not making the argument that the state's power to compel attendance is settled. The entire quote declares that;

> The power of the State to compel attendance at some school and to make reasonable regulations for all schools, including a requirement that they shall give instructions in English, is not questioned. Nor has challenge been made of the State's power to prescribe a curriculum for institutions which it supports. *Those matters are not within the present controversy.*

262 U.S. at 402 (emphasis added).

27. 262 U.S. at 400.

28. 347 U.S. 483 (1954).

29. *Id.* at 493. For a general overview of compulsory attendance laws including the criminal status of parents who refuse to submit their children to the reach of those laws, *see* 78A Corpus Juris Secundum §§ 697-725 and §§ 734-743 (St. Paul, MN: West Publishing Co, 1995).

30. Wayland *supra* note 18 at 324. In "Politics, Markets and America's Schools," John E. Chubb and Terry Moe argue that "existing institutions cannot solve the problem, because they *are* the problem -- and that the key to better schools is institutional reform." Instead of turning to the unalienable and natural rights of parents as does Wayland, however, the authors declare that "[t]he fundamental point to be made about parents and students is not that they are politically weak, but that . . . the public schools are *not meant* to be theirs to control and are literally *not supposed* to provide them with the kind of education they might want. The schools are agencies of society as a whole, and everyone has a right to participate in their governance." Though their analysis of the present institutional situation is perceptive, they fail to consider the unalienable rights of parents and entirely misapprehend the object of civil government.

Their basic approach is a free market theory of education revolving around parental choice. This may sound appealing, but there can be no real choice (or free market) in education until compulsory attendance and compulsory exposure to state approved and regulated curriculums are abolished. Until that happens, the application of a market theory to education is inappropriate, since choice is irrelevant if one may only choose among schools within the state's educational monopoly or among schools subject to that monopoly's regulation or control. *See* John E. Chubb and Terry Moe, Politics, Markets and America's Schools (Washington, D.C.: The Brookings Institution, 1990) 3, 32.

31. Montgomery, Question *supra* note 1 at 52.

32. Meyer v. Nebraska, 262 U.S. 390, 401 (1923).

33. Nothing is so opposed to consent as force and fear.

34. Of course, when children become of age they may make the decision regarding what teachers if any, they will retain. Such is the case with college or university instruction. These institutions, however, are not based on compulsory attendance laws. The present discussion of compulsory education laws involves minor children who are not legally emancipated from their parents.

Chapter 5

State Approved Citizens

The burden of proof rests with the civil government to document that its system of governmental education--established, operated and financed on the palladium of force and coercion--can produce a citizen whose mind is free from regulation, whose labor and its fruit are his choice and doing, and whose genuine acts of citizenship spring from true volition.[1]

The Arguments

The last Chapter examined the unalienable right of parents and asserted that civil government's compulsory attendance and education laws abridged such rights. Subsequent Chapters will explore other State education laws relating to compulsory financial support, teacher certification and approved curriculum. But this Chapter pauses to consider the rationales which undergird and prop up all such laws and are usually raised in objection to the type of parental rights so far examined.

The general arguments (including countless variations thereof) are that civil government's control of education is necessary for 1) ensuring democracy, 2) transmitting common values, and 3) education of the poor. These may be stated in proposition format as follows:

1) State control of education is necessary, because an educated populous is essential to good citizenship and the perpetuation of our democratic government, and

2) State control of education is necessary, because it ensures the transmission of commonly held American cultural values essential to the perpetuation of our institutions, and

3)   State control of education is necessary, because the rich will never voluntarily pay for the education of the poor.

The Guarantee of "Democracy"

The first proposition is that state control of education is necessary, because an educated populous is essential to good citizenship and the perpetuation of our democratic government. It is certainly true that an educated citizenry is necessary to perpetuate our form of government, but does it follow that such a result is ensured by governmental control, regulation or oversight of public and private K-12 education, rather than by parental control, regulation or oversight of their own child's education?

The Supreme Court has consistently parroted the doctrine that the sole guarantor of an educated citizenry is the state approved public or private school. In a parade of its own opinions (why look for any other "authority") the Court has affirmed that:

> Education is perhaps the most important function of state and local governments.   Compulsory school attendance laws and the great expenditures for education both demonstrate our recognition of the importance of education to our democratic society. It is required in the performance of our most basic public responsibilities, even service in the armed forces. It is the very foundation of good citizenship. Today it is a principal instrument in awakening the child to cultural values, in preparing him for later professional training, and in helping him to adjust normally to his environment. In these days, it is doubtful that any child may reasonably be expected to succeed in life if he is denied the opportunity of an education. Such an opportunity, where the state has undertaken to provide it, is a right which must be made available to all on equal terms.[2]

The Court is arguing that the civil government is responsible for awakening the child to cultural values, preparing the child for professional training, and helping the child to adjust to the social and political environment. (The qualification, "where the state has undertaken to provide it" is gratuitous). Cultural values recognized by the state, have replaced parental values.   The responsibility of preparation for a job or future labor has been taken from the parents and given to the state. The state, and not parents, will conform the child to the civil government's social and political image.

The Court adds the patronizing comment that "[i]n these days, it is doubtful that any child may reasonably be expected to succeed in life if he is denied the opportunity of an education." Parents, do you hear what the Court thinks of your abilities to direct the education of your own child without its coercive apparatus? The Court says it is "doubtful" your child can succeed in life if denied the opportunity of an education. Of course the Court means an "opportunity" for an education provided by state and local governments and backed by "compulsory school attendance laws" and "great expenditures" of public money.[3]

✓ Key Idea:

☞ OF WHAT VALUE IS A "FREE" PUBLIC EDUCATION IF A CHILD'S MIND IS *CONFORMED* TO THE GOVERNMENT'S POINT OF VIEW AND *ALIENATED* FROM HIS OR HER PARENT'S VALUES OR TRAINING?

The Court's confidence in governmental controlled schools, however, is misplaced given the fact that every year in this country many children *graduate from governmental controlled public high schools who can neither read nor write.* If doubt is to be expressed, then let the Court rather say: "It is doubtful that any child may reasonably be expected to succeed in life where he or she is subjected to compulsory attendance at a state influenced, regulated or controlled school." Moreover, the Court's use of the phrase "[i]n these days" to preface its doubts, also indicates that the Court believes that changes in social conditions warrant an increase in the power of the state to compel education, and thereby implicitly warrant a further decrease in the rights of parents. It is not, however, for the Court to adjust unalienable rights to the ebb and flow of history.

The Court has navigated far from the law into unadulterated social policy and has made preposterous assertions in support of its policy. For instance, it has asserted that historic "perceptions of the public schools as inculcating fundamental values necessary to the maintenance of a democratic political system have been confirmed by the observations of social scientists."[4] The laws of nature, however, do not speak of the unalienable rights of social scientists to confirm fundamental values. Nor does the Declaration allude to it. The duty, right and opinions of parents, however, arise from nature and are evenly implied in the Declaration. The opinions of social scientists who do not regard the Declaration are useless, as is the opinions of those who quote them.

A closer examination of the proposition that state control of education is necessary because an educated populous is essential to the perpetuation of good citizenship and our democratic government, suggests that it can be broken down into two components. That, 1) an educated populous is necessary to perpetuate our democracy, and 2) such an educated populous can be best ensured by governmental control of public and private education. These propositions presuppose that educational content currently is, or should be, related to citizenship, our form of government and the law of the land. They also presuppose that civil government is an objective and neutral provider of knowledge about itself and its actions. Both of these presumptions are, however, against every bit of reason and all experience.

The Guarantee of Republican Government

Is an educated populous necessary for the perpetuation of our democracy? The question itself amply illustrates the modern problem. The characterization of the United States as a democracy is quite alien to its form of government. The United States is not a democracy but rather is a limited Constitutional Republic by design. The clear language of Article IV, section 4 of the Constitution also ensures that the United States will guarantee to each and every state a "republican form of government."

That the Court presently regards the divine object of education to be the perpetuation of democracy is an embarrassing byproduct of governmental control. Such control has superimposed over the history of American government a mistaken evolutionary paradigm in which the United States is evolving from whatever it was to something much better than what it is. This march of democracy is thus more accurately a decline of the Republic. So the question "Is an educated populous necessary to the perpetuation of our democracy?" is simply the wrong question. It is an uninformed question. Yet, it is the common chorus line of a government educated citizen.

✓ Key Idea:

☞   PERPETUATION OF OUR REPUBLICAN FORM OF GOVERNMENTAL IS *JEOPARDIZED* BY GOVERNMENTAL CONTROL OF PUBLIC AND PRIVATE EDUCATION.

How is it, that the modern state control of education has produced a judiciary and citizen who can not distinguish between the American Republic and a democracy? How can such a coercive enterprise as governmental control of education have failed to produce even a basic understanding about the very nature and form of our government? The civil government must be a very poor communicator. One can imagine that its transmission of more ambiguous cultural values is mangled far worse. This wretched condition suggests the actual rule to be stated as follows:

    1) that an educated populous is necessary to perpetuate our American form of limited Constitutional government and,

    2) perpetuation of that republican form of government is clearly *jeopardized* by governmental control of public and private education.

In fact, the citizens of this country as well as its republican form of government have been *compromised and jeopardized* by governmental control of public and private education.

The burden of proof is on the civil government. Can the civil government best ensure freedom through a closed and coercive monopoly of state dictated ideas, state approved teachers, state mandated attendance and state economic subsidization? The civil government must demonstrate that its system of government education--established, operated and financed on the palladium of force and coercion--can produce a citizen whose mind is free from intimidation, who can choose his or her profession free from government "assistance" and enjoy the fruit of that labor, and whose genuine acts of citizenship spring from volition. A government which tramples any of these rights or choices is not a good government.

✓ Key Idea:

☞   GOOD CITIZENS CANNOT BE PRODUCED BY BAD GOVERNMENTS.

It is written that a good tree bears good fruit, and a bad tree bears bad fruit. Can we honestly expect that a system of education built on state force and coercion will generally bear the fruit of individual freedom and volition? There are many who believe that a system of coercion makes men free, but the truth is that these disciples of coercion earn their living from the fruit of governmental edicts confiscating money from their neighbor's pocketbook.

On its face, the governmental objective of educating the citizenry about citizenship and the preservation of the principles of our government has failed miserably. The public school populous is not educated in citizenship at all. As a result of their government coerced education, they have come to disrespect the Declaration of Independence and Constitution as meaning exactly what they state. The Declaration grounds the entire American experiment on the "Laws of Nature and of Nature's God." It affirms that our Creator gives to all persons certain unalienable rights. It recognizes that civil governments have one cardinal purpose--to secure these rights on an equal basis. It charges the people--the educated populace, the citizens--with instituting a government on such principles and in such a form as will secure those rights. It recognizes that the citizens of this country may also alter or destroy their governments. The Constitutions of the states and the federal Constitution followed these principles. This is what an educated citizenry should know.[5]

The laws of nature's God, the Creator, equality, unalienable rights, and the right to create and abolish their civil governments, however, are not the subject matter of governmental controlled public and private schools. It can hardly be expected that those who teach--who dismiss the key documents of the United States, who are mortified with public discourse of their actual texts, and who have a vested financial stake in perpetuation of the present system--are able to rise above their own self-interest and educate their neighbor's children in the preservation of the principles of our government. The issue is not their *qualifications*, but rather of their *self-interest*. Like every financially animated special interest group, the self-interest of the professional educator has time and again, come well ahead of any notion so ambiguous as the preservation of democracy or transmission of cultural values.

Parents nevertheless, are less motivated from self-interest and more inclined to educate their own flesh and blood from a natural desire to see their own child's future usefulness and happiness in life secured. In this context of love and parental desire is the seed for teaching a child the meaning of freedom and citizenship. But the context of coercion administered by paid professionals, propped up by state force, state mandates and state compulsion, cannot systematically produce any such result. Those who hope to the contrary, do so in vain. It is only profound arrogance which insists that a parent will not render an education to his or her own child which is due from familial love, but that a paid professional educator is uniquely qualified to render the same (as long as the latest round of collective bargaining goes their way).

Transmission of Cultural Values

The second assertion is really the social equivalent of the first contention just examined. It is argued that state control of education is necessary, because it ensures the transmission of commonly held American cultural values. The Supreme Court has also advanced this proposition. In *Ambach v. Norwick*,[6] the Court approvingly observed that other authorities "have perceived public schools as an 'assimilative force' by which diverse and conflicting elements in our society are brought together on a broad but common ground."[7] The "other" authority to whom the Court refers is John Dewey and a full quotation of the Court's reference discloses much about the Court's lunge into the assimilation abyss. The full quotation is as follows:

> The assimilative force of the American public school is eloquent testimony to the efficacy of the common and balanced appeal.
>
> The school has the function also of coordinating within the disposition of each individual the diverse influences of the various social environments into which he enters. One code prevails in the family; another, on the street; a third, in the workshop or store; a fourth, in the religious association. As a person passes from one of the environments to another, he is subjected to antagonistic pulls, and is in danger of being split into a being having different standards of judgment and emotion for different occasions. This danger imposes upon the school a steadying and integrating office.

In other words, it is the governmental controlled public school, and not the family, which provides the steady influence preventing a child from "having different standards of judgment and emotion for different occasions." In the government regulated world of Dewey and the Court, every family, every employer and every religious institution is suspect in creating a world of dangerous contradictions, while the government school alone stands free from this influence and danger! The Court's belief that the school stands free from the influence and danger of antagonistic pulls is absurd.

In reality, it is the governmental controlled school which is guilty of antagonistic pulls and which inculcates different standards of judgment and emotion for different occasions. This danger in turn imposes upon the family, employer, church and criminal courts a steadying and disintegrating force. Many parents have recognized the danger of assimilation. Parents who seek to impart their ethnic, cultural, linguistic or religious values and outlook to their children must realize that government oversight of education is designed to result in comprehensive assimilation of family and religion into the government's cultural construct.

✓ Key Idea:

☞ JOHN DEWEY THOUGHT THAT CULTURAL DISINTEGRATION AROSE FROM ASSOCIATION WITH FAMILY, FRIENDS, THE EMPLOYER, AND RELIGION. HIS SOLUTION, GOVERNMENTAL CONTROL OF EDUCATION, HOWEVER, HAS PROVEN THE REAL BREEDING GROUND OF CULTURAL DECAY.

Exposing the minds of children to those ideas which obtain the approval of the state is the sum and substance of assimilation. Assimilation of a child's way of thinking to the state's way of thinking is accomplished by exposing a child to ideas that either exclude God's relevance to all of life, exclude ideas which simply differ from the ideas parents wish to impart or communicate to their child, or exclude ideas entirely inconsistent with those of the child's parents. Textbook selection in particular is intended to assimilate a child's way of thinking to the government's conception of a "broad but common" way of seeing the world. The phrase "broad, but common" means broad enough to include many ideas parents object to, and common enough to keep out the ideas many individual parents want to convey. Education related laws are not designed by any stretch of reason or the imagination to help *parents* educate their children.[8]

Predictably, in *Plyler v. Doe*,[9] the Court reaffirmed that public schools are "the primary vehicle for transmitting 'the values on which our society rests.'"[10] This is most certainly a falsehood. Public schools more often than not, teach students to reject the values of their parents. "Our children are being brainwashed with the latest ideological fashions -- whether about homosexuality, environmentalism, multiculturalism or a thousand other non-academic distractions."[11] These are not the values upon which our society rests. Our society rests on the self-evident truths found in the Declaration of Independence-- the laws of nature and nature's God, equality, unalienable rights, government by consent and the unalienable right to alter or abolish civil government.

The arguments previously advanced in the section discussing education for democracy also apply here equally. Recall that the family and voluntary organizations such as private philanthropy and religion are the legitimate transmitters of commonly held cultural values, not the civil government which has a vested self-interest in reducing its citizens from freemen to employable tenants and tax paying underlings. Thus, a state educated citizen is a slave to its master.

Compassion for the Poor

It is also argued that state control of education is necessary, because the rich will never voluntarily show compassion and pay for the education of the poor. At the root of this argument is an assumption that lack of compassion, or selfishness and self-dealing are vices. These vices ought not be tolerated by society and, therefore, society may impose upon the general populous taxation for the support of public schools, teachers and administrators.

From a legal and jurisdictional point of view, the vices of selfishness and self-dealing are neither criminal nor civil offenses. The civil government has no jurisdiction to punish such attitudes. The civil government may not punish wrong thoughts or wrong values. Under the law of nature, civil government's authority is limited to punishment of certain wrongful *conduct* alone. A selfish man may be guilty of a sinful state of mind, but unless his selfishness breaks out into overt acts against the public peace and order (such as theft), his state of mind is not subject to the phoney moralizing of governmental officials about compassion.

Selfishness and self-dealing are none the less vices which affect *all* men and women in common whether or not they are rich or poor. The consequences of these vices suggest that both rich and poor must suffer from lack of compassion. Both rich and poor share equally in the vices because both are human beings. Such vices affect *all* men and women including parents, elected officials, school board members and professional teachers. These are all human beings and so they must likewise be subject to the same vices as their fellow man.

Thus, when "Person A" demands that "Person B" open his pocketbook to "Person A" as a sign of "B's" compassion, "B's" response ought to be an absolute refusal followed by the charge that "A" is attempting to perfect the vices of covetousness and selfishness. So too when state lawmakers or local school board members *compel by law*, that local citizens open their pocketbooks to fund education as a sign of the community's care and compassion, the community ought to respond with an absolute refusal and then charge state lawmakers and local school board members with the vices of covetousness and selfishness.

Yet, this is hardly ever the response. It does not seem to occur to the average person that such demands by governmental officials are both petty and selfish. A demand that "Person B" support "Person A's" educational goals cannot be said to reflect either "B's" generosity or "A's" compassion. Rather than expressing an unselfish concern for the welfare of others (such as "the children"), the demands of state lawmakers or local school board members actually embody a selfish concern for their own happiness, gain and political viability.

Such demands are *petty* because governmental officials do not want to eliminate the vice they profess to disdain. As a matter of fact their entire argument for continued expansion of the government's educational monopoly is premised on the enlargement of the vice of selfishness. Were the vices of self-dealing and lack of compassion actually reduced, so too the pretended legitimatizing rationale for the educational monopoly would decrease.

In other words, government extraction of money from both rich and poor through property, sales, and income taxes, does not seek to extinguish the vice of selfishness at all. The petty humanitarianism of governmental officials and school board members has nothing to do with reducing the vices of selfishness or lack of compassion. Their petty altruism, however, has everything to do with propagating a convenient pretext for the state to obtain money from those who have it.

✓ Key Idea:

☞ THE STATE'S MISUSE OF "COMPASSION" AS A JUSTIFICATION FOR FINANCING ITS SYSTEM OF COMPULSORY EDUCATION, IS A PRETEXT FOR THE STATE TO TAKE MONEY FROM THOSE WHO HAVE IT, IN ORDER TO BRIBE THOSE WHO COVET IT.

Moreover, official moralizing about compassion is not only petty, but it is *selfish* as well. Such moralizing fails the cardinal test of altruism. Altruism involves an unselfish concern for the welfare of others. Government claims of "compassion" fall short of altruism because governmental officials are being generous with someone else's money. A man is regarded as generous or unselfish where he freely gives money to others from his own pocketbook, without any expectation of something in return. If a man, however, offers another person money from his *neighbor's* pocketbook and not his own, then he is a thief. Moreover, if he offers someone else his neighbor's money and expects a favor in return, then that man is a thief offering a bribe.

Yet, when state governmental officials, in cooperation with local school boards, presume to impose governmental control of public and private education upon a local community and moreover, they establish a system of compulsory support by offering parents of school aged children, money from their *neig . no 's* pocketbook and not from the official or member's own pocketbook, then such officials and members do not practice either compassion, altruism or generosity at all.[12]   Despite all the government's petty moralizing about the general taxpaying public's aversion to showing compassion for the poor, human society is not so reprobate as to fail to provide private assistance in the education of others. Religious, private and philanthropic organizations abound and have shown compassion by *giving* beyond their ability in order to help others.

Compassion by its very nature involves a volitional act. If compassion is compelled by force, then it is not compassion which is being expressed, but rather it is malice.   If compassion is to be the universal rule of conduct, then civil government itself ought to practice compassion with respect to parents who seek to educate their own children without any of the state's interference, oversight, regulation or control. The compassionate approach would not force parents into the state's system against their will or belief.[13]

✓ Key Idea:

☞   COMPASSION EMPHASIZES FREELY GIVING TO
        OTHERS, NOT FORCEFULLY TAKING FROM OTHERS
        UNDER THE THREAT OF PUNISHMENT.

What about Parents who Neglect their Duty?

It is true that some children will be denied a proper education because of the irresponsible and profligate lifestyle of their parents. Moreover, some children will not receive a complete education because their conscientious parents are not able to spend the necessary time or do not have the financial wherewithal to hire a teacher to educate on their behalf. Some families will invariably fall through the cracks. The remedy for such a situation, however, is certainly not that the state should compel *all* children to be educated in its schools! The parental inability of some parents is no argument for governmental control of all education.

But the threat of children falling through the cracks will no doubt be absorbed in principal part by teacher union free schools. For teachers' unions have been assuring parents for years that they have been operating public school at peak efficiency, with superb results and in a spirit of genuine public service. Surely these venerable public spirited organizations will step forward to ensure that every parent has the help they need, even at some financial cost to a union's own welfare. Let parents also approach those political parties who advocate compassion for the financially poor, seeking to convert those representations into voluntary assistance. Certainly the unions and politicians will not turn needy parents away where their *own* personal wealth is at stake, for they heaped lavish assistance upon others when their neighbor's pockets were being emptied through coercion.

The argument that "compassion" warrants the compulsory education of a child where the parent neglects same suggests the following rule. It has already been observed that the failure of a parent to provide any education for their own children whatsoever, is not evidence in regards to a parent's unfitness. Such conduct *standing alone and unaccompanied by an additional judicial finding* of material cruelty or abandonment, habitual drunkenness, or criminal depravity, is under the laws of nature, and ought to be under the laws of the states, insufficient to establish parental unfitness or neglect. In fact, it is no more neglect or criminal to fail to teach one's child to read his ABC's, than it is neglect or criminal to fail to teach one's child to read his catechism or religious doctrines. If parents fail to educate their own child, they may not be subject to loss of custody or punishment by the civil government, any more than if they fail to teach their child about God or religion.

What about Teachers who Neglect their Duty?

But *if* the failure to educate *were within the power of the legislature to punish*, then many teachers, administrators, and professional educators ought to be adjudicated habitual criminals. Every functionally illiterate high school graduate would be able to establish a *prima facia* case of a pattern or practice of abuse, neglect or other criminal conduct. This would be especially true for public school teachers since the teacher-child relationship arises by the force of statute law alone and is not a natural one.

State imposed criminal sanctions, however, are no more proper for parents than for teachers. The true sanction against parents who simply neglect their educational duty is for their neighbors to privately confront them and then openly criticize them. Moral persuasion and public shame, not civil punishment, is the correct sanction. But parents are not uncaring villains. By and large, parents want an education for their children: they will not leave them ignorant.

To the mocker who scoffs: "Well what about the children? -- You would keep them ignorant and illiterate!" it may be inquired, "Well, what *about* the children? What civil remedy *presently exists* for the child who has been instructed compulsorily by the state, but can neither read nor write?" Shall the state legislature grant a legal cause of action to a child against his public school teacher, because his grammar and spelling are inferior? What student would not have a cause of action on some count?[14]

Recognition of the fact that there will be some children who are not going to be formally educated, is simply to recognize and admit that the same situation under the present educational arrangement already exists. The present system of governmental control has not achieved perfection. It is absurd to demand perfection from a free system. If the natural love of parents both rich and poor, for their own children is left free from governmental constraint, the probability their children will receive a good education is better than under the present system. The probability can also be increased when local, state and federal taxes which are presently taken from poor and rich alike to support education, are eliminated.

★ HYPOTHETICALLY SPEAKING . . . .

Problem #1: There were two men in a certain town, one rich and the other poor. The rich man had a very large number of sheep and cattle, but the poor man had nothing except one little lamb. He raised it and it grew up with him and his children. It was virtually a member of the family.

Now a hungry traveler came into town and stayed with the rich man. But instead of preparing meat to eat from his own herds, the rich man *took* the lamb that belonged to the poor man and prepared it for the traveler and himself. It was a fine meal.

You are a judge and the poor man comes to you for a remedy. What will you say and do?

Problem #2: There were two men in a certain state, one was the Governor and the other was a parent. The former controlled the administration of justice, but the parent controlled the education of his own child.

Now a special interest group came to town and stayed with the Governor. They encouraged the Governor to also take control of the education of children. So, not satisfied with the administration of justice which was rightly his, the Governor *took* the education of children away from the parent. The Governor educated the parent's child in the Governor's own schools and in the philosophy of the special interest group.

You are a judge and the parent comes to you for help. What will you say and do? *See* 2 Samuel 12:1-14.

Notes

1.   This text is the author's own words.   To a similar effect see *Hafen, The Constitutional Status of Marriage, Kinship, and Sexual Privacy-Balancing the Individual and Social Interests,* 81 Mich. L. R. 463, 480-81 (1983).

In the text, the word palladium refers to an idea or principle upon which the safety or security of a City or Nation depends. The word palladium also describes a sacred statue or image, and in ancient Greece and Rome referred to any statue of the Greek goddess of wisdom, Pallas Athena. As used herein, the palladium of force refers to our several civil governments' use of force and coercion, rather than reason and conviction, as its argument for control of education. From force and coercion civil government defends its control of American public and private education. While Greece turned to wisdom for its principles, America has turned to force and coercion as the basis for our National security. The state says, "Force, not reason is our argument."

2.   Plyler v. Doe, 457 U.S. 202, 222-23 (1982) quoting Brown v. Board of Education, 347 U.S. 483, 493 (1954).

3. When Mr. Justice McReynolds wrote in Meyer v. Nebraska, 262 U.S. 390 (1923) that compulsory laws are instituted to enforce the natural educational obligations of parents, he well described only one-half the correct legal rule. He neglected to consider whether any civil government has jurisdiction to compel a parental duty arising from the laws of nature and of nature's God. No civil government has such power. No state or national government has jurisdiction to act as a parent where the parents are not under a legal disability. No state or national government has jurisdiction over a child's mind by virtue of the child's birth or residence within its borders. If it were otherwise, the civil government could also claim jurisdiction to abridge the child's intellectual liberty *after* the child became an adult.

On the other hand, the duty of a parent to educate his or her child exists by virtue of their natural relationship. The means by which that duty is to be discharged is based on that natural relationship. The period of time over which the obligation is due is also governed by that relationship. The means by which a parent teaches his child is regulated by the terms of that relationship. These matters are governed not by the coercion of the civil government, but by the laws of nature, the bonds of parental love and the nature of their relationship.

The civil government, however, is not empowered to employ love as a vehicle for the administration of justice. It cannot and should not be thought that the use of civil coercion and force is a proper means by which ideas should ever be conveyed.

4. 457 U.S. at 221 quoting Ambach v. Norwick, 441 U.S. 68, 77 (1979).

5. Quite candidly, however, those who believe that a system of coercion makes free citizens and who employ the argument of an educated democracy as their pretense, are desperately torn between following some of the framer's *practices* with respect to colonial education, and adherence to the legal *principles* which the framers articulated.

6. 441 U.S. 68 (1979).

7. *Id.* at 77, citing JOHN DEWEY, DEMOCRACY AND EDUCATION, AN INTRODUCTION TO THE PHILOSOPHY OF EDUCATION, (New York: The MacMillan Company, 1916) 26 (quotation marks omitted).

8. For a legal analysis of state education laws as creating an impermissible presumption of guilt upon home schooling parents, *see* Alan P. Reed, *State Education Laws and the Irrebuttable Presumption of "Vlandis v. Kline"*, (Masters Thesis, Regent University, 1989).

9. 457 U.S. 202 (1982).

10. *Id.* at 221, quoting Ambach v. Norwick, 441 U.S. 68, 76 (1979).

11. Thomas Sowell, *Non-academic Classroom Distractions*, The Washington Times, June 1, 1992 at E1.

12. Does this mean, therefore, that state education and government officials, local school board members, and school teachers are all thieves offering a bribe? What it means is that when the civil government imposes governmental control of public and private education upon a local community, and establishes a system of compulsory support by offering local parents of school aged children money from their neighbor's pocketbook, that those who *benefit from this arrangement* are either knowing principals or unwitting accessories to theft and bribery.

For instance, elected legislative officials who support such an arrangement certainly benefit as principals to theft and bribery because they force money from their neighbor's pocket into their own pocket. (Their defense that such money is an appropriate tax used for the legitimate object of promoting the general welfare is unpersuasive, since it has already been shown that the suppression of unalienable rights is never in the general welfare.) Local school board members benefit from such an arrangement as accessories to the extent they are willful and willing players in the compassion con game. Public school teachers also benefit as accessories to the extent they remain silent when they ought to speak up against the immoral manipulation of parents and the local community by their educational unions and political operatives who propagate the falsely contrived drumbeat of showing "compassion for our children, our community and our future" or some other equally manipulative slogan. Private school teachers are also accessories to the extent their neighbor engages them in conversation about schools and education, and they fail to discuss the matter from the perspective of parental rights and limited state power.

13. In fact, true compassion for helping poor children receive the benefits of an education and rise above their circumstances must first begin with helping parents to see the nature of their rights and duties and then second, helping those parents who desire it, obtain private aid and resources available to them in their local community. With respect to the first, every parent rich or poor, has the right and duty to direct the education of his children. This right is to be exercised commensurate with the financial means available to a parent and with an appreciation of the child's abilities. Financial abundance or financial need does not alter or modify this right. Simply because parents are poor, suffer from adverse social attitudes, or suffer from the vestiges of past discrimination, does not diminish their unalienable right.

Francis Wayland has helped parents whether rich or poor, disadvantaged or advantaged, to understand their relative duties and rights. He says of a father for instance, that:

1. He [the father] is bound to inform himself of the peculiar habits, and reflect upon the probable future situation, of his child, and deliberately to consider what sort of education will most conduce to his future happiness and usefulness.

2. He is bound to select such instructors as will best accomplish the results which he believes will be most beneficial.

3. He is bound to devote such time and attention to the subject, as will enable him to ascertain whether the instructor of his child discharges his duty with faithfulness.

4. To encourage his child, by manifesting such interest in his studies as shall give to diligence and assiduity all the assistance and benefit of parental authority and friendship.

5. And, if a parent be under obligation to do this, he is, of course, under obligation *to take time to do it*, and so to construct the arrangements of his family and business, that *it may be done*. He has no right to say that *he has no time for these duties*. If God ha[s] required them of him, as is the fact, *he has time exactly for them*; and the truth is, he has not time for those other occupations which interfere with them. If he neglect[s] them, he does it to the injury of his children, and, as he will ascertain when it shall be too late, to his own disappointment and misery.

FRANCIS WAYLAND, THE ELEMENTS OF MORAL SCIENCE, 4th ed. (Boston: Gould, Kendall and Lincoln, 1841) 318-19 (emphasis in original).

In other words, parents whether rich or poor, must review their lifestyles and priorities. If a father, for instance, examines his family's financial picture and determines to put the education of his children in proper perspective, but still finds that he has neither the time or the money to educate, he should again consider whether "the truth is, he has not time for those other occupations which interfere with them." Single parents must also examine their household finances in the same way.

Parents must be able to turn to family, neighbors, private philanthropy or religious benevolence for help. They should approach such organizations and seek to work out temporary arrangements by which their parental obligations can be financially met. Such organizations also have a need to be good stewards of their finances and are entitled to review the financial habits of applicants in making a determination of their need. This is an opportunity for family, friends and local religious organizations to help each other, and not for the government to usurp control of education or try to make parents dependent upon itself. Moreover, the opportunity for teacher union operated schools to offer parents what they need will be present and will serve as the true test of professed unionized devotion to education absent the club of a state operated monopoly.

14. Let the public school teacher or governmental administrator who is without fault cast the first stone at these parents. But first, let that teacher recall that no child is fined for failing to pass an exam, and no public teacher is jailed for students who fail to learn. In fact, many teachers, regardless of their individual performance or the literary abilities of their graduates, receive a pay raise according to their union contract. In many instances, however, the parents of students who are home schooled without the permission of the civil government are jailed, irrespective of their child's performance. *See e.g.,* Jernigan v. State, 412 So.2d 1242 (Ala. 1982)(Criminal conviction of Catholic parents affirmed who did not send child to state approved public or private school). The Jernigan court expressly relied on the careless dicta of the Supreme Court in Meyer v. Nebraska, 262 U.S. 390, 400 (1923), that "[p]ractically, education of the young is only possible in schools conducted by especially qualified persons who devote themselves thereto" as a legal basis for state certification of home based teaching. *See* 412 So.2d at 1247.

Chapter 6

Public Servants and Public Masters

Now the teacher of a child is simply a person who, for the time being, acts as a substitute for its parents. But if a majority [of a community] has no right to select the principal, what right has it to select the substitute?[1]

Historical Background

Who really believes, as suggested by the above passage, that "the teacher of a child is simply a person who, for the time being, acts as a substitute for its parents?" Or perhaps the better question is: "Does a public school teacher believe that he or she is acting as a substitute for a child's parent, or instead that he or she is acting as an agent of the State?"

If these questions were examined in a detached intellectual sense, perhaps many teachers would acknowledge that they are temporary substitutes for the parent while the student is under their instruction. If the questions are considered in a legal sense, however, the waters begin to part very quickly. Examination of the demise of the idea that the teacher is the *sole agent* of the parent, will demonstrate how professional educators have been transformed from our public servants to our public masters through state compulsory attendance and education laws.

In reviewing the history of state involvement in education, the Supreme Court observed in *Abington School District v. Schempp,* that "[i]n the North American Colonies, education was almost without exception under private sponsorship and supervision . . . . This condition prevailed after the Revolution and into the first quarter of the nineteenth century." The Court noted that "[i]t was not until the 1820s and 1830s . . . that a system of public education really took root in the United States."[2] The Court is not saying that education was

73

neglected in the colonies. The colonists simply did not develop a system of education. More significantal, however, they did not develop a *governmental system* that controlled education. Colonial education was in fact decentralized, individualized, and voluntary.

The Puritans developed some of the first schools based on parental rights and decentralized control.[3] Although not perfect (nor claiming to be perfect), their Massachusetts Company was a notable example of voluntary education that came the closest to being a "system" if it could be called that.[4] Later on, northern states such as Massachusetts, followed the system approach and were more inclined toward instruction through a centralized system of education which in turn yielded itself more easily to governmental control.

Southern states on the other hand retained a decentralized approach to instruction and were more resistant to governmental control of education. Thus, the principal difference in education between the two regions pertained to the existence of a centralized system in the North as distinguished from a decentralized approach in the South. It is quite incorrect to conclude, however, that the South had no regard for education because it did not develop a centralized system or embrace governmental control.[5] Nor is it true "that Southerners had no interest in providing their children with an education"[6] simply because they were less inclined to rely on the civil government to mandate it.

On some occasions, particularly in the South, free schools taught students whose parents did not contract with tutors. These free schools were financed by civic-minded citizens, who voluntarily established such schools from their own private beneficence.[7] The teacher instructed the children according to the parents' direction and was paid either by the parents, or in the early part of the 18th century, by contributions from "Literary Funds." For example, in Virginia, such a fund was underwritten by civil fines and by escheats, not by property or general taxation.

✓ Key Idea:

☞ THE STATES' ADOPTION OF COMPULSORY ATTENDANCE LAWS IS A RELATIVELY MODERN EXERCISE OF STATE POWER.

It was not until 1852, however, that Massachusetts became the first state to enact a *compulsory attendance* law. The District of Columbia followed suit in 1864 and set off a chain reaction of enacting such laws among northern and western states. By 1890, 27 states (including the District of Columbia) had laws requiring compulsory attendance or education. But even these laws only required attendance generally between 12 to 20 weeks and only a portion of that time needed to be consecutive. The Southern states, however, did not adopt such laws until Tennessee and North Carolina authorized compulsion on a county by county basis in 1905 and 1907 respectively. Though Southern states such as Alabama, Georgia, Florida, Mississippi, South Carolina, Texas and Virginia did not legislate compulsion in attendance, this changed so that by 1929, every state in the Union (48 at that time) had one form or another of compulsory attendance or education law. Since that time, such laws have been strengthened, expanded, and in many instances constitutionalized. The length of attendance has been extended to 35 weeks in many states and the age for attendance has been expanded to often include 6 to 16 year old children. Thus, the compulsory attendance or education movement is quite a modern state establishment.[8]

In Loco Parentis

As previously discussed, the relationship between the parent and the teacher was not one defined by or grounded in the context of state compulsion. Rather, the relationship arose and was established in the soil of mutual voluntary association--an association between the teacher and parent grounded in the legal common law doctrine of *in loco parentis*. *In loco parentis* is a Latin term meaning, "in the place of a parent" or "in the stead of a parent." The doctrine applies in situations where parents delegate their parental authority to another. Pursuant to the doctrine of *in loco parentis*, a teacher could acquire the legal authority to teach a child. The authority or right was derivative, meaning that it flowed from a parent who alone had the authority to give it. The right was also intended to protect the teacher from interference from all other persons while acting *in loco parentis* (in the place of the parent). Of course the teacher's right was not intended to prevent interference from the parent who gave it!

Under this doctrine, the education of students proceeded without many problems. The lines of authority were clear. The teacher was charged with the responsibility of educating the child consistent with the authority delegated by the parent. Francis Wayland provides a very clear picture of this relationship, and his insight is worth a careful reading. He states:

> The authority of *instructors* is a delegated authority, derived immediately from the parent. He, for the time being, stands to the pupil *in loco parentis*. Hence the relation between him and the pupil is analogous to that between parent and child; that is, it is the relation of superiority and inferiority. The right of the instructor is to command; the obligation of the pupil is to obey. The right of the instructor is, however, to be exercised, as I before stated when speaking of the parent, for the pupil's benefit. For the exercise of it he is responsible to the *parent*, whose professional agent he is. He must use his own best skill and judgment in governing and teaching his pupil. If he and the parent cannot agree, the connection must be dissolved. But, as he is a professional agent, he must use his *own* intellect and skill in the exercise of his own profession, and in the use of it, he is to be interfered with by no one.[9]

In other words, the specific authority of the teacher was directly ascertained by referring to the written or verbal agreement existing between the teacher and the parent. If the right of the teacher was uncertain, the agreement between the teacher and the parent would be consulted. This agreement did not, however, modify or diminish the authority of a parent. It was predicated on the idea that parents were fully empowered by the laws of nature to hire tutors or agents to discharge a portion of their educational obligation. Wayland stated that the parent's "obligation requires that it be done either by a parent himself, or that he procure it to be done by another" with the caveat that "it can be done *only in part*" by the agent of the parent.[10]

✓ Key Idea:

   ☞   A TEACHER MUST FIRST OBTAIN THE PERMISSION OF THE CHILD'S PARENTS BEFORE BEGINNING TO TEACH THAT CHILD. A TEACHER'S KNOWLEDGE, ABILITY OR "STATE CERTIFICATION" ESTABLISHES NO RIGHT TO DIRECT A CHILD'S EDUCATION IN ANY WAY, AT ANY TIME, IN ANY PLACE, OR IN ANY MANNER.

Wayland did not say that an instructor could disregard the will of the parent. He recognized that the teacher's authority extended only as far as the parent permitted. That seems simple enough. Wayland pointed out that the "teacher is only the *agent*; the parent is the *principal*. The teacher does not remove from the parent any of the responsibility of his relation."[11] Thus, neither public or private school teachers possess a "right to teach." A school teacher's "right" is only derivative. That is to say, it is completely dependent on the pre-existing unalienable right of a parent. It is only derived from parental rights. Since the teacher can only be the agent of the parent, it also stands to reason that the teacher possesses only that authority with respect to a student which is delegated by the student's parent.

Moreover a teacher has no inherent or unalienable right (as a teacher alone) apart from the authority delegated by the parent. The teacher's authority to teach does not come from teacher organizations. Nor does it spring from the education, knowledge or certification of the teacher. In no instance ought the authority of the teacher to teach *in loco parentis* come from the state or federal government. For neither the state nor the federal government has an unalienable right to teach a child, and therefore neither the state nor the federal government has any jurisdiction to give such a right to another *in loco parentis*. A teacher is expected to utilize his or her professional experience to educate the child. That is why he or she was hired. This freedom, however, does not extend beyond what the parent directed or desired. Thus, the teacher is not "academically free" to violate parental authority to educate.

Application of the common law principle of *in loco parentis* to the parent-teacher-child relationship, however, was thwarted by virtually all the state legislatures in the early part of this century. As previously noted, the states adopted laws and often state constitutional provisions establishing public schools. The federal courts then relied upon these state legal provisions to untie the education of students from the teacher as an agent of the student's parents, thus undermining the doctrine of *in loco parentis*. In the place of parents, the courts instead tied the education of students directly to their teachers as agents of the state government (and not parents). For instance, it has been observed that the leading case of *Dixon v. Alabama State Bd. of Education*,[12] "implicitly rejected the in loco parentis concept, under which the law had bestowed on schools all the powers over students that parents had over their minor children."[13]

Parens Patriae

While the doctrine of *in loco parentis* in education was shrinking in scope, another common law doctrine was in expanding--the doctrine of *parens patriae*. *Parens patriae* literally means "Father of the country", "Parent of the country" or as King James I used the term "the political father of his people."[14] In England, the king was not only the government, but the king also claimed to be the father or parent of the people. The legitimate doctrine of *parens patriae* recognizes that the civil government may exercise the power of *wardship* over certain types of persons. The civil government's power of wardship may legitimately extend to persons who are under a disability, such as insanity and those who are lawfully declared mentally incompetent persons. The doctrine also takes into account minor children, but only under certain specific circumstances.

Joseph Story, a Justice of the United States Supreme Court from 1811 to 1845 and a legal scholar, traced the origin of the doctrine and found that is was presumably justified upon the notion that:

> the king is bound by the law of common right to defend his subjects, their goods, chattels, lands, and tenements; and therefore, in the law, every royal subject is taken into the king's protection. For which reason an idiot or lunatic, who cannot defend or govern himself, or order his lands, tenements, goods, or chattels, the king, of right, as *parens patriae*, ought to have in his custody, and rule him and them. And for the same reason, the king, as *parens patriae*, ought to have the care of the persons and property of infants, where they have no other guardian of either.[15]

When Story refers to idiots and lunatics, he means those persons who cannot defend or govern themselves. Thus, a person without understanding from birth would be considered an "idiot," while a person who was born sane but thereafter lost his memory or understanding would be regarded as a "lunatic." The whole point, however, of the King asserting authority over such persons, is that their defect in understanding warrants the civil government to care for and rule over such persons and to administer any property such persons may hold for their benefit. The modern legal equivalent of an idiot or lunatic is roughly someone who is mentally incompetent or insane.

But what about application of the same principle to infants or minors? Do they possess a defect in understanding in relation to their person or property? It cannot be maintained that a minor's lack of knowledge is the legal equivalent of an idiot or lunatics' lack of understanding. So the use of *parens patriae* jurisdiction on this point is defective. But more significantly, do minors universally lack "no other guardian" of either their person or property?

Story consistently affirms that the jurisdiction or authority of the civil government does not spring to life with respect to its *parens patriae* power over minors, except and unless such minors "have no other lawful protector."[16] Certainly, to the extent that the idiot or lunatic have no one who, on their behalf, will exercise understanding with respect to their person and property, then the civil government may employ its *parens patriae* power. But where parents stand in their natural relationship with their own children, then no *parens patriae* jurisdiction exists to superintend, supersede, or nullify that relationship.

Story's definitive historical review of *parens patriae* confirms this limitation on civil power. Story recognizes first of all that "in general, parents are intrusted with the custody of the persons, and the education of their children." He grounds this trust "upon the natural presumption, that the children will be properly taken care of, and will be brought up with a due education in literature, and morals, and religion; and that they will be treated with kindness and affection."[17] Thus, the legal presumption of the doctrine of *parens patriae* is that parents have the duty and right to direct the education and upbringing of their own children, and to do so without any interference, regulation or control interjected into the parent-child relationship by the state.

Compare this to the use and the *mis*use of *parens patriae* in the modern judicial context. For instance, in *Prince v. Massachusetts*,[18] the Supreme Court reasoned that "neither rights of religion nor rights of parenthood are beyond limitation. Acting to guard the general interest in youth's well being, the state as *parens patriae* may restrict the parent's control by requiring school attendance, regulating or prohibiting the child's labor and in many other ways." At issue in *Prince*, was not school attendance but rather a state child labor law which prohibited a child from working after hours (which in this case prevented her from the "work" of proselytizing or handing out religious literature.)

Whether the Court correctly states that "neither rights of religion nor rights of parenthood are beyond limitation" is not the point. Some rights are unalienable and as such in their legitimate exercise are in fact without limitation. Other rights are merely civil and as such may be limited. In point of fact, a parent's right to direct the education of his or her child is unalienable and without limitation in its sphere of exercise.

But conceding for a moment just for the sake of argument, that the right of parenthood is not beyond limitation, the controlling legal question is whether the doctrine of *parens patriae* empowers the state to "restrict the parent's control by requiring school attendance?" Recall that Justice Story recognized that the doctrine of *parens patriae* was grounded in the "natural presumption, that the children will be properly taken care of, and will be brought up with a due education" by their parents, not by the state. Story indicated that this presumption could be overcome by the state, but only if *it* carried the burden of production and proof establishing

> that a father is guilty of gross ill-treatment or cruelty toward his infant children; or that he is in constant habits of drunkenness and blasphemy, or low and gross debauchery; or that he professes atheistical or irreligious principles; or that his domestic associations are such as tend to the corruption and contamination of his children; or that he otherwise acts in a manner injurious to the morals or interests of his children.[19]

While the profession of atheistical or irreligious principles are morally counterproductive, they certainly constitute no basis for legal unfitness. With this acknowledgment, the rule is that absent a specific case by case finding of unfitness of the type described by Story, the doctrine of *parens patriae* cannot warrant loss of parental custody.

✓ Key Idea:

☞ THE STATE'S PURPORTED *PARENS PATRIAE* INTEREST IN UNIVERSAL COMPULSORY EDUCATION, IS UNQUESTIONABLY A LEGAL FRAUD UPON THE UNALIENABLE RIGHT OF PARENTS TO EDUCATE THEIR OWN CHILDREN.

Of more significance to the present discussion, however, is that as a matter of law, *parens patriae* has no bearing on compulsory school attendance. Thus, when the Supreme Court in *Prince* concluded, that "the state as *parens patriae* may restrict the parent's control by requiring school attendance," the Court misapplies and abuses the doctrine, and stretches it far beyond its legitimate purpose, context or meaning.[20]

When the state restricts the parent's control by requiring school attendance, it does so only by *usurpation* of the legitimate exercise of a parent's unalienable right to direct the education of their children free from state interference, regulation or control.[21]

The fact is, that modern compulsory attendance laws entirely reverse the legal presumption that parents enjoy the duty and right to direct the education of their own children, unless and except the state proves in a court of law on a case by case basis that a given parent has committed some act that warrants removal of the presumption. Rejecting this presumption categorically, state compulsory attendance laws adopt the opposite presumption, often irrebuttable, that parents do not enjoy the duty or right to direct the education of their own children, unless and except they comply with its compulsory attendance, compulsory certification, compulsory curriculum and compulsory financing schemes.

Parens patriae has been distorted to permit civil government to exercise a general jurisdiction over children. Once this legal sham was begun, the right and authority of parents became subordinated to the civil government. The doctrine of *in loco parentis* also became confused since the teacher began looking to the state for a derivative right to teach. The fountainhead of educational authority became the state rather than the parent or the teacher *in loco parentis*.

The School Board--From Servant to Master

Because American education was grounded historically in the doctrine of *in loco parentis*, it tended to be administered at a very decentralized level. When groups of parents who lived near each other joined together to educate their children, an organizational scheme responsive to parents in a locality was sought. Rather than individual parents contracting with individual teachers, parents now voluntarily delegated some responsibility to educate their children to a group of people chosen or elected by them. Thus, the idea of a local school board resulted. It was created to serve parents whose agent it was. The school board eventually became a widespread mechanism to assist parents in the education of their children. The school board was considered a means to assist parents to inculcate a set of *common values shared by the parents* in a locale or community. Thus, the school board was both accountable and responsive to the parents residing in that community. Their relationship was contractual as well as community based. The school board was representative of and responsible to the parents as their trustees much in the same way in which the teachers were held responsible to the parents as previously discussed. A trustee is one who acts on behalf of another for a specific purpose and is responsible to that person to perform all of the agreed obligations in a manner consistent with the trust or the agreement.

In the case of the school board, the agreement between the parents *at large* and the board with respect to the education of children, established the terms and obligations of their trust relationship. The board was therefore answerable to the parents who lived in the same local area or district. As teachers had no inherent authority to educate except pursuant to authority delegated by the parents, so too the school board had only that authority which parents in the community gave it. Teachers in turn became responsible to the school board as per agreements or contracts created between the school board and themselves, and the school board was subject to the parents as noted.

✓ Key Idea:

☞ TEACHERS, SUPERINTENDENTS AND SCHOOL BOARDS HAVE NO AUTHORITY OVER ANY CHILD UNLESS IT IS FREELY AND VOLUNTARILY DELEGATED BY A CHILD'S PARENT.

Needless to say, this entire arrangement of accountability (teachers to the school board and the school board to the parents of students) has been utterly lost or rejected. This relationship and accountability have become completely reversed, sometimes in a grotesque and frightful way. School boards rarely serve parents. School boards are no longer public servants of the student's parents. In many urban areas such as New York, they no longer even serve the community at large.[22]

Now what if a parent in the community objected to a school board's educational policy, but all the other parents wanted that policy? What if the common community values turned out to be not so common after all? What then? Well, if one parent objected to what the board was doing, but the rest of the parents in the locale approved of the board's action, the objecting parent had the option to withdraw his delegated authority from the school board and proceed to teach his child consistent with his own point of view. An alternative for such a parent was to retain a teacher or tutor directly or to relocate to a different locality.

This burden was not contrary to common sense, since the parent had the original responsibility to educate his or her child *in the first place*. This is very important since many have incorrectly assumed that the right of parents *is to have their children educated by the state*. This is the common absurdity of our day and reflects the passion of a slave for his master.

In times past the school board represented the majority of parents in their educational objectives, but even this has been turned on its head. It is not uncommon to have the majority of a community object to a given curricular decision and then watch the school board reject the will of that majority of parents in favor of a policy which promises certain political or financial rewards (what Thomas Jefferson would have characterized as a system of giving and taking bribes).[23]

To summarize, the right of a teacher was historically grounded in a contract delegating some of the authority of parents to direct the education of their children.[24] The right of a teacher was solely a function of the nature and extent of the delegated authority flowing from the parent. If the teacher objected to what a parent required, he or she would be under no obligation to remain in their employment. Once the agreement was struck, however, both parties were bound as with any contract. No one was forced to teach what they did not want to teach, but by the same token, parents were free to teach or have their children instructed as they wished. When the school board came into widespread use, the same principle applied. The teachers' rights were defined by their relationship with the school board which in turn was directly answerable to the majority of the parents within a given community.

Eventually these unique aspects of American public education, with its parent-directed and localized character, became suppressed. The legal right of parents to direct the education of their children through a teacher or school board based on the laws of nature was lost, forgotten or subverted. It was never refuted. In its place were substituted the powers of the state to educate. State governments began to assert that they had a vested interest in ensuring that all of *their citizens* were enlightened. That is to say, educated in a "broad, but common" *government-dictated outlook*. This approach assumed that the civil government is authorized or required to produce good citizens.[25]

To make a long historical story short, the school board was transformed from public servant to public master. Now the school board has become the public master of parents. School boards and teachers now tell parents what their children will learn whether parents like it or not.[26] The local school board was created to serve parents as their agent in matters of education but now parents must serve the school board. Unfortunately, neither political conservatives nor liberals seem to disagree over the basic premise that the state and the federal government should control or oversee education.[27]

★ HYPOTHETICALLY SPEAKING . . . .

Problem: A man had two employees. He said to the first: "Go and work in my field," to which the first employee said "yes," but he didn't go. Then the man said the same to his second employee, but the second said "no," though afterward he relented and went.

Which employee did the will of his employer? The one who said "yes" but didn't work for him or the one who said "no" and did work for him?

Answer: The one who worked followed the employer's will. So too, a school board which says "yes" to parents, but does not follow their will with respect to the education of their children, does not honor parents. A school board does the will of parents by first obtaining their permission before beginning to teach a parent's child.

Moreover the civil government which says "yes" to the people, but does not do the will of the people as declared in the Declaration (when it says that governments are instituted to secure unalienable rights), dishonors the people. The government which does the will of the people with respect to

education, is the one which secures the God-given unalienable rights of parents to direct the education of their own children.

Notes

1. ZACH MONTGOMERY, COMP., THE SCHOOL QUESTION FROM A PARENTAL AND NON-SECTARIAN STAND POINT, 4th ed. (Washington: Gibson Bros., 1889; reprint ed.; New York: Arno Press, 1972) 57.

2. 374 U.S. 203, 238-39 n.7 (1963)(Brennan, J. concurring).

3. In 1642 and then again in 1647/8 the Company enacted "The Old Deluder Satan Act." The Act's preamble declared the purpose of encouraging knowledge: "It being one chief project of that old deluder, Satan, to keep men from the knowledge of the Scriptures . . . and that learning may not be buried in the graves of our forefathers in Church and Commonwealth. . . ." THE LAWS AND LIBERTIES OF MASSACHUSETTS OF 1648 (Reprint ed., Birmingham: The Legal Classics Library, 1982) 47.

The purpose of education according to this law was two-fold: knowledge of Scripture and perpetuation of that knowledge. The means to achieve knowledge of the Scripture was also expressed by the law. The General Court ordered "That every Township . . . shall then forthwith appoint one within their town to teach all such children as shall resort to him to write and read . . . ." *Id.* This law did not require or compel parents to send their children to be educated. All that was required was that the *opportunity* for their education be made available. Parents who voluntarily sent their children to the locally appointed tutor, could have them taught to write and read the Scriptures. This was "public education" in a nutshell. Thus, the families in each township retained authority to teach their children.

4. "The Old Deluder Satan Act" provides that compensation of the tutor should be paid "either by the parents or masters of such children, or by the inhabitants in general by way of supply, as the major part of those that order the prudentials of the town shall appoint. Provided that those which send their children be not oppressed by paying much more than they can have them taught for in other towns." *Id.* Does this mean that all inhabitants were taxed for the education of a few, or that each *participating* parent could be required to bear a part of the costs of educating the children of the township? The language is admittedly confusing because it gives the power to decide the question to a majority of the local government. The text, however, seems to favor the view that general financial support could be ordered. Such a mandate for general support would come from an appointed committee which managed "prudentials" or the subordinate discretionary concerns and economy of the Massachusetts Bay Company. (Massachusetts did not become a Royal Colony until 1684.) Thus, the Puritans appear to have accepted the idea that civil government could compel each inhabitant to pay for the education of their neighbor's child. Such coercion does not square with the lawful scope of civil power under the laws of nature and of nature's God. *See* LAWS AND LIBERTIES *supra* note 3 at 47. *See also* ELLWOOD P. CUBBERLEY, PUBLIC EDUCATION IN THE UNITED STATES (New York: Houghton Mifflin Co., 1919) 17.

5. Prior to and after the Civil War, though northern and western states utilized civil power to establish school systems and tended to centralize that power, centralization was only required at a local community level.

In various southern states, however, parents did not delegate their responsibility to local government. Parents retained their God-given authority to educate their own children or obtained tutors under contracts. One author notes that "there were few towns in the colonial South. Its agricultural way of life, with widely scattered farms and plantations, made the establishment of an effective school system impossible." AVERY CRAVEN, WALTER JOHNSON, & F. ROGER DUNN, A DOCUMENTARY HISTORY OF THE AMERICAN PEOPLE (Ginn & Co.: New York, 1951) 119. *See also,* CHARLES W. DABNEY, UNIVERSAL EDUCATION IN THE SOUTH, VOL. 1: FROM THE BEGINNING TO 1900 (Chapel Hill: University of North Carolina Press, 1936).

6. CRAVEN, DOCUMENTARY HISTORY *supra* note 5 at 119.

7. *See* CRAVEN, DOCUMENTARY HISTORY *supra* note 5 at 119.

8. *See* PAUL MONROE, ED., A CYCLOPEDIA OF EDUCATION (New York: The Macmillan Press, 1919) 1:285-95; ELLWOOD P. CUBBERLEY, PUBLIC EDUCATION IN THE UNITED STATES, 2ND ED. (New York: Houghton Mifflin Co., 1934) 563-64. Both Monroe and Cubberley provide interesting and readable discussions on the development of state legislation.

9. FRANCIS WAYLAND, THE ELEMENTS OF MORAL SCIENCE, 4th ed. (Boston: Gould, Kendall and Lincoln, 1841) 324 (emphasis in original).

10. *Id.* at 318 (emphasis in original).

11. *Id.* (emphasis in original). Wayland continues:
Several duties devolve upon the [parent], which cannot be rightfully devolved upon the [teacher]. For instance,--
> 1.   He [the father] is bound to inform himself of the peculiar habits, and reflect upon the probable future situation, of his child, and deliberately to consider what sort of education will most conduce to his future happiness and usefulness.
> 2.   He is bound to select such instructors as will best accomplish the results which he believes will be most beneficial.
> 3.   He is bound to devote such time and attention to the subject, as will enable him to ascertain whether the instructor of his child discharges his duty with faithfulness.
> 4.   To encourage his child by manifesting such interest in his studies as shall give to diligence and assiduity all the assistance and benefit of parental authority and friendship.
> 5.   And, if a parent be under obligation to do this, he is, of course, under obligation *to take time to do it,* and so to construct the arrangements of his family and business that *it may be done.* He has no right to say that *he has no time for these duties.* If God ha[s] required them of him, as is the fact, *he has time exactly for them*; and the truth is, he has not time for those other occupations which interfere with them. If he neglect[s] them, he does it to the injury of his children, and, as he will ascertain when it shall be too late, to his own disappointment and misery.

Id. at 318-19 (emphasis in original).

12. 294 F.2d 150 (5th Cir. 1961). *Dixon* involved college students at Alabama State college who were expelled from school for misconduct without due process of law. The due process principle, however, was also applied in the secondary school context. *See also* Goss v. Lopez, 419 U.S. 565, 579 (1975) (Public secondary school students faced with suspension of less then 10 days is entitled to Fourteenth Amendment due process notice and hearing) and Tinker v. Des Monies School District, 393 U.S. 503 (1969) (First Amendment right to non-disruptive protest in public high school was not punishable by suspension).

13. WILLIAM A. KAPLIN AND BARBARA A. LEE, THE LAW OF HIGHER EDUCATION, 3rd ed. (San Francisco, CA: Jossey-Bass Publishers, 1995) 371 (quotations omitted).

14. Lawrence B. Custer, *The Origins Of The Doctrine of Parens Patriae*, 27 EMORY L. J. 195 (1978) 201. *See also* JOHN LOCKE, TWO TREATISES OF GOVERNMENT, (Awnshan & John Churchill, 1698; reprint ed., New York, The Legal Classics Library, 1994) chapters II and VI.

15. JOSEPH STORY, COMMENTARIES ON EQUITY JURISPRUDENCE (London: Stevens and Haynes, 1884; reprint ed., Birmingham, Al: Legal Classics Library, 1988) 919.

16. *Id.* at 921.

17. *Id.* at 929.

18. 321 U.S. 158 (1944).

19. STORY *supra* note 15 at 929.

20. English courts have even recognized that parents enjoy the legal right to control and direct the education and upbringing of their children *even where they are wards of the court.* The court will not interfere with the parent in the exercise of his paternal authority unless the parent commits gross moral turpitude, abdicates parental authority or attempts to remove the child from the court's jurisdiction. Agar-Ellis v. Lascelles, 24 Ch. D. 317 as cited in STORY *supra* note 15 at 930.

21. Though the Supreme Court was willing to acknowledge that this trampling effect was not warranted under the doctrine of *parens patriae* in Wisconsin v. Yoder, 406 U.S. 205 (1972), the Court limited its holding to religious parents and the education of children only after the eighth grade. In other words, the Court simply engaged in a balancing of rights and interests and not any solid application of the doctrine. For nothing in the doctrine of *parens patriae* differentiates between a religious and non-religious parent, nor does it warrant that the state as *parens patriae* may restrict the parent's control before the eighth grade by requiring school attendance. Unless a parent has committed some act that warrants removal of the legal presumption recognized by the doctrine, the requirement of school attendance either before or after the eighth grade is not warranted.

22. A classic and famous example of school boards and teacher unions ganging up against parents occurred in 1968 in New York. The School Board for the city of New York had agreed to permit the Oceanhill Brownsville school district to experiment with community based control of their children's education. The Ford Foundation made some monies available and the City's school board endorsed the idea.

The American Federation of Teachers (AFT) under the leadership of Albert Shanker also gave the demonstration project its approval, but only tentatively. The AFT was concerned that parents would be making the curricular choices for their own children and that this might not result in their best interest. The AFT's real misgivings, however, surfaced when the superintendent for the Oceanhill Brownsville school district transferred several union teachers out of the district because those teachers were not in full accord with the goals and philosophy of the project. The transferred teachers objected and appealed to the union. The union backed the teachers and demanded that the School board overrule the superintendent's decision and permit the teachers to stay. The Board refused and so the union ordered a City-wide teacher's strike.

Eventually the school board caved in to the teacher's demands leaving the parents and the idea of local or community based schools to die a sudden financial and political death. The teacher's union had won. The parents had lost. Unfortunately, the entire conflagration was not understood in terms of parental rights versus the power of the unions and the state.

Moreover, much of the discussion was carried on in racial and religious terms. The parents and superintendent in the Oceanhill Brownsville school district were largely black and hispanic. The teacher's union was generally white and largely Jewish. These factors blurred the real issue of parental rights. The opportunity to empower parents would have to wait another generation.

This example bears out the fact that school boards tend to serve their own political interest. Many school boards also serve the latest educational pedagogy upon its approval by teacher unions. These unions reveal they are no servant of parents when their promotional materials challenge: "WE TEACH THE CHILDREN."

23. Perhaps the greatest irony is that the will of the community where almost all are of one mind with respect to what their children should be taught, may be defeated by the single objection of one parent where religion is merely implicated in the curriculum. A single objecting parent can make the entire system of education conform to his will alone! *See* Wallace v. Jaffree, 472 U.S. 38 (1985). In Wallace, the Supreme Court struck down an Alabama statute that attempted to designate a one-minute period of silence in all public schools "for meditation or voluntary prayer." The Court sanctioned voluntary student-initiated prayer but found the statute's one-minute designation an unconstitutional attempt to return prayer to the public schools.

24. *See* AUBERON HERBERT, THE RIGHT AND WRONG OF COMPULSION BY THE STATE (Indianapolis: Liberty Classics, 1978) Essays 2 and 4. *See also,* JOHN W. WHITEHEAD, PARENTS' RIGHTS (Westchester, IL: Crossway Books, 1986). *See generally,* WILSON SMITH, ED., THEORIES OF EDUCATION IN EARLY AMERICA 1655-1819 (Indianapolis: Bobbs-Merrill Co., 1973); and CLIFTON JOHNSON, OLD-TIME SCHOOLS AND SCHOOL-BOOKS (Toronto: Dover Publications, 1963).

25. More recently this rationale has expanded into the *federal* government's desire to produce efficient New World Order worker-citizens in order to fulfill *speculative* employment goals in the year 2000 and beyond. *See generally* National Center for Education Statistics, "Projections of Education Statistics to 2000," Office of Education Research and Improvement, U.S. Department of Labor (NCES 89-648) 1989; Bureau of the Census, "Projections of The Population of the United States, by Age, Sex, and Race: 1988 to 2080," in Current Population Reports - Population Estimates and Projections, U.S. Department of Commerce (Series P-25, No. 1018) Jan. 1989; Bureau of Labor Statistics, "Outlook 2000," U.S. Department of Labor (Bulletin 2352) April 1990; Bureau of Labor Statistics, "Projections 2000," U.S. Department of Labor (Bulletin 2302) March 1988; Employment Standards Administration, "Opportunity 2000: Creative Affirmative Action Strategies for a Changing Workforce," U.S. Department of Labor, September 1988.

26. *See* DAVID RUBIN & STEVEN GREENHOUSE, THE RIGHTS OF TEACHERS, THE BASIC ACLU GUIDE TO A TEACHER'S CONSTITUTIONAL RIGHTS (New York: Bantam, 1984) 115-40.

27. As far as liberal versus conservative views on federal intervention into education are concerned, neither object to (indeed neither question), the expanded jurisdiction of the federal government. For contemporary examples of how federal jurisdiction over education is justified on the basis of expediency reflecting a liberal agenda, *see* FRANCIS KEPPEL, THE NECESSARY REVOLUTION IN AMERICAN EDUCATION (New York: Harper & Row, 1966) and JOSEPH A. CALIFANO, JR., GOVERNING AMERICA (New York: Simon & Schuster, 1981). For a contemporary example of how federal jurisdiction over education is justified on the basis of expediency reflecting a conservative agenda, *see* STUART M. BUTLER, ED., MANDATE FOR LEADERSHIP II (Washington, D.C.: The Heritage Foundation, 1984) 49-62. Though some have suggested that the 1994 electoral transfer of Congressional power to a Republican majority may change this condition, the fact remains that neither party recognizes the Constitutional limitations on Congressional power. The Republicans simply prefer to exercise less radical usurpation in the area of education, than their more radical usurping Democratic counterparts.

It is interesting to note that the Heritage Foundation's recommendations tout the "necessity" of federal funding, statistical record keeping and moral pressure in "reasonably accommodating the nation's interest in education." *Id.* at 54-56. Of conservatives in general, this rule of political action appears to have been well-described by theologian Robert L. Dabney when he said: "American conservatism is merely the shadow that follows Radicalism to perdition. It remains behind it, but never retards it, and always advances near its leader. This pretended salt hath utterly lost its savor . . . . It is worthless because it is the conservatism of expediency only, and not of sturdy principle. It intends to risk nothing serious for the sake of the truth . . . ." Quoted in *The Chalcedon Report*, (Vallecito, CA) August 1990, page 12. A conservative agenda is no different than a liberal one if parental liberty and the Constitution are suppressed in the process.

For salt of a more substantial savor, see J. GRESHAM MACHEN, EDUCATION, CHRISTIANITY, AND THE STATE (Jefferson, Maryland: The Trinity Foundation, 1987); GORDON H. CLARK, A CHRISTIAN PHILOSOPHY OF EDUCATION, 2nd rev. ed. (Jefferson, Maryland: The Trinity Foundation, 1988); and NATHAN TARCOV, LOCKE'S EDUCATION FOR LIBERTY (Chicago: University of Chicago Press, 1984).

Chapter 7

What is Intellectual Freedom?

[T]he opinions of men, depending only on the evidence contemplated by their own minds, cannot follow the dictates of other men.[1]

Thinking about Thinking

The unalienable right of parents to direct the education of their own children is not the only educational right found in the law of nature. Intellectual freedom or freedom of the mind is also a significant unalienable right. What is intellectual freedom and how does it translate into a discussion about real choice and real freedom in American education? This Chapter will concentrate on this right and consider its relationship to parental and governmental education.

According to nature, the mind contemplates ideas to which it is exposed. If one is told to picture a tree in the mind, the mind tends to picture a tree. The mind is created in such a way that it *automatically* considers the ideas to which it is exposed, assuming it is paying attention. Thus what a man thinks *about* is a function of that to which he is first *exposed*. Every man's mind testifies to itself that it considers that to which it is exposed. It can be no other way.

The Bible recognizes that God is the Creator of all things visible as well as invisible.[2] He created mankind, male and female in His own image.[3] He created their mind to think.[4] The Creator gave mankind the faculty of reason to sufficiently know and understand the Creator and the creation,[5] including the laws God impressed upon the heavens and earth.[6] God also recognizes that mankind can abuse reason and pollute the mind, and that mankind's thinking is often at odds with reality.[7] He therefore exhorts each person to renew his or her mind, though He does not force any person to do so.[8]

A relationship exists between those ideas which a man first takes into himself through his thoughts, and the effect of those ideas on his life. "For as he thinks in his heart, so *is* he."[9] This Biblical understanding of the mind affirms what nature and reason teach: what one thinks about, is that to which one is exposed. Moreover, what one thinks about on an ongoing basis will result in shaping his or her thoughts, character and eventually actions.

✓ Key Idea:

☞   AS A MAN THINKS, SO IS HE.

Given the serious implications of ideas on the mind and action, it is curious that so little attention has been paid to the subject of *mandatory* exposure to ideas. For, if ideas shape thoughts and thoughts shape character and eventually character shapes action, it is of utmost importance to carefully examine the authority of those persons who claim a right or power to expose others to *their* ideas in the first place.

In the context of childhood education the concern is even greater. Children are more impressionable than adults. Those who claim a right or power to control the education of a child and thus to ultimately shape his or her thoughts, character and, indirectly, his or her actions, bear an extraordinary burden. They must convincingly prove they hold the legal authority under the laws of nature and of nature's God to expose children to the state's ideas.

Ideas have consequences. A relationship between ideas and actions exists. Ideas are inextricably tied to thoughts, character and ultimately action. Exposure to that which is right tends to lead to right action, and wrong tends to wrong action. What is sown will be reaped.[10] But the question of more immediate importance for this book and Chapter is not *what* mental seed should be sown, but *who* has the legal right, power and authority to sow such mental seed?

Who May Lawfully Renew the Mind?

Where does the civil government get its authority to renew the mind or forcibly expose the mind to its approved ideas or curriculum? The civil government cannot claim an original authority to direct the mind because it did not create mankind nor did it create the mind of any child. Moreover, both nature and reason demonstrate that the mind was created free from the reach of the civil government's power. The civil government lacks any mechanism to truly know what is in someone's mind. Torture can sometimes elicit a desired response but there is no "lie detector" test that can truly reveal a person's thoughts.

Nor has God given the mind of man to civil government as one of its legitimate objects upon which force or coercion may operate. Instead, every man is individually responsible for renewal of his own mind.

The laws of nature and nature's God, therefore, do not extend any general authority to the civil government with respect to renewing the mind *vis-a-vis* punishment for failure to be exposed to government sanctioned ideas. Neither nature, reason or Revelation warrant that the civil government has the authority to compel children to be exposed to government approved ideas or to face a civil penalty for their refusal. Neither nature, reason or Revelation indicate that the civil government is granted the authority or power to either awaken the minds of children, nationalize students into "model citizens," or transmit cultural values. Nor has it the power to impose upon parents, a civil penalty for failure to ensure that their children be so awakened, nationalized or conformed. Civil government fails in its burden of proof to make out any case whatsoever for its claim to compel children to be mandatorily exposed to its approved ideas including state approved curriculum, tests and textbooks.

✓ Key Idea:

☞ CIVIL GOVERNMENT LACKS THE AUTHORITY TO RENEW OR INSTRUCT THE HUMAN MIND.

While the civil government cannot sustain the right to compel exposure to ideas, ample evidence for parental empowerment exists. Nature, reason and Revelation recognize that parents are endowed with the unalienable right to care for their children and to continue that care and oversight until their children become adults. Nature teaches that children are the offspring of their parents. A parent's duty to care for his child includes the obligation to instruct the child's mind. The mind of a child needs instruction and the responsibility of *instructing* the minds of children falls exclusively to their parents.[11] Parents are to teach their children to embrace the truth, to understand what is right and reject what is wrong.[12] Of course parents cannot "make" their children believe what they teach. They may require exposure, but parents cannot mandate belief, and in this sense parents share in the universal limitations that preclude all others from compelling belief.

✓ Key Idea:

☞ PARENTS HAVE THE AUTHORITY AND RIGHT TO INSTRUCT THE MIND OF THEIR CHILDREN.

That parents can compel exposure, however, without trampling the intellectual freedom of their own children, is based on the fact that parental exposure is appropriate to the context of being a parent. That context is one of education through the means of love, training and discipline, not force and coercion. If children are viewed outside of their familial context, it could be said that any compulsory exposure to ideas, either by the civil government *or* parents with respect to the education of their children, violates the intellectual freedom of a child. This is similar to the approach taken by children's rights activists and various United Nations resolutions.

This Chapter, however, does not assume that children are independent free agents or have no mother or father to educate them or that the family is a creature of the state.[13]   While parents, like civil government, cannot compel belief, parents, unlike civil government, may require exposure to parent approved ideas. Parents may ensure that their children are properly *instructed* because this exercise of parental discipline and training fits within the acceptable parameters of parental love.[14]

While the adult who wants to enjoy intellectual freedom must be free to refuse compulsory exposure to government approved ideas, the rule for children is that parents are empowered to instruct them. Thus, parents and not the civil government may instruct the minds of their own children. The way the mind operates, according to the way it is created, according to the rule of reason and according to the Bible, all testify in favor of this conclusion. When we think about this situation, we would do well to also remember that not even God himself exercises the power to make men believe in ideas, at least not in this life.[15] Who then is the civil government to exercise such a power?

Compelling Exposure is No different than Compelling Belief

With this background in mind, perhaps some examples of intellectual freedom will serve to illustrate the legal boundaries as well as how intellectual freedom has been abused by the civil government in the context of education. Consider this proposition: If I now direct the content of what you think about, then I now direct your thoughts. I don't have to make you believe what I say. I only have to expose you to what I say, in order to get you to think about what I say. Now if I get you to think about what I say, because you want to think about it, then all is fine and well. [Hopefully, you are reading this because you want to.]   I offer the idea and you agree to accept exposure to it.   I say intellectual freedom is a good thing and you say (by continuing to read on) "Tell me more." Indeed, you may even go on to say whether or not you believe what is being said. *The distinction that is material, however, does not focus on exposure versus belief, it turns on compulsion verses freedom in choosing to be exposed to an idea in the first place.*

So when the additional element of coercion or force is added, the equation is significantly changed. In the first situation you voluntarily agreed to expose yourself to what I have said (and perhaps to also believe it) and thus you freely made the decision to trigger the operation of your mind--from ideas to thinking (and possibly from thinking to character to action).   But now coercion is introduced into the equation. Your previous voluntary decision to expose your mind to this Chapter's ideas is taken away from you and given to another. Forced control or exposure to this Chapter is what you would experience, *i.e.*, you *must* read this book because another told you to do so and civil punishment will follow if you don't.

✓ Key Idea:

☞ INTELLECTUAL FREEDOM INCLUDES THE RIGHT TO VOLUNTARILY CHOOSE THE IDEAS ONE RECEIVES.

If the civil government commands your exposure to ideas and imposes a civil penalty on you if you fail to follow its directive, then freedom of the mind is flagrantly violated. If a minor child's parent commands the same exposure and then disciplines the child for disobedience because of a failure to follow their instruction, then that does not violate intellectual freedom. Parents have this duty and right from God; the civil government does not. Moreover, when the civil government forces you to receive its instruction under threat of civil penalty, then it has also undertaken to substitute its judgment for yours as it pertains to matters of choice in exposing one to ideas. Such forced exposure to ideas, however, is contrary to the unalienable right of intellectual freedom simply because it takes away an indispensable element of the right--your choice in the matter--a choice that God himself endowed within every person and which the civil government may not take away. Penalizing a person for *refusing* to be exposed violates intellectual freedom because it imposes a civil penalty for exercising your choice.

In understanding the right of intellectual freedom, it is crucial to understand that the right is not a freedom *from* being *incidentally* exposed to things we dislike. People are incidentally exposed to many things they dislike everyday simply because they eat, work and participate in our society. It is not uncommon for the mind to be exposed to another's conversation while waiting at the check-out line. We are exposed to advertising billboards, bumper stickers and other drivers which honk at us while we operate our cars on the highway. There are many things that we do not especially want to see or hear but because we must live and work, we are exposed to these things regardless. That is part of life.

The right of intellectual freedom is not a freedom *from* being *incidentally exposed*. It is a freedom from being *compulsorily exposed*. Intellectual freedom is a freedom from being compulsorily exposed where civil penalties attach for failure to submit to the compulsion. The right of intellectual freedom is violated when the civil government chooses ideas to which we shall be exposed and it subjects us to a penalty, fine or imprisonment if we refuse to submit our children to those ideas. In practice, compulsion and penalties generally go hand in hand.[16]

For example, suppose the civil government says to you; "You must *believe* what we tell you. If you don't believe then we will punish you!" This is clearly a case where intellectual freedom has been abridged. The state cannot tell you what ideas to *believe*. The state violates the right of intellectual freedom when it chooses ideas and subjects us to a penalty if we refuse to believe.

✓ Key Idea:
>   INTELLECTUAL FREEDOM INCLUDES THE RIGHT TO
       REFUSE COMPULSORY EXPOSURE TO IDEAS.

Now suppose the state is more cunning and says; "You must *sit there and listen* to the ideas we tell you. If you don't listen to these ideas, *then* we will punish you!" This coercion also violates your intellectual freedom. The state violates the right of intellectual freedom when it chooses ideas and subjects us to a penalty if we refuse to submit our minds to those ideas. Both of these situations involve denial of the unalienable right of intellectual freedom. Both involve government forced exposure with government penalties for failure to be so exposed. The former approach is called "compulsory education," and the latter "compulsory attendance." Both approaches lie at the foundation of state control of the mind.

Three Examples
Three historical images may serve to define the various contexts in which the state has said in effect; "You must *believe* what we tell you" or "You must *sit there and listen* to the ideas we tell you, or else . . . ." These examples focus on the debilitating effect of physical coercion, intellectual coercion and prolonged exposure to government approved ideas, on the unalienable right of intellectual freedom.

A. Changing the Mind through Physical Coercion
When thinking of governmental oversight of ideas--where the civil government tells someone what they must listen to and think about--recall a scene from an old movie. You know the one. Picture an abhorrent looking man with an evil countenance. He is usually down in the King's dungeon groping around a torture machine. He has some poor human being tightly bound to the device and is stretching him to death.

While all this is going on, the evil one says to the man on the rack (who is at an obvious disadvantage): "Renounce your beliefs. Promise you will renounce your writings and swear allegiance" to this or that. "Then you will be set free." There are variations on the terminology but the general idea is, "Look, if you just say you believe what we want you to believe, then you can walk out of here unharmed (relatively speaking)." Of course, the evil one would always add something ludicrous like: "The choice is yours." Then the one being physically tortured says something like: "No. I will never believe that. I won't renounce. You can't make me believe." At this point he is either rescued or the movie comes to an hasty end.

It is amazing that the torturer would tell the one tied up that the choice was up to him--that he could renounce his beliefs and live in shame or keep them and die in honor. Why not let him live in honor with his own beliefs? Why not let him read what he wants to read? Why does the civil government think it has to expose this fellow to its point of view for his own good?

The phrases "governmental control of the mind" or "governmental violation of intellectual freedom" may lead one to think of the human being on the rack, but perhaps a second image will serve us better.

B. Controlling the Mind through Intellectual Coercion

Picture this in your mind. A public school teacher enters a room of fifth graders. She says cordially: "Today we will study history and then we will have an examination." Some of the students moan. "Of course," she adds, "If anyone doesn't approve then we can go down to the principal's office and work it out." Then out of nowhere comes that line: "The choice is yours" or "It is up to you." Is she serious? Is that really a choice--a trip to the school principal's office or sit and listen to the civil government tell you its official view of history?

Remember, the teacher *is* the voice of the civil government. She may be religious and worship where you worship. She may be an atheist or your best friend or neighbor. She could be the kindest, sweetest person you have ever known. But there is no getting around the fact that she is required to teach your kids those ideas which the state legislature has approved and she is precluded from teaching what the legislature prohibits. Now your children must listen to the state say: "You will *sit here and listen* to what we tell you. If you refuse to listen or don't come to school, then you are a delinquent and need to be removed from the home." Moreover the state says to parents: "You parents should be fingerprinted, photographed and prosecuted. A fine and a little time in jail is in your future. Better plead *no contest* or *guilty*, or else we will make it tough on you and your child. The state can't expect a parent to educate his or her child-- why democracy would fail if you parents had your way." Suddenly, that sweet public school teacher or truant officer, is the voice of belligerent nationalism. Arrogance, hysterical moralizing and petty altruism mark her lecture.

The first scene in the dungeon is essentially nonexistent in the United States, the second is the reality. Yet they both have at least one thing in common. The civil government has ventured into the area of telling children what they must listen to and what they must think about. If the child refuses to sit and be exposed to it, then he or she will either be disciplined (a problem child--a delinquent) or the parents will be incarcerated in a modern dungeon. Controlling the mind through intellectual coercion is the school teacher's way of enlightening a room of fifth graders. But in so doing, she tramples on parental rights and intellectual freedom because she is an agent of the state.

C. Dominating the Mind Through Prolonged Exposure

Consider one more image. Picture a quiet town in 18th century Virginia. It is Sunday. All the town is at church except one aimless man. The townspeople are hearing a sermon designed to instill the "broad, but common" values of this religious community. They are required to hear these viewpoints for the rest of their lives, every week. The man who refuses to go to church differs from those who attend in two distinct ways. First he has to pay a fine to the minister for his failure to attend. After all, skipping church is against the law.

Second, he isn't exposed to the minister's sermon like everyone else. (That's why he is regarded as aimless, not broad minded, and probably dangerous at that!) In any event, don't feel too sorry for this man, because after all the choice is his. He can go and be exposed to his state-approved minister and his state-approved ideas or he cannot go, pay the fine and presumably remain as he will. The choice is his.

Of course, hardly anybody these days would say that this is a choice that one should have to make. They would scream and bellow about how the rights of this man were violated by the civil government. Most people today would say: "You should have a choice to go or not to go. That's his choice, not the other option of paying a fine." They would say that no one should be compelled to be exposed or fined for the rest of his or her life adding that "Whether you support the church or don't support is your choice." Or maybe, "If you want to support this minister or that one, that's your business and not the civil government's business." But one thing is clear: those that obey the government and attend every week will soon come to adopt many of the ideas to which they have been forcibly exposed over a prolonged period of time.

Now when we examine the law today, it is clear that people have real choice and real freedom to attend or not to attend, to support or not to support the ideas, people and religious institution of their choice. It is also equally clear that in the United States at least, the government doesn't put you in jail if you don't want to go hear a minister or a sermon or if you don't believe what the government believes about religion.

But what about those fifth graders and that nice teacher and those compulsory attendance laws that throw parents in jail if they don't meet all of the civil government's rules, regulations and requirements for a "broad, but common" assimilating education? What about real choice and what about this take it or leave it, "the choice is yours" mentality? While we enjoy real choice in matters of religion (as far as indicated here), we have been told to live with something less than real choice in matters of education. Why? Why not real intellectual freedom followed by real choice in American education, just as in American religion?

The preceding Chapters have discussed the idea that "all men are created equal, that they are endowed by their Creator with certain unalienable rights." The Chapters have also considered the Declaration's recognition that the laws of creation establish the duty of civil government to secure those rights. This Chapter asserts that acknowledgment of the laws of nature also leads to a recognition of the right to intellectual freedom, including intellectual freedom in education. Intellectual freedom means freedom to think without threat of physical punishment. It means thinking, free from government-compelled exposure.

✓ Key Idea:

☞ INTELLECTUAL FREEDOM INCLUDES THE RIGHT TO
THINK ABOUT IDEAS FREE FROM GOVERNMENTAL
COMPELLED EXPOSURE.

Real Freedom and Choice in Religious Thought

Thomas Jefferson understood the right of intellectual freedom most plainly in the context of government regulation of religion in 1786. He swore "upon the altar of Almighty God" eternal hostility against *every form* of tyranny over the mind of man. (Not even those who profess to worship God in our day and age are this committed). What historical situation faced Jefferson when he made this vow? In addressing this question it is important to examine the history of Virginia's regulation of religious ideas and the unalienable right of intellectual freedom that emancipated the people from that regulation. What is more important, however, is to identify the principle that led Jefferson and Virginians from "choice" in religion to "real choice" in thinking about religion.

Prior to 1786, Virginians lived with an established or official church. The Commonwealth also sanctioned an official "textbook" of common prayers. The people were compelled to attend the official church or else pay a fine. They were compelled to support its ministers financially. Their ministers were required to be licensed by the civil government. Taxes also went to construct and maintain church buildings. The people were compelled to attend a government approved church and be exposed to the government's approved version of the Gospel and Protestant theology by a government licensed minister. It made no difference whether the people agreed with those religious ideas or not.

The people of Virginia thus did not enjoy intellectual freedom. They did not enjoy the right to be free from government influence of their minds. They lacked the freedom to choose that to which they should be exposed. They lacked real choice and real freedom over when, where, by whom and in what manner they exercised their religion. In short, the state established church held a monopoly over the teaching and preaching of religious ideas in the colony and Commonwealth--a monopoly not even God enjoys.

Thus, the classic state-established religion reflected four elements "established" by either state approval or state coercion:

1)   State approved preachers;
2)   State approved doctrine;

3)   State compelled attendance laws;

4)   State compelled tithing.

Virginia followed this pattern to the letter. Its religious teachers, the clergy, were licensed by the Crown. Only those persons who taught the official Anglican doctrine and liturgy (the curriculum) were eligible for a license. To preach or teach without a state license was punishable by incarceration. Not only were the clergy and curriculum approved and mandated by the civil government, but persons failing to attend church services (classes) were punished by the civil government, often through fines. Finally, the salaries of the clergy (teachers) were financed by a mandatory tithe or tax.

But in 1785 a powerful coalition of religious groups and denominations joined together to change this situation. With the help of James Madison's irrefutable *Memorial and Remonstrance Against Religious Assessments*,[17] this coalition was able to persuade the Virginia General Assembly in two very important ways. First, they persuaded the Assembly to reject a compromise bill which sought to expand the state's monopoly to different societies and sects of the Christian faith. The compromise measure, entitled *A Bill Establishing A Provision For Teachers of the Christian Religion*,[18] was an attempt to bring many of the differing Christian sects under the jurisdiction of the civil government. The proposed bill permitted each of the sects or groups to enjoy a little less harassment as well as a certain degree of financial support from the civil government. This scheme is a classic bribe. Today, its called a voucher.

✓ Key Idea:

☞   COMPULSORY   SUBSIDIZATION   OF   THE
     PROPAGATION   OF   IDEAS   IS   CONTRARY   TO
     INTELLECTUAL FREEDOM.

In effect, the bill would have allowed the civil government to bring all of the major sects under its roof. The government would then have collected a special property tax that otherwise would have gone to the original state-established church, and instead distribute it to those additional churches now approved by the government. The distribution would be according to the choice of the one paying the tax. This was the only "choice" the taxpayer enjoyed-- designate the tax for an approved church or pay the tax for the established church. Not much of a choice. The bill proposed a religious voucher program. Property owners must pay the tax, but may designate the religious recipient as long as that recipient was approved in its doctrine by the civil government. This scheme is the legal father of a modern school voucher plan.

The bill also indicated that approved recipients were limited to certain Christian denominations.   If your denomination was not acceptable, the government did not approve it and you did not enjoy the choice to designate your title accordingly. You had no choice. The bill also limited the purposes to which the money could be put. The government controlled the money even after it left the public treasury. Furthermore, the money could only be used to pay the minister or provide a place to worship. No other use was permitted. Unappropriated monies went to encourage seminaries of learning within those counties wherein the sums were collected.

Stop and think about all this for a minute. Isn't it obvious that many of the solutions being proposed for the problems of modern education are following this exact approach, particularly when we are dealing with government vouchers for *approved* private schools? Property taxes go to support the schools. Only qualified (government licensed) schools get the money. The money can only be used for certain official and approved purposes.[19]

Now, do not draw the superficial conclusion that "Well, the 18th century bill dealt with religion and today's laws deal with education." You will have missed the whole point. Both the 18th century bill and today's laws have the same underlying assumption. They both assume that the civil government has a right to compel its people to financially subsidize approved teachers who profess approved ideas and to only subsidize those teachers and ideas approved by the civil government. The voucher bill, however, did not pass because the legislature rejected this underlying assumption. Instead of accepting this assumption, they embraced the underlying basis of intellectual freedom.

This basis was elucidated in James Madison's *Memorial and Remonstrance Against Religious Assessments*. The *Remonstrance* is an excellent defense of intellectual freedom. Madison drove to the heart of the matter when he declared religious liberty to be an unalienable right, "because the opinions of men, depending only on the evidence contemplated by their own minds, cannot follow the dictates of other men."[20] In other words, when someone dictates or compels you to think about this or that, he violates the unalienable right you possess to select the evidence or ideas which you alone wish to consider.

✓ Key Idea:

☞ INTELLECTUAL FREEDOM MEANS THAT THE OPINIONS OF MEN CANNOT BE MADE TO FOLLOW THE DICTATES OF THE CIVIL GOVERNMENT.

Some people think that they can force others to be exposed to their ideas because their ideas are true, are traditional, are held by a majority of the community or because they *should* be held by the community. This is the temptation. It is natural that someone who has an idea they believe is right, should want others to believe it also. The usual and accepted way of getting others to believe what you believe is through reason and free debate. The established church and the established school, however, rejected this option and used force and compulsion. This is the temptation that must be avoided: to achieve a good end through a prohibited means. The means of reason and voluntary persuasion are good. The means of force and coercion in matters of ideas are not good. This limitation on the means of conveying ideas applies to all men and women, religions, institutions and governments. All of them.

The principle of avoiding force and violence is as true in the context of religious liberty as it is in the context of educational liberty. The right of religious liberty involves the duties which men owe to God and is therefore unalienable. A parental right in education involves the duties which parents owe to God with respect to their children and is also unalienable on the same basis. This understanding of intellectual freedom is the common thread that when pulled, will undo the entire fabric of government involvement in education.

A Political Strategy of Disestablishment

The idea of religious freedom was not discovered in 1786. Colonial agitation for freedom had been brewing for at least 15 years prior. Samuel Davies "had won the right of toleration for all dissenters in Virginia who were willing to register their ministers and carry out the somewhat onerous provisions of Virginia law."[21] The Virginia legislature passed an Act on December 9, 1776 that "exempted dissenters from all taxes and levies for the support of the Established Church and that suspended the levy for members of the established church until the end of the next session."[22] (If education reformers who favor incremental changes need an historical pattern to follow, this is it). But complete disestablishment still eluded the people until 1786 when Virginians passed *A Bill for Establishing Religious Freedom.*[23] It is important to point out some of the dynamics which accompanied the passage of the religious freedom bill and then we will see how Madison's recognition of intellectual freedom in his *Remonstrance* was incorporated into Thomas Jefferson's disestablishment bill.

Several special interest groups emerged in the fight. First there were the clergymen associated with the official religious establishment. These clergymen had received the lion's share of continued favor and financial support. They enjoyed a legal monopoly over religious ideas. They had a powerful union of sorts, which represented their interests overseas before the King and Parliament before the revolution, and in Virginia's General Assembly thereafter.

Some of the clergy believed there was a real need for change, but were uncertain whether a partial or complete disestablishment was necessary or even wise. Most of these men were good ministers. They loved their religion and church. They were not certain how it would fare without the props of the government's treasury or its stamp of approval. Other ministers thought only of themselves and how their own future and financial security would fare. They knew it would be difficult for them if they became economically dependent on the approval of their local parish, rather than the tenure offered by their superiors.

Perhaps you may recognize that the same divisions exist today within teacher unions and educational institutions.

A second group was made up of the religiously disestablished. In Virginia this included some Quakers, Jews, Roman Catholics and the Mennonites, but mainly consisted of Baptists and Presbyterians. The Baptists took a straightforward position. They argued that *no church* should be propped up by the civil government. They didn't want to be part of the government's system of financial support. They didn't want to give up their control to the government. The Baptists wanted all religious ideas and institutions to stand on equal footing-- equally without government "strings attached."

The Presbyterians took a little bit different approach. They were originally willing to accommodate and consider the plan for the civil government to support all major Protestant religions and sects. In other words, they favored the bill that Madison's *Remonstrance* had demolished. They wanted to be part of the system, not tear it down. But eventually they sided with the Baptists' approach. Both denominations had always sought greater liberty in matters of religious thought and expression. Now they were finally agreed on a means.

A third major group involved the civil government--the Virginia General Assembly. As with all political bodies, money and power interests were tied up in the whole affair. Very few delegates were willing to disinvest themselves of political power. Madison's *Remonstrance* turned up the political heat in that department.[24] The people began to demand a complete disestablishment across the board and they were preparing to make their views known at the polls.

It has been observed that the more things change the more they remain the same. The struggle for disestablishment of governmental control over ideas is a constant and timeless theme. The context then was compulsory religion. The context now is compulsory education. There was a religious establishment then and there is an educational establishment now. The major difference between then and now, however, is that then Virginia disestablished government influence over religious ideas, financing and practice. At the present time, state governments have established their control over non-religious ideas, financing and practices in the education of children.

It will help to keep these points in mind as the next chapter examines the legislation Thomas Jefferson proposed in order to free the mind from government oversight of religious ideas and practices. If the principle that necessitated Virginia to free its people from government oversight of religious ideas is universal, then it applies with equal strength to freeing the people of every state and nation from government influence and oversight of any idea.

★ HYPOTHETICALLY SPEAKING . . . .

Problem: The people living in the Nation of Blackacre are very religious. Their institutions presuppose the existence of a Divine Being. The people

believe that the mind can only be free when it is educated in the knowledge of God and true religion.

The people have just elected you their sole ruler. They now demand that you pass a compulsory education law. They want you to establish and institute a "school system of religious instruction that will educate the children of Blackacre in the knowledge of God and true religion." They also demand you require attendance at the school and punish those who do not attend, otherwise the people fear that the Nation will soon become irreligious and will degenerate. If you meet their demand, they will give you an honorary Doctorate of Divinity degree. If you refuse their demand, the people of Blackacre will say you are against religion and impeach you.

Should you pass the law?

Answer: No. The people, in effect, want you to pass *A Bill Establishing A Provision For Teachers of the Christian Religion.* You must refuse to pass such a law on the grounds that "the opinions of men cannot follow the dictates of the government." While it is true that education in knowledge of God and true religion is related to the security of a Nation, it is not true that the civil government has any jurisdiction to compel people to know about God and religion by *penalizing* them for failure or refusal to be instructed.

Notes

1. ROBERT L. CORD, SEPARATION OF CHURCH AND STATE (New York: Lambeth Press, 1982) 244 quoting James Madison's Memorial and Remonstrance Against Religious Assessments.

2. *See* Genesis 1:1.

3. *See* Genesis 1:26-28.

4. Philippians 4:8 indicates that "Finally, brethren, whatever things are true, whatever things are noble, whatever things are just, whatever things are pure, whatever things are lovely, whatever things are of good report, if there is any virtue and if there is anything praiseworthy; meditate on these things."

5. *See* I Chronicles 28:9, Isaiah 26:3, Matthew 22:37, Romans 12:2, Philippians 2:5 and II Corinthians 3:5.

6. Hebrews 8:10 states; "For this is the covenant that I will make with the house of Israel after those days, says the Lord: I will put My laws in their mind and write them on their hearts; and I will be their God, and they shall be My people."

7. *See* Colossians 2:18, Romans 1:28, 7:23 and 8:7.

8. Romans 12:2; "And do not be conformed to this world, but be transformed by the renewing of your mind, that you may prove what is that good and acceptable and perfect will of God."

9. Proverbs 23:7.

10. This approach does not embrace either an environmental or intellectual determinism to mitigating fault.

11. *See* Genesis 18:18-19; Exodus 10:2; Deuteronomy 4:5-10; Deuteronomy 6:1-9; Deuteronomy 11:18-21; Deuteronomy 31:12; Deuteronomy 32:45-46; Psalms 34:11; Psalms 78:1-11; Proverbs 1:8; Proverbs 2:1-5; Proverbs 3:12; Proverbs 4:1; Proverbs 4:20-27; Proverbs 6:20-23; Proverbs 13:1; Isaiah 38:19; Joel 1:3; Ephesians 6:1-4; Colossians 3:20, and 1 Thessalonians 2:11.

12. Parents are to instruct their children's mind in things that are true, honest, just, pure, lovely, of good report, virtuous, and praiseworthy. Parents are not to instruct their children's mind in those things that are at enmity with God, but parents are the judge of which ideas are true and which are false, not the civil government.

13. Both civil government and parents derive their authority from the laws of nature and of nature's God. The functions of both, however, and the means of fulfilling those functions differ. Parents use love and discipline to fulfill their obligations. Civil government uses force and coercion to achieve its valid ends. In matters of the mind, love and discipline are permissible if not the exclusive means to achieve the legitimate education of a child. Civil force and coercion, however, are not valid means to educate children. Consequently, in the case of parents, God has directed them to instruct their child. The means of this instruction are to be undertaken in the context of love, training and discipline.

14. To the degree that such discipline is viewed as "punishment" then it could be said to also violate the prohibition against coercion, but discipline and training properly applied have no resemblance to the civil pains and penalties typically applied by the civil government when its commands are not observed: i.e., deprivation, fines and imprisonment. We should do well to keep the apples separate from the oranges when discussing "punishments" for refusal to be exposed to ideas. *See* Ephesians 6:4.

15. God does not force men to believe what He tells them. *See* Romans 1:28; "And even as they did not like to retain God in their knowledge, God gave them over to a debased mind, to do those things which are not fitting."

16. Of course the right of intellectual freedom could be asserted as a right to expose oneself to any idea that one desires. Under this approach, an individual could claim that he or she voluntarily desired to be exposed to pornographic or obscene ideas and that when the government punishes them for such exposure, the government violates their intellectual freedom. The government is thus called upon to prove how it comes into the jurisdiction to determine which ideas are protected and which are not protected.

This inquiry is of interest, but wholly beyond the context of parental education. It has already been observed that a parent's right is not a license to engage in criminal wrongs. Moreover with respect to ideas, the state has not declared that the ideas parents generally wish to convey to their children (religious, cultural etc.) are criminal and so the argument is a poor offense for those who seek to negatively equate parental rights with intellectual anarchy or those who wish to positively equate intellectual liberty in the parent-child context with an unbounded license to print and sell pornography or obscene materials.

It may be sufficient here to simply note that the immediate purpose of examining the right of intellectual freedom is to understand its historical recognition in the context of state-compelled exposure to ideas (with corresponding punishment for failure to be exposed). Left to another day is an analysis of whether the right to intellectual freedom is broader than simply a right to be free from being *compulsorily exposed,* in those circumstances where civil penalties attach for failure to submit to the compulsion.

17. CORD *supra* note 1 at 244-49. Madison wrote that: "The Religion then of every man must be left to the conviction and conscience of every man; and it is the right of every man to exercise it as these may dictate. This right is in its nature an unalienable

right. It is unalienable; because the opinions of men, depending only on the evidence contemplated by their own minds, cannot follow the dictates of other men: It is unalienable also; because what is here a right towards men, is a duty toward the Creator." *Id.* at 244.

18. CORD *supra* note 1 at 242-43.

19. Many persons think vouchers are the answer to our educational problems. But, extending power to civil government to pre-approve a school's educational options and operations is never a good solution, and government approval is the only way the civil government is going to subsidize, fund or approve education or anything else. A voucher is a funding mechanism that presumes the validity of compulsion in subsidizing state propagation (directly or indirectly) of approved ideas. Forced financial subsidization of state approved ideas, however, does not bode well whether those ideas are religious or otherwise. They are all ideas just the same.

20. CORD *supra* note 1 at 244-49.

21. ERNEST T. THOMPSON, PRESBYTERIANS IN THE SOUTH, VOL. 1: 1607-1861 (Richmond, Virginia: John Knox Press, 1963) 98.

22. *Id.* at 101.

23. *See* CORD *supra* note 1 at 249-50.

24. For background on Virginia's disestablishment *see* CHARLES F. JAMES, DOCUMENTARY HISTORY OF THE STRUGGLE FOR RELIGIOUS LIBERTY IN VIRGINIA (Lynchburg: J. P. Bell Co., 1900; reprint ed., New York: Da Capo Press, 1971). *See generally,* ISAAC A. CORNELISON, THE RELATION OF RELIGION TO CIVIL GOVERNMENT IN THE UNITED STATES OF AMERICA (New York: G. P. Putnam's Sons, 1895; reprint ed., New York: Da Capo Press, 1970).

Chapter 8

Securing Intellectual Freedom

Almighty God hath created the mind free, . . . that all attempts to influence it by temporal punishments, or burthens, or by civil incapacitations, tend only to beget habits of hypocrisy and meanness, and are a departure from the plan of the holy author of our religion, who being lord both of body and mind, yet chose not to propagate it by coercions on either, as was in his Almighty power to do.[1]

Legislation to Free the Mind

In the previous chapter, it was learned that Thomas Jefferson was the principal author of *A Bill for Establishing Religious Freedom.* In that bill he identified an immutable law of nature. He said "that the opinions and belief of men depend not on their own will, but follow involuntarily the evidence proposed to their minds."[2] Where did Jefferson get this idea that the mind will necessarily consider that which is put before it?

Jefferson identified the source of his controlling legal premise in clear and unambiguous terms. He said that intellectual freedom was based on recognition that "Almighty God hath created the mind free."[3] The Declaration also proclaimed that God created human beings and endowed them with certain unalienable rights. Now Jefferson worked that proposition out in another dimension, namely, that God created the mind of man to be free of coercion by the civil government. Jefferson's observation that "the natural rights of mankind" included those rights which flow from the idea that God created man and made his mind, was entirely consistent with the laws of nature and nature's God and their prior reflection in the Declaration of Independence.

What does it mean when we say "the mind is free?" When Jefferson says "free" he means free from the oversight and coercion of the *civil government*, not parental authority. Intellectual freedom and parental rights must be construed in *pari materia*. Construing rights in *pari materia* means construing them with reference to each other, not in derogation of each other. Thus, intellectual freedom demands limits on the jurisdiction of civil government as well as recognition of the jurisdiction of parents to direct the education of their minor children as discussed in prior Chapters.

✓ Key Idea:

☞   THE MIND WAS CREATED TO BE FREE FROM THE
      COMPULSION AND FORCE OF CIVIL GOVERNMENT.

The Commonwealth of Virginia accepted Jefferson's observation about intellectual freedom and eventually disestablished its control over the church. Virginia repealed its practice of forcibly exposing the people to state-approved religious ideas and opinions. The General Assembly not only rejected the notion that it had power to shape the ideas, opinions, and minds of the people, but it also rejected the idea that it could compel them to subsidize those ideas or finance those who promoted such ideas. Why should the same rule not apply in the case of education?

A Word about Thomas Jefferson and Education

As we proceed through this Chapter, Thomas Jefferson's views on freedom of the mind in the context of religion will be examined point by point. This approach will identify and examine the underlying principles he applied to state religious establishments such as churches. This examination will be followed with the statement or assertion that the same principles should also apply to state educational establishments such as schools.

Perhaps, the reader may then conclude that Jefferson himself applied, for instance, the underlying principles of unalienable rights and intellectual freedom in an equal fashion to both religion and education. That conclusion would be a mistake in at least one dimension. Jefferson was clearly of one mind where the principles of unalienable rights and intellectual freedom applied to religion. He was divided, however, on the application of the principles of unalienable rights and intellectual freedom to education.

It is clear that he consistently applied the principle of unalienable rights to *both* religion and education. He asserted that *religion* was "of the natural rights of mankind" and that if the legislature impaired it in any way, that such would "be an infringement of natural right."[4] Likewise, he also supported the unalienable rights of parents to direct the *education* of their children free from civil punishment. He asks:

Is it a right or a duty in society to take care of their infant members, in opposition to the will of their parents? How far does this right and duty extend? [T]o guard the life of the infant, his property, his instruction, his morals? The Roman father was supreme in all these; we draw the line: but where? Public sentiment does not seem to have traced it precisely. Nor is it necessary in the present case. It is better to tolerate the rare instance of a parent refusing to let his child be educated, than to shock the common feelings and ideas by the public asportation and education of the infant against the will of the father.[5]

Thus, to the civil government in general and to state governments in particular, Jefferson said that it *may not and ought not compel instruction in either religion or education*--it is better to tolerate a parent refusing to let his child be educated by the civil government, than to compel education against the will of the parent. Unfortunately, the current system of governmental control of education says it is better to incarcerate the rare instance of a parent refusing to let his child be educated in a state approved public or private school, than to shock the teaching profession by permitting just one child to escape the reach of the coercive education monopoly. Jefferson said show some tolerance. The modern educated man says intolerance is mandatory, incarceration is required, and force is essential.

With respect to *state mandated taxation*, however, Jefferson held a different view on religion than he did on education. He abhorred and rejected on the principle of intellectual freedom, state financial compulsion in the support of religion and churches. He declared that "to compel a man to furnish contributions of money for the propagation of opinions which he disbelieves, is sinful and tyrannical" and "that even the forcing him to support this or that teacher of his own religious persuasion, is depriving him of the comfortable liberty of giving his contributions to the particular pastor whose morals he would make his pattern, and whose powers he feels most persuasive to righteousness."[6]

But no such equal application of the principle to education is to be found. To compel a man to furnish contributions of money for the state educational propagation of opinions, was not according to Jefferson, sinful, tyrannical or even a deprivation of "comfortable liberty." According to Jefferson, such compulsion was justified, not on any principle, but simply on utility. To the objection that it is unjust to take the property of one man to educate the children of another, Jefferson responded with a circular argument. He first observed that the rich will benefit from the education of the poor because the sons and grandsons of the rich themselves may one day become poor. They may become poor because of the abolition of primogeniture. Primogeniture is the practice whereby the first-born male child takes the estate of his ancestors, in right of his seniority by birth, to the exclusion of younger siblings. Thus, younger siblings were less likely to inherit wealth and therefore more likely not to retain it.

To this premise Jefferson then added that the sons and the grandsons of the poor will one day be rich as a result of *gratis* (free) education. Thus Jefferson concluded, that the future poor sons of the present rich will derive an equal advantage of education throughout the generations, *i.e.*, they too having become poor will become rich again through free education.[7] The merits and demerits of primogeniture and the cycle of wealth and poverty, are left to the reader to sort out. Have poor children become rich because of "free" government education? Have the sons of the rich become poor because of the abolition of primogeniture? Or is it more plausible to instead believe that the future usefulness and happiness of both rich and poor children, are more likely a function of the oversight and direction of their own parents?

✓ Key Idea:

☞   THOMAS JEFFERSON SAID THAT IT IS BETTER TO TOLERATE THE RARE INSTANCE OF A PARENT REFUSING TO LET HIS CHILD BE EDUCATED BY THE CIVIL GOVERNMENT, THAN TO COMPEL PUBLIC EDUCATION OF THE CHILD AGAINST THE WILL OF THE FATHER.

In essence Jefferson didn't apply his own professed principles against coercive financing to education like he could have. He stopped short in this respect. While Jefferson is quoted extensively in this Chapter, it is not the man himself which is due ultimate deference, but the principles he correctly identified. It is the principle of intellectual freedom and freedom from coercive subsidy, *which is to be applied to teacher unions and state educational establishments, with the same intensity which Jefferson specially reserved for the clergy and religious establishments.*

While Jefferson did not reject certain forms of state taxation to support education, he clearly rejected a state controlled *system* of education such as is common today. In a letter to Joseph Cabell dated February 2, 1816, Jefferson discussed his recent legislative proposal to call each local community (as defined by militia company districts) to decide whether they would even have a local school supported chiefly by tuition of those who attended. Jefferson added that "Should the company, by its vote, decide that it would have no school, let them remain without one." Far from state mandated mass public education, Jefferson cautioned against the state assuming to force a system of education on its inhabitants. He mocked the notion of state control of education where education related legislation was being considered. He observed:

[i]f, however, it is intended that the State Government shall take this business into its own hands, and provide schools for every county, then,

by all means, strike out this provision of our bill. I should never wish that it should be placed on a worse footing than the rest of the State. But, if it is believed that these elementary schools will be better managed by the Governor and Council, the Commissioner of the Literary Fund, or any other general authority of the Government, than by the parents within each ward, it is a belief against all experience . . . . No, my friend, the way to have good and safe government, is not to trust it all to one; but to divide it among the many, distributing to every one exactly the function he is competent to.[8]

Thomas Jefferson was a defender of parental rights and real freedom in education. He was no champion of the state controlled mind or of state controlled public education or religion. His views are momentous and sobering to those who have only known him in their own unionized image.

The argument that we must have an educated citizenry and ergo that means a state controlled system of education was rejected by Jefferson. He says that the way to have good and safe government, is not to trust it all to one--to the civil government. He says do not give education to the State or its agents, its department of education, the state school board, paid professionals in our schools of education, the County, township, school district, charter school or any government corporation. The way to have good government (not the proverbial American democracy) is to distribute to every parent exactly the function he is competent to--the education of his or her own child.

Jefferson reasoned that we do not entrust the government to run our businesses, food distribution, housing, health etc., so why should we extend our child's education in the same manner. He advanced this argument in the context of his school bill. He mocks "[t]ry the principle one step further, and amend the bill so as to commit to the Governour and Council the management of all our farms, our mills, and merchants' stores." He then answers his own mocking in a jurisdictional, and not evolutionary vein, stating:

Let the National Government be entrusted with the defence of the nation, and its foreign and federal relations; the State Governments with the civil rights, laws, police and administration of what concerns the State generally; the counties with the local concern of the counties, and each ward direct the interests within itself. It is by dividing and subdividing these republics from the great national one down through all its subordinations, until it ends in the administration of every man's farm and affairs by himself; by placing under every one what his own eye may superintend, that all will be done for the best.[9]

The administration of every man's household and educational affairs *by himself* and under his own superintending eye is what Jefferson believed. He is not the pro-public education idol his pretended eulogizers have made him out to be. Jefferson was willing that the state take the people's money, but not their children or their freedom. We, however, ought not be willing to let the state take any of these three.

Jefferson concludes in politically incorrect fashion that: "I do believe, that if the Almighty has not decreed that man shall never be free, (and it is blasphemy to believe it,) that the secret will be found in the making himself the depository of the powers respecting himself, so far as he is competent to them."[10]   This belief--that parents are competent to govern their own household and that this competence is a function of God's decree--is the basis upon which parental rights is grounded.

Coercing The Mind

With this accurate understanding of Jefferson in mind, we may now return to the original discussion of the disestablishment of religion. In support of this approach, Jefferson advanced a series of logical arguments for his major legal premise that God made the mind free, and his major legal conclusion that the opinions of man cannot be forced to follow the dictates of civil rulers. Let us examine these arguments in some detail since coercion is also at the core of modern state education.

Jefferson laid the foundation for his views by declaring that "all attempts to influence it [the mind] by temporal punishments, or bur[d]ens, or by civil incapacitations, tend only to beget habits of hypocrisy and meanness, and are a departure from the plan of the holy author of our religion . . . ."[11]   In other words, free thought was disregarded by the civil government when it sought to use compulsion in things of the mind.

Jefferson outlined the rationale for this position. He said that God "who being lord both of body and mind, yet chose not to propagate it [religion] by coercions on either, as was in his Almighty power to do, *but [chose] to extend it by its influence on reason alone* . . . ."[12]   In other words, God himself does not employ force or coercion where he desires mankind to consider or accept certain ideas, though God certainly has the power to coerce. If God doesn't use his power to coerce man to consider certain ideas, then just who is the civil government to invoke such a power? The state legislature's arrogance rushes in where God doesn't even tread.

Remember, Jefferson expressed this view at a time when the Virginia civil government used religion as a powerful vehicle of influence and control. Religion and religious ideas were propped up by a regulatory structure. Punishments and other legal disabilities were imposed upon those persons who did not want to be subject to the state's self-appointed power to direct their thinking. The self-appointed advocates of controlling American religion were no doubt outraged that Jefferson would "attack religion." They probably demanded to know: "Why is Mr. Jefferson against the religious instruction of the people?"

When confronted with the simple notion that God made the mind free and that the opinions of men are not subject to the dictates of another, the self-appointed apostles of American education plagiarize their historical brethren. They are outraged that someone would "attack education." They demand an answer to the same question which could have been asked two hundred years ago: "What reasonable person can be against the education of children?"

✓ Key Idea:
☞   OPPOSITION TO COMPULSION IN RELIGION IS NOT OPPOSITION TO RELIGION. OPPOSITION TO COMPULSION TO EDUCATION IS NOT OPPOSITION TO EDUCATION.

God made the mind as free in 1786 as He does today. The opinions of men were not subject to the dictates of the civil government in 1786 and they are not subject to the dictates of civil government today. All ideas *whether religious or secular*, are beyond the jurisdiction of the civil government to compel exposure to at any time in history. These facts require legislative steps to bar civil government from using force, compulsion or coercion to direct the education of our children.

The Temptations of Virginia

Having laid the foundation that God made the mind free, Jefferson then proceeded to analyze the four elements of state established religion:

1)   State approved preachers/teachers;
2)   State approved prayers/curriculum and textbooks;
3)   State compelled attendance/truancy laws;
4)   State compelled financing through tithes/taxation.

Jefferson examined each of these elements point by point and illuminated their legal and intellectual defects. Let us examine his analysis and then redirect his arguments from the state established church to the state established school.

Virginia had already succumbed to the temptation to violate intellectual freedom through four practices:

1) Virginia licensed its clergy. Only state approved clergy could teach and preach. Only clergy which taught state approved doctrine could receive a license. In general, all others were barred and punished for unauthorized teaching and preaching. Today state governments license teachers through teacher certification requirements. Only state approved teachers (most often those who have graduated from a state approved or accredited institution) may teach. Approved teachers must teach the state's minimum curriculum. Uncertified teachers are not recognized as valid teachers.

2) Virginia practiced compulsory exposure to state-approved religious ideas and opinions. Historically this practice included forced use of the state-approved prayer book; today it involves forced use of the state-approved curriculum, tests and testing, and outcomes.

3) Virginia enforced compulsory attendance laws. Historically this practice involved mandatory church attendance; today it is mandatory school attendance and accompanying truancy laws.

4) Virginia required compulsory financial support. In the 18th century this requirement included escheats and compulsory taxation. Today it includes development fees and all types of taxation such as millages, income and property taxes.

Thomas Jefferson offers an evaluation of these practices. His views on compulsory exposure and attendance laws will be considered first. His analysis reveals why these practices are dangerous and unlawful. He also reveals something of the *character* of those who participate in the state's systematic abuse of intellectual freedom. The character of government officials really mattered to him and it should matter to us as well. We are not merely interested in the legal basis of intellectual freedom. We are also interested in the character of those who claim to power to forcibly dictate what our children should think.

Compulsory Exposure and Attendance

In the context of religion, Jefferson offered severe and astringent criticism for those persons who imposed their opinions and ideas on others through the force of law. After all is said and done, this is what is at issue: the power of the civil government is used to force one man's ideas on another's child. Yet are those who force their ideas infallible? Do they see truth better than the child's parents? Jefferson asserted:

> [T]he impious presumption of legislators and rulers, civil as well as ecclesiastical, who, being themselves but fallible and uninspired men, have assumed dominion over the faith of others, setting up their own opinions and modes of thinking as the only true and infallible, and as such endeavoring to impose them on others, hath established and maintained false religions over the greatest part of the world and through all time.[13]

In other words, it was the *legislators* who imposed their own opinions or modes of thinking on the people. It was the legislators who sponsored, directed, regulated or controlled religious ideas and faith. Jefferson describes their character: impious, fallible and uninspired. And what is the character of today's local, state and federal officials in light of the same principle? Are not such officials, school board members, local superintendents and government lawmakers also impious, fallible and uninspired? Do these public officials disrespect parental rights, usurp parental authority, and (with the aid of local judges) fine and punish parents for their children's truancy? They are all these and more if they have assumed the oversight of our children's minds.

But legislators are not the only public servants guilty of setting up their own opinions as officially "true and infallible" and then imposing them on others. The judiciary has been equally at fault. In the educational context, the Supreme Court has specifically approved of the use of civil power to compel the mind to be exposed to a government inspired state-approved curriculum. In *Board of Education v. Pico*, the Court stated that "[t]he school is designed to, and inevitably will, inculcate ways of thought and outlooks."[14] In other words, if the mind is exposed long enough (depending on the person) to the same content or ideas, then the opinions and beliefs of that person will tend to accept the content proposed to the mind. This is simply human nature. It is the way God created the mind to work.

The result of this legislative and judicial presumption has taken the form of laws requiring compulsory attendance or education at schools owned, controlled or regulated by the government. Such laws apply to state schools as well as private schools. For instance, state regulation of both curriculum and instruction in private and parochial schools has been held to be a valid exercise of the state's police power. While private schools have a judicially declared Constitutional right to exist and parents have a right to send their children to them, it has also been held that the state legislature has a right to regulate such schools in the public's interest.

Governmental regulations which have been found to be permissible include compulsory school attendance, state certification of private school teachers, state approval of minimum curricular standards, the requirement that private schools maintain a course of study approved by the state commissioner of education, use necessary equipment and materials, maintain a specified pupil-teacher ratio, and submit to state licensing and supervision of such schools and school courses.[15] This is not exactly freedom of choice.

These laws and regulations are examples of arrogant impious presumption. Courts and legislatures have arrogated to themselves the power to establish their own opinions and modes of thinking as the only official point of view. They have imposed them on others with the understanding that their imposition is "designed to and inevitably will inculcate ways of thought and outlooks."

State statutes have claimed to regulate private schools in order "to ensure that children be exposed to other attitudes, values, morals, lifestyles, and intellectual abilities by having contact with children outside their immediate family."[16] This is no different in principle than the Supreme Court's approval in *Ambach v. Norwick*[17] that the states' public schools are "an assimilative force by which diverse and conflicting elements in our society are brought together on a broad but common ground."[18]

Through compulsory attendance laws, state governments have told parents what ages of children must be forced to listen to the government's curriculum.

The civil government has told parents whether or not they are eligible to teach their own children by requiring teacher certification. They have told parents what their child must learn by requiring state approval of minimum curricular standards and through requiring private schools to maintain an approved course of study. They have told parents what is an acceptable educational setting by requiring private schools to maintain a specified pupil-teacher ratio. They have told parents how to socialize their children properly by defining the "other attitudes, values, morals, lifestyles, and intellectual abilities" to which they shall be exposed. What is arrogance and usurpation of rights if not this? And yet we still pretend that these usurpers will teach our children "character" and that they are "role models."

✓ **Key Idea:**

> ☞   INTELLECTUAL FREEDOM IS DENIED WHEN THE CIVIL GOVERNMENT MANDATES EXPOSURE TO ITS APPROVED IDEAS.

The legislature which does these things, substitutes its will for that of parents. The legislature, however, has not borne the child. It possesses no inherent virtue or expertise that is not also available to parents. Where does it claim to be endowed by the Creator with a right to dominate the thinking of its youngest citizens? State governments have no inside track on the "best way" to educate children. Indeed, if the civil government's track record on education were considered, one would be forced by the sheer weight of evidence to conclude quite the opposite--that its efforts are a remarkable failure.

By legislating in this way, however, the government has "assumed dominion" over our children. It has set up its "own opinions and modes of thinking as the only true and infallible" ones. If parents lack the discernment or the discretion to decide what is best for their own children, how much less competent and discerning are their neighbors who happen to sit in the legislature?

As God gave children to parents and not the civil government, then parental judgment must control, not the teachings of the legislature. Let the evidence be submitted to a candid world. Have not the state legislatures violated the unalienable right of parents to choose that to which their own children shall be exposed?[19] Think back to Jefferson's critique of impious religious leaders. Did that criticism effortlessly flow through your mind? How did the same critique as applied to education flow? Was it a little harder to circulate? Consider some other applications of this "natural right" and its extension to education.

Financial Compulsion

Jefferson's challenge to governmental oversight of ideas ran deeper than just objecting to the civil government setting up its own curriculum and excluding all other ideas. He was also concerned about money.[20] He said "that to compel a man to furnish contributions of money for the propagation of opinions which he disbelieves, is sinful and tyrannical." He added "that even the forcing him to support this or that teacher of his own religious persuasion, is depriving him of the comfortable liberty of giving his contributions to the particular pastor whose morals he would make his pattern, and whose powers he feels most persuasive to righteousness."[21]

This is plain language. His meaning cannot be mistaken. He is saying that no one should be compelled to finance the teaching or dissemination of ideas, opinions or publications. No one should be compelled to finance teaching or ideas which he or she disbelieves, considers offensive or simply does not wish to support, irrespective of its worthiness. The use of the taxing power to finance teaching or the inculcation of ideas violates the unalienable right of every person to support *voluntarily only* those opinions and ideas that he or she desires to support.[22]

Whether one agrees with those ideas is not the point. Agreement or disagreement is not relevant in this context. The point is that the right to give voluntarily to those who espouse ideas that you support is being trampled upon by the civil government. If this principle is applied to governmental control of American education, it is easy to see just how deep the abuse runs. Where the local government levies property taxes on its residents and then applies those taxes to support this or that teacher or educator, then that local or county government deprives each of its property-owning residents of their unalienable right to support *voluntarily only* those opinions and ideas that each resident individually desires to support.[23]

✓ Key Idea:

   ☞   INTELLECTUAL FREEDOM IS DENIED WHEN THE CIVIL GOVERNMENT MANDATES FINANCIAL SUPPORT FOR THE TEACHING OF IDEAS.

These property owners are deprived of giving their individual contributions of money to the particular printing house, school or teacher whose concern and perspective each would support. Each property-owning *parent* is deprived of his unalienable right to support *voluntarily only* those teachers and schools they think will impart to their own child those opinions and modes of thinking that each parent believes are most persuasive to their child's individualized needs and character. Coercion by way of taxation contravenes this right in every respect when the civil government undertakes the forcible propagation of ideas.[24] This is also the situation when the civil government levies an income or any other type of tax on its citizens and then applies any or all of that tax to the propagation or maintenance of this or that idea or educational institution. The controlling principle is that if those who attend an institution do not, will not, or cannot financially support it, then those who do not attend the institution ought not be forced to support it.

✓ Key Idea:

☞   IF THOSE WHO ATTEND AN INSTITUTION DO NOT
VOLUNTARILY SUPPORT ITS FINANCIAL DEMANDS,
THEN WHY SHOULD THOSE WHO *DO NOT* ATTEND,
BE FORCED TO SUPPORT IT?

It is clear that Jefferson construed the principle to prohibit compelling a man to subsidize religious opinions contrary to one's own point of view. Compelling a man to subsidize opinions contrary to his own point of view is certainly unlawful. The principle also prohibits *compelling* him to subsidize opinions that are *consistent* with his own opinions. This type of compulsion is also unlawful. It deprives the individual of the right to support *voluntarily only* those opinions and ideas that he desires to support. It is the same right and principle whether or not the state compels one to aid what one approves or aid what one opposes. It is the same principle whether the state-established church or state-established school is involved. The unalienable right of intellectual freedom applies equally across the board even though Jefferson himself did not apply the principle to education *per se.*

Equitable Financial Compulsion

Moreover, the principle of intellectual freedom is not laid aside simply because the *form* of financial compulsion is "equitable." Thus, a state legislature or supreme court may not escape the reach of the principle merely by increasing or reappropriating tax dollars out of the treasury for equal *per capita* redistribution throughout the state. This trend is one of the more distressing movements in state school funding--equalization of per pupil expenditures across districts.[25] What does this mean? To use a real-life example: In 1989-90, Princeton, New Jersey raised $8,346 per student at a tax rate of 67 cents per $100 of assessed property value. Camden taxed its residents at $1.62 per $100 but raised only $4,186 per student. Reliance on the assessed value of local property varied widely and produced diverse results in the amount of money available for students on a comparative district basis. The remedy for this spending gap was to raise state taxes in order to equalize expenditures across districts, making them roughly equal in every part of the state.

Prior discussion of the Declaration of Independence has indicated that equality is something to be embraced, so what is the danger in equalization? The rule or principle of equality requires equal opportunity. In the context of parental rights equality of opportunity means the opportunity for every child to be educated by their own parents or their voluntarily obtained agent. The principle of equality does not mean equal results. It does not mean that every parent is equal in ability or financial capacity. The amount of money one has is not a function of some immutable characteristic. The principle of equality should not become a pretext for state centralization or governmental control of education and educational funding.[26]

In the context of *equalization,* however, the greater resources of some districts are made to support the lesser resources of other districts *across school district lines.* While this transfer of money is interesting, it is not the central defect. This sort of equalization occurs everyday *within districts* and was first accepted when the idea that each individual parent need not be financially responsible for the education of their own child was accepted by the community.

The real abuse in financing education emerged when the old idea that each parent should pay his own child's way was rejected. The new idea became: "Let the district pay the way." Now the idea is becoming: "Let the people of the State pay the way." Soon it will be: "Let the people of the United States pay the way." The push for statewide equalization is simply the next logical extension of the idea that civil government (first one's neighbor, then the district, then the States and then the United States) must pay the way.

The only other objection to equalization beyond loss of parental rights is principally that equalization centralizes control. Equalization is dangerous in and of itself because it takes control one more step away from parents. It is deceptive because it extends more control to the state, thereby consolidating education even more than it presently is centralized.[27]

State laws which require the attendance or education of children at any government-run-or-regulated school, which interfere or regulate parents or the parent-teacher relationship, or which compel financial support of the government's propagation of ideas, are contrary to the civil government's obligation to secure intellectual liberty. Such educational laws accomplish the opposite result. They aid and abet forcible exposure and support. Such laws must be repealed by the state legislature. They are contrary to the intent and purpose of civil government under the Declaration. In states where state constitutions define or intimate that the people posses certain unalienable, inherent or natural rights, their state courts should also be prevailed upon to strike statutory provisions down as contrary to the state's own constitution, provided the courts truly interpret the written text and do not make up its meaning to serve personal bias.

Jefferson also noted the dangerous effect of financial subsidies on the recipient. He said that the tendency of these subsidies is to "corrupt the principles of that religion it is meant to encourage, by bribing, with the monopoly of worldly honors and emoluments, those who will externally profess and conform to it." With respect to those who are so bribed, he notes "that though indeed these are criminal who do not withstand such temptation, yet neither are those innocent who lay the bait in their way."[28]

What forceful language! He is speaking of elected officials as engaging in bribery! And of the public officials who offer the bribe, Jefferson says they are acting like criminals. Moreover, those who conform to teaching the civil government's approved curriculum are also charged with *accepting* a bribe.

✓ Key Idea:
> ☞   THE FINANCING OF PUBLIC EDUCATION IS BASED
>   ON A SYSTEM OF GIVING AND TAKING BRIBES.

In the context of education, it can be said with equal force that the state legislature bribes with a monopoly of worldly honors (pay raises), those teachers and school districts who will externally parrot its will and conform their pupils to the ideas or curriculum approved, certified and accredited by the legislature. Whether those ideas are in the form of an "outcome based" curriculum, "prayer in the schools" or otherwise, it is bribery all the same.

Moreover, just as the state religious establishment was built on conformity and bribes, so by analogy the state educational system is also built on conformity and bribes. If this statement rings true in the context of religion, should it not reverberate just as clear in the context of education? The unalienable right of intellectual freedom is universal. Jefferson summarized his argument by saying:

> [T]hat to suffer the civil magistrate to intrude his powers into the field of opinion and to restrain the profession or propagation of principles on supposition of their ill tendency is a dangerous fallacy, which at once destroys all religious liberty, because he being of course judge of that tendency will make his opinions the rule of judgment, and approve or condemn the sentiments of others only as they shall square with or differ from his own.[29]

By the same principle, when parents permit the civil authorities, their local school board or the Secretary of Education to intrude their power into the field of composition, writing and teaching, they permit a dangerous and deceptive practice. They permit the civil government to destroy freedom of the mind as well as undermine parental rights.[30] The pushing and prodding of the federal government for national testing and examinations now becomes clear for what it truly is--destruction of intellectual freedom, usurpation of parental rights and centralization of control. Such is the face of tyranny, not freedom. Do not let the smiling face of a politician confuse the difference.

In closing his discussion on the subject of intellectual freedom, Jefferson affirmed:

[T]ruth is great and will prevail if left to herself; that she is the proper and sufficient antagonist to error, and has nothing to fear from the conflict unless by human interposition disarmed of her natural weapons, free argument and debate; errors ceasing to be dangerous when it is permitted freely to contradict them.[31]

What does it mean to say that "truth can be disarmed of her natural weapons" by human interposition? Jefferson is saying that as long as a human authority does not prevent free argument and debate on ideas, then truth will be able to overcome that which is false. When the government controls the curriculum, however, whether religious or otherwise, only those ideas that the government permits into the discussion can be considered. But to assume that the civil government has a monopoly on truth or true ideas is dangerous--it is "an impious presumption." Indeed such a claim is genuinely arrogant irrespective of whether it comes from the political right, left or otherwise.

Statutory Freedom and Choice in Thought

In response to these insights, the 1786 General Assembly of Virginia decided to yield to temptation no longer. It consequently enacted a law that prohibited compulsion in attendance and financial matters. The legislature declared that:

[N]o man shall be compelled to frequent or support any religious worship, place, or ministry whatsoever, nor shall be enforced, restrained, molested, or bur[d]ened in his body or goods, nor shall otherwise suffer, on account of his religious opinions or belief; but that all men shall be free to profess, and by argument to maintain, their opinions in matters of religion, and that the same shall in no wise diminish, enlarge, or affect their civil capacities.[32]

Equal strength of the principle and of the rights involved requires that today's state legislatures apply the same rule to education.[33] The legislative remedy for such an abuse is to free up education from the civil government by enacting legislation repealing the present practices of compulsory influence, exposure, certification and financial support. The right to educate free from government influence, control or regulation lies at the heart of real parental choice and real intellectual freedom.[34]

The unalienable right of intellectual freedom must be revived and asserted. This right includes freedom of every person to choose what to believe, the freedom to choose that to which one shall be exposed, and the freedom to finance or support voluntarily only those ideas and teachers one would follow. It is time to abolish the state school and repeal governmental control over private and home-based education.

★ HYPOTHETICALLY SPEAKING . . . .

Problem: The people living in the Nation of Blackacre are very secular. Their institutions presuppose the existence of human history since time immemorial. The people believe that they can only achieve their greatest potential when they are educated in the knowledge of man and his world.

The people have just elected you as their sole ruler. They now demand you pass a compulsory education law. They want you to establish and institute a "school system of secular instruction that will educate the children of Blackacre in the knowledge of man and his world." They also demand you require attendance at the school and punish those who do not attend, otherwise the people fear that the Nation will soon become illiterate and ignorant and will not be able to compete in a global economy. If you meet their demand, they will give you an honorary Doctorate of Philosophy degree. If you refuse their demand, the people of Blackacre will say you are against education and impeach you. Should you pass the law?

Answer: No. You must refuse to pass such a law on the grounds that "the opinions of men cannot follow the dictates of the government." While it is true that education in the knowledge of man is important and is related to the security of a Nation, it is not true that the civil government has any right to compel people to know about "man and his world" or to penalize them for failure to know.

Notes

1. ROBERT L. CORD, SEPARATION OF CHURCH AND STATE (New York: Lambeth Press, 1982) 250, quoting Thomas Jefferson's "A Bill for Establishing Religious Freedom."

2. CORD *supra* note 1 at 249.

3. *See also* An Act for Religious Freedom, adopted by the Virginia General Assembly on January 16, 1786, VA. CODE ANN. § 57-1 (1950).

4. An Act For Religious Freedom *supra* note 3. *See* CORD *supra* note 1 at 250. For an excellent analysis applying freedom of the mind to endowments for the arts, sciences and public broadcasting *see* Daniel R. Blackford, *The Extent of Civil Authority over Opinions and Ideas,* (Masters Thesis, Regent University, 1986).

5. J. W. RANDOLPH, EARLY HISTORY OF THE UNIVERSITY OF VIRGINIA, AS CONTAINED IN THE LETTERS OF THOMAS JEFFERSON AND JOSEPH C. CABELL, (Richmond, VA: C. H. Wynne, Printer, 1856) 97. See also CHARLES F. ARROWOOD, THOMAS JEFFERSON AND EDUCATION IN A REPUBLIC, (New York: McGraw-Hill Book Co., Inc., 1930) 61-62. The legal term "asportation" means the wrongful or felonious removal of goods from the place where they were deposited. As used by Jefferson, the "public asportation and education of the infant against the will of the father," means the wrongful or felonious removal of a child from his or her parent by the state.

6. An Act for Religious Freedom *supra* note 3. *See also* CORD *supra* note 1 at 249-50.

7. RANDOLPH *supra* note 5 at 105. *See* ARROWOOD *supra* note 5 at 62-63.

8. RANDOLPH *supra* note 5 at 54.

9. RANDOLPH *supra* note 5 at 54.

10. To the modern state educated mind, this is all embarrassing "religion."

11. An Act for Religious Freedom *supra* note 3.

12. *See* CORD *supra* note 1 at 249. The text in italics was deleted by Senate amendment on January 16, 1786.

13. An Act for Religious Freedom *supra* note 3. *See also* CORD *supra* note 1 at 249.

14. 457 U.S. 853, 879 (1982)(Blackmun, J., concurring in part).

15. *See* Dale R. Agthe, *Validity of State Regulation of Curriculum and Instruction in Private and Parochial Schools*, 18 AMERICAN LAW REPORTS 4TH, 649 (1982 and 1994 Supp.) In certain limited instances, courts have held some of these regulations to be invalid, generally on grounds of religious liberty and due process of law. Though the religious liberty claims of some parents have prevailed, they have usually been limited to situations where parents convince a court that the beliefs of their church or religion prohibit them from submitting to the regulation at issue, that such beliefs are sincerely held, that the state's interest is not compelling and that parental rights cannot be otherwise accommodated (or some combination thereof). *See* People v. DeJonge, 442 Mich 266, 501 NW2d 127 (1993)(religious parents enjoy unalienable right to educate free from state requirement mandating use of state certified teachers).

This approach however, does not do justice to the principle that *all* parents are endowed with certain unalienable rights, and that among these is the right to direct and control the education of their children free from state intervention, regulation or control. The religious freedom approach takes this right and destroys its universal feature. It regards parental rights as valid only when a parent can qualify on religious grounds. While some parents have been freed from state control of their child's education on a religious basis, the principle upon which their freedom rests does very little to aid all parents generally. More significantly, this approach does nothing to advance unalienable rights and actually undermines its potential in future litigation. For other "successful" cases in this area see, Kentucky State Board for Education & Secondary Education v. Rudasill, 589 SW2d 877 (1979), *cert. denied*, 446 U.S. 938; State of Ohio v. Whisner, 351 NE2d 750 (1976); State of Vermont v. La Barge, 357 A2d 121 (1976); and Nagle v. Olin, 415 NE2d 279 (1980).

16. *See* Strosnider v. Strosnider, 101 NM 639, 686 P2d 981 (1984 App). *See also In Re* Kilroy, 121 Misc. 2d 98, 467 NYS2d 318 (1983)(Home visitation by public school education committee whose duty was to evaluate non-public schools was considered a permissible requirement for home schoolers).

17. 441 U.S. 68 (1979).

18. *Id.* at 77, citing JOHN DEWEY, DEMOCRACY AND EDUCATION, AN INTRODUCTION TO THE PHILOSOPHY OF EDUCATION, (New York: The MacMillan Company, 1916) 26 (quotation marks omitted).

19. The only limited deviation from this practice appears to be found among those States in which the legislature or courts have enacted or construed compulsory attendance provisions to allow "equivalent instruction" elsewhere than in a school. While some limited exceptions exist, the general rule is that the,

> contention that instruction in the home is instruction in a "private school" has been rejected in several cases, either because of the difficulty of governmental supervision or for the reason that the place of instruction must be a duly organized and existing educational institution.

14 AMERICAN LAW REPORTS 2ND 1369 (1950).

Courts which have ruled in favor of parents have not done so on the basis of their unalienable rights, but rather on the basis that home instruction or instruction by a parent's agent complied with the spirit and the letter of the law. For instance, in People v. Levisen the court held that a child was attending a school within the meaning of the statute "where it appeared that the mother, who had received training in various educational fields, was giving her child instruction corresponding to that which she would have received in the public schools, with regular hours of study and recitation." 14 AMERICAN LAW REPORTS 2ND 1369, 1371 citing People v. Levisen, 90 NE2d 213 (1950). It was also observed in State v. Peterman that:

> The result to be obtained, and not the means or manner of obtaining it, was the goal which the lawmakers were attempting to reach. The law was made for the parent who does not educate his child, and not for the parent who employs a teacher and pays him out of his private purse, and so places within the reach of the child the opportunity and means of acquiring an education equal to that obtainable in the public schools of the State.

14 AMERICAN LAW REPORTS 2ND 1369, 1371 citing State v. Peterman, 70 NE 550 (1904).

Both of these cases, though ultimately favorable to the parents, nevertheless required parents to maintain minimum standards determined by the state. To that extent they run roughshod over the right of parents to say what, when, where, and by whom their children shall be educated.

More recently, the cases seem to have favored state qualification of private schools in three distinct areas; 1) the age and duration of attendance, 2) the approval of curriculum, and 3) the certification and competency of the teacher. *See generally*, Allan E. Korpela, *What Constitutes a Private, Parochial, or Denominational School Within Statute Making Attendance at Such School in Compliance with Compulsory School Attendance Law*, 65 AMERICAN LAW REPORTS 3RD 1222 (1975 and 1994 Supp.)

20. In Virginia, where Jefferson resided, the laws relating to state intervention into education prior to 1870 permitted the state to provide money from the literary fund, established in 1810. These monies went to local authorities to assist in paying the expenses of education of indigent children and school construction. The literary fund's purpose was solely for the education of poor children. The fund obtained its revenue by looking to escheat, confiscations, forfeitures, and abandoned personal property. No local taxation or direct state appropriation was considered. Albert L. Garrison, *Legislative Basis for State Support of Public Elementary and Secondary Education in Virginia since 1810*, (Masters Thesis, Duke University, 1932) 1-5.

21. An Act for Religious Freedom *supra* note 3. *See also* CORD *supra* note 1 at 249-50.

22. Jefferson's proposal for public education was reduced to a "Bill for the More General Diffusion of Knowledge" and introduced into the Virginia House of Delegates in June, 1779. It is true that the Bill would have committed some public funds to educate children and pay instructors whose parents indicated that they lacked the means to provide for their schooling. It is clear, however, that "Jefferson never advocated public schools like those operating in the nation today. The grammar schools under his plan were still largely supported by tuition." ANDREW M. ALLISON, THE REAL THOMAS JEFFERSON, VOL. 1, THE AMERICAN CLASSIC SERIES (Washington, D.C.: National Center for Constitutional Studies, 1983). "Jefferson also expressed both fear and scorn when contemplating a centralized state authority in education." JAMES B. CONANT, THOMAS JEFFERSON AND THE DEVELOPMENT OF AMERICAN PUBLIC EDUCATION (Berkeley: University of California Press, 1962) 30-31.

Joseph Cabell and Thomas Jefferson were the principal founders of the University of Virginia. This university also received money from the Commonwealth's Treasury for the "propagation of opinions." The University opened on October 7, 1822 with Mr. Jefferson as its first rector. It is crucial to note that no one is compelled to attend a University, though the people of the Commonwealth were compelled to support its professors and maintain its facilities, irrespective of whether the people concurred or dissented from the ideas expressed therein.

The principles of the Declaration and the Constitution are our guide, not necessarily the historical examples of past generations. There is no reason why precedent should prevail when shown to be contrary to principle. The framers of the Constitution recognized this, for example, when they realized that the Articles of Confederation were inconsistent with the principles of the Declaration of Independence. Even though that same generation had drafted both of these documents, they did not abandon the principles of the former in order to legitimate the defects of what followed. We should be ready to learn from their example.

23. A faint reflection of Jefferson's principle of freedom from financial compulsion surfaces from time to time in Supreme Court cases. The reflection is "faint" since the principle is only extended to bar compulsory support of *political* ideas. *See* Keller v. State Bar of California, 496 U.S. 1 (1990)(State Bar's use of compulsory dues to finance political and ideological activities with which petitioners disagreed violates First Amendment right of speech when such expenditures are not necessary or reasonably incurred for the purpose of regulating the legal profession or improving quality of legal services). The Court apparently approves of compulsory support for regulating the legal profession or improving the quality of legal services irrespective of whether one wants to fund those objects through another organization. Far from defending the unalienable right of every person to support *voluntarily only* those opinions and ideas which he or she desires to support, the Court balances away the right and lets compulsory association and financial coercion prevail. It is unfortunate that these types of decisions are hailed as victories when they strike at the very heart of the one principle that can result in real freedom from the compulsion of governmental monopolies such as a state bar association.

24. Jefferson does not rest with a criticism of the state-controlled curriculum or coercive taxation to support teachers of religion. He notes that these deprivations of liberty also demean religion and the clergy. He says that the clergy are now more likely to seek after the honor associated with position and power, rather than embrace the rewards of genuine service. The natural result of state control and support leads to "withdrawing from the ministry those temporary rewards, which proceeding from an approbation of their personal conduct, are an additional incitement to earnest and unremitting labors for the instruction of mankind . . . ." In other words, because the clergy is paid money forced from their neighbor's pocket, it is unlikely that their neighbor will then voluntarily pay additional sums out of genuine thankfulness for the clergy's labor. Only a fool makes a gift to a thief after he steals your money. See An Act for Religious Freedom *supra* note 3. The same rule also applies to state established education and its state-paid teachers and professors.

25. The Supreme Court has held that relative differences in taxation and spending levels between school districts located in the same state do not violate the equal protection clause of the Constitution or entitle strict scrutiny by the courts of statewide schemes of school finance. *See* San Antonio Independent School District v. Rodriguez, 411 U.S. 1 (1973).

26. The State of Michigan embraced this approach through reduction of high local property taxes and a corresponding increase in sales and income taxes. The net effect was to further centralize financial control of Michigan education in the state government.

27. What the state proposes to do with equalization of funding is to *guarantee a minimum* level of *equal results* to which everyone is entitled as a matter of right. The state set this level when it established minimum graduation requirements. Now the state is trying to set a minimum financial level as well. The point is, however, that the state should not act as a minimum level guarantor. Certainly where state action is involved it is under an obligation to apply the law even-handedly, but the education of a child is a parental, not a state function. Therefore, the funding of a child's education is a parental, not a state function.

If the process of equalization were carried to its natural and national conclusion, the federal government would require every state to spend at least $5246 per child which was the 1989-90 average expenditure nationwide. Tom Snyder and W. Vance Grant, "1989 Back to School Forecast," press release, National Center for Education Statistics, August 24, 1989. If the logic of equalization (in other words -- guaranteed minimum results) were valid, it should then be extended not only to funding, but also to advancement to the next grade. For a student who is held back a year will not have the equal opportunity as a classmate who is promoted. This line of reasoning can be applied in perpetuity. If pushed to the next step, if a student is not graduated then he or she does not have an equal opportunity to obtain employment as do others. And again, if a person does not have a two or four year college degree, the same can be said -- he lacks equal opportunity. If he does not have a guaranteed first job, how will he compete with those already employed on an equal basis? This logic, however, would require equal *results* across the board and has nothing to do with equal *opportunity* based on ability and merit.

Equalization is not only invalid in terms of equality, but it requires a centralized bureaucratic structure to implement, oversee and control. With centralization, comes standardization of ideas and the mind, loss of real choice for parents and loss of real freedom. Consider that in 1945-46 the United States contained 101,382 public school districts. In 1986-87 these were consolidated into only 15,713 districts. Far from encouraging diversity, the consolidation of these districts resulted in uniformity of curriculum and thought. Equalization would merely continue this trend resulting in only 50 school districts. One district for each state would serve simply as an administrative convenience to the federal government! Centralization does not lead to diversity or choice--it leads to uniformity and control. *See* National Center for Education Statistics, Office of Educational Research and Improvement, Digest of Education Statistics, 1988 (Department of Education, 1988) p. 83.

28. An Act For Religious Freedom *supra* note 3. *See* CORD *supra* note 1 at 250.

29. An Act for Religious Freedom *supra* note 3.

30. Jefferson, of course, acknowledged "that it is time enough for the rightful purposes of civil government for its officers to interfere when principles break out into overt acts against peace and good order . . . ." An Act For Religious Freedom *supra* note 3. *See* CORD *supra* note 1 at 250. But this is not an invitation to usurp the freedom of the mind. It is a recognition that when the people engage in *overt acts* to subvert the peace and order of the community, the government may properly arrest such actions.

31. An Act For Religious Freedom *supra* note 3. *See* CORD *supra* note 1 at 250.

32. An Act For Religious Freedom *supra* note 3. *See* CORD *supra* note 1 at 250.

33. Virginia also recognized that the universality of these rights was not limited to a colonial period or mere application to religious ideas. The Virginia Assembly observed this when it declared:

> And though we know well that this Assembly, elected by the people for the ordinary purposes of legislation only, have no power to restrain the acts of succeeding Assemblies, constituted with powers equal to our own, and that

therefore to declare this act irrevocable would be of no effect in law; yet we are free to declare and do declare, that the rights hereby asserted are of the natural rights of mankind, and that if any act shall be hereafter passed to repeal the present or to narrow its operation, such act will be an infringement of natural right.

The Virginia Assembly declared that the rights protected by the law were the natural rights of mankind. If any law were later passed to repeal or narrow these rights, it would be an impermissible infringement of natural rights.

34. State and federal enactments touching education constitute an infringement of natural right. Present day state educational enactments are clearly acts that infringe the unalienable rights of parents and tie the intellectual freedom of all to the millstone of state-approved curriculums. State statutes that regulate or interfere with the education of children at home or at private schools are also contrary to natural right. In addition, government education in the public sector, both at the state and federal level, wrongfully compels the taxpayers to support the erection and maintenance of a physical building. It wrongfully compels them to support state school teachers whether they agree with them or not. Most importantly, most state laws wrongly compel parents to send their children to be exposed to ideas and opinions approved and propagated by the government.

Chapter 9

Religion and Pure Religion

Pure religion and undefiled before God and the Father is this, To visit the fatherless and widows in their affliction, and to keep himself unspotted from the world.[1]

Commitment of Religion to First Principles

Having identified both the unalienable right of parents and the unalienable right of intellectual freedom in the law of nature, we then established that civil governments are duty bound to guard and defend those rights in the context of education. This Chapter pauses to consider whether or not activist religious organizations have defended and advanced these unalienable rights in a judicial context. What is their general litigation track record? Should these groups undertake such a defense? Should they work toward disestablishment? Are they intellectually and legally equipped to do so?

Our examination need not be extensive in order to capture the flavor of present litigation tactics and principles. Two contexts, one historical and one modern, will suffice to show how religious organizations have unfortunately, not only abandoned parental rights and intellectual freedom, but have also shown a remarkable unfamiliarity with the law of nature itself. The first context considers the central place that religious organizations once held with respect to the education of children, especially children from poor families. The second context jumps to the more or less harmful effect which has resulted from the litigation of education cases under the First Amendment of the U.S. Constitution. Much of this Chapter discusses cases and legal theory. The non-legal reader may be inclined to move to the next Chapter. To the extent, however, such a reader also tends to also be a financial contributor to religious litigating organizations, this Chapter might be helpful in understanding the actual principles one's money is advancing.

The first context examines the crucial involvement of churches and religious organizations in providing children with an education, especially when the child's parents were poor or mother widowed. Churches and religious organizations recognized the need and acknowledged their obligation to help their neighbor as themselves. The need in the South was particularly significant. Religious bodies initially "attempted to meet the need for elementary education on the part of the masses of the [southern] people by establishment of Sunday schools."[2] These Sunday schools taught children to read and spell, instructed them in sound morals and the "first principles of natural and revealed religion." They also "taught gratuitously, did not take children from their work, did not belong exclusively to any religious sect, were successful in discipline, in elevating the minds and manners of the poor, and in extending the reign of love between rich and poor."[3]

The churches provided a crucial service in educating children of poor parents. The education was basic, privately endowed and free of governmental control.[4] The social movement for a free *public system* of education recognized this situation but characterized it as a limitation. The state also argued that education by itself through a *system* of instruction could be more beneficial.

✓ Key Idea:

☞   RELIGIOUS ORGANIZATIONS SHOULD REEVALUATE
      HOW THEY CAN BEST MEET THEIR OBLIGATION TO
      ASSIST POOR PARENTS IN THE EXERCISE OF GOD-
      GIVEN PARENTAL RIGHTS.

The move to a *state system* of instruction attracted many supporters. The rationale for a state system was well represented in a letter from James H. Thornwell, President of the State College of South Carolina, to Governor Manning on the subject of "Public Instruction in South Carolina." Thornwell said that:

> There are those among us who admit that no complete *system* of popular education can be instituted without the intervention of the State, and yet maintain that the true method is simply to supplement individual exertions [of parents and churches]; that is, they would have those who are able to do so educate their children in schools sustained by themselves, and solicit the aid of the Legislature only for paupers.[5]

Thornwell was not simply content with educated children. He wanted more. He wanted a *system*. But he especially wanted a *state system*. He explained why *only* a state system would be acceptable:

It is obvious, in the first place, that in this there is no system at all; the schools are detached and independent; they have no common life, and the State knows nothing of the influences which may be exerted within them. Education is too complicated an interest, and touches the prosperity of the Commonwealth in too many points to be left, in reference to the most important class of its subjects, absolutely without responsibility to the Government. The homogeneousness of the population can only be sustained by a general system of public schools.[6]

From his point of view, the people were subjects of the government, not citizens who created the government. The government could not leave the people to their own instruction but needed to check up on them and approve their influence. The people did not create their common culture; the government created culture. A state system of education alone (it was argued) could achieve the state's desired homogeneous result. Though Thornwell acknowledged a system was not necessary for education *per se,* a system could achieve other results deemed politically useful. Thus, the place of religion in providing for the education of the poor was soon superseded by the power of the state to standardize children.

The Strategy of Religious Litigation

Jump now to the present and consider a second context. What has been done in order to recover the right of parents to control education and the authority of religious organizations to offer education to the needy, unregulated by the state? One may ask if court litigation involving religious organizations and educational issues has been undertaken for the purpose of freeing parents and private religious schools from the control of the civil government. More importantly one might ask if litigation to free parents has been based on the fact that parents have an unalienable right from God to direct the education of their children free from state interference, regulation or control? Has litigation to protect intellectual freedom been based on the fact that the opinions of men cannot follow the dictates of other men because God made the mind free?

✓ Key Idea:

☞ RELIGIOUS AND LEGAL ORGANIZATIONS SHOULD ADOPT A LITIGATION STRATEGY WHICH BY ITS VERY NATURE, DOES NOT SUPPRESS GOD-GIVEN PARENTAL RIGHTS OR INTELLECTUAL FREEDOM.

One might expect this overview to review the herculean efforts of religious organizations to articulate and litigate God-given rights and freedoms. Unfortunately, the defense of God-given rights and freedom has not been the litigation priority of most activist religious organizations. The priority has rather focused on winning cases with legal arguments that ignore and sometimes suppress these God-given rights and freedoms.

In considering a litigation strategy one should be immediately aware that an immense volume of First Amendment establishment clause litigation is tied up with various laws relating to public education. Most litigation has come to the same result--neither religious control, influence, presence, or religious symbols are not welcome in state schools. The courts have declared that, generally speaking, religion in the public schools is unconstitutional.

One should also recognize that judicial opinions reflect an historical context. The steady direction of education in the last 150 years has been away from parental rights and decentralized familial education, and toward state centralization. The state now uses education to enforce the secular will of the community on its students. A predominantly secular community prescribes through their legislative representatives, the curriculum, funding arrangements and services which state schools will mandate. The community or state defines who must attend and for how long. They define who may teach and determine their qualifications. Generally, when a religion/education case comes before the Supreme Court, one of these legal prescriptions, regulations or mandates has come under attack. The Court usually responds with an establishment clause analysis and finds the policy, action, or statute either valid or unconstitutional.

From the point of view of parental rights, however, it is quite irrelevant whether a secular majority or minority of the state's citizens, or a religiously minded majority or minority of its citizens, enforce their respective will as it pertains to curriculum, funding, taxation, teacher qualifications and school services. It is irrelevant because to the extent that *any* majority or minority of the community interferes with the unalienable rights of a parent (or of intellectual freedom), then to that extent an individual parent is divested of his or her unalienable rights to say when, where, by whom, and in what manner his or her child shall be educated.

Likewise when a religious minority or majority sense that their childrens' public school education is *too* secular or insufficiently religious, they respond by pressuring the school or legislature to accommodate their desire to infuse some measure of religion into the curriculum, or through a variety of arrangements they infuse some type of state aid into religious or church-run schools. This reaction to secularization, however, also attempts to use the public schools to carry out the will of the community irrespective of specific parental rights. To the extent that a religiously minded minority or majority make the decisions about the education of any parent's child, that parent is also deprived of the unalienable right to say when, where, by whom, and in what manner his or her child shall be educated.

Consequently, First Amendment education establishment cases are not usually fought over whether education should be controlled by the government, but over *how much* control the civil government should have. The only active players in the contest are churches, church operated schools, teacher unions, interests and the state. The right of parents to control the education of their own children, is more often than not, generally ignored by all players.[7]

Judicial Response to Religious Organizations

A review of several Supreme Court opinions over the last decade amply indicate the inability of religious parties to recognize the significance of a parent's unalienable right in religion/education litigation. For instance, in the recently overruled case of *Grand Rapids School District v. Ball*,[8] the Court was presented with a challenge to the use of tax funds to pay public school teachers to teach non-public school students at church operated schools leased by the city during the time of instruction. The students were taught secular remedial subjects. The Court ruled that the use of public tax funds to pay public school teachers to teach at leased church schools was an unconstitutional establishment of religion in that the program unduly entangled and promoted religion.

Likewise in the also overruled case of *Aguilar v. Felton*,[9] the use of federal funds to pay public school teachers to visit church operated schools in order to teach remedial secular subjects was also held unconstitutional. In both cases public funds made their way to church schools contrary to the three part test for establishment[10] announced in *Lemon v. Kurtzman*.[11]

In *Wallace v. Jaffree*,[12] the Court struck down an Alabama statute that attempted to designate a one-minute period of silence in all public schools "for meditation or voluntary prayer." The Court sanctioned voluntary student-initiated prayer but found the statute's one-minute designation an unconstitutional attempt to return prayer to the public schools. Consequently, the law did not advance a secular purpose and therefore failed the establishment clause test announced in *Lemon*.

Another case, *Edwards v. Aguillard*,[13] involved an establishment clause challenge to a Louisiana law which required equal time for teaching creation science and evolution. Creation science holds that God created the earth including mankind and that evidence of a creation scheme is supported by the scientific method. It differs from evolution which emphasizes gradual development of mankind from lower forms of life and non-life. The Court struck down the equal time provision because it lacked a clear secular purpose. The Court, however, did not preclude the state from requiring the teaching of alternate theories of origins other than evolution under certain circumstances.

And in *Stone v. Graham*,[14] the Court struck down a state law requiring the posting of the Ten Commandments on the wall of every public school classroom. The Court held that the law had an insufficient secular legislative purpose and thus violated the establishment clause. The Court, however, did not bar the use of the Ten Commandments as well as the Bible where it constituted an appropriate study of history, civilization, ethics, or comparative religions.

The general issue sought to be illustrated by these cases is not that the respective practices were unconstitutional. The issue of immediate interest is that the "religious" defense of the statute or law at issue (tax-funding, equal time for creationism, moment of silence and ten commandments) was necessarily justified on the suppression of a God-given right or liberty. For instance, in *Grand Rapids School District* and *Aguilar,* the use of tax funds to pay public school teachers to teach disadvantaged children was never questioned in light of the power of the state to compel its citizens to financially subsidize education irrespective of the choice of parents. The fact that both of these cases were subsequently overruled in *Agostini v. Felton*[15] to now allow public school teachers to offer supplemental remedial instruction of disadvantaged children in a religious school, does not change the fact that the state still retains the power to compel its citizens to subsidize governmental control of education, both public *and* religious.

Edwards v. Aguillard attempted to promote equal time for teaching creation science and evolution in public schools. This argument is based on the idea that the state and not a parent, has the right to compel students to be forcibly exposed to ideas irrespective of the choice of parents. Parents who want their children to learn only one, the other or neither view would be subject to interference with their unalienable rights. The state has neither the right or authority to teach a child either view because it lacks the authority to teach ideas by coercion in the first instance. *Wallace v. Jaffree* attempted to designate a one-minute period of silence in all public schools. This argument is also based on the idea that the state, and not parents should determine the content or context of education. *Stone v. Graham* (Ten Commandments on the wall) involved the same idea--the state, and not parents should determine the content or context of education.

Far from defending the God-given unalienable rights of parents, more often than not, the religious party or litigant sought to secure his or her own prerogative or advantage. Some may say that the foregoing arguments are petty since we are simply dealing with one minute of silence and a posting which nobody has to read. What's wrong with a little religion? Nothing is wrong with a little religion--but this is not the right question. The right question is "What's wrong with a little coercion--whether religious or secular?" The answer is, that any *degree* of coercion on the unalienable rights of parents to define the context of their child's education, is objectional. It is objectional because it assumes that the state may define the content or context of education in *any* degree whatsoever.

These cases all focus on the relationship between religion and the state as they battle each other over curriculum and money in the context of education. The cases have not sought to limit the civil government from encroaching upon the God-given "essential and unalienable rights" of parents with respect to the education of their children. Instead, the Court has gotten bogged down with judicial adjustment of curriculum, funding and redistribution of power (which, if such matters were legitimate civil objects, they would be legislative functions).

If unalienable rights were considered by the parties involved in these cases, they would result in an effort to bar all statutory attempts to utilize public schools to carry out the will of the state, whatever its beliefs or outlook, religious or secular. The emphasis would be on returning the choice over education and funding to each parent for his or her own child's education to the extent unalienable rights had received statutory or constitutional protection.[16]

Even in cases where a religious party has prevailed, the decision has been at the expense of the rights of parents to give to those organizations which they alone deem worthy of their financial support, and the right of the people to have tax dollars spent on the legitimate jurisdictional objects of the civil government.

For instance, in *Committee for Public Education & Religious Liberty v. Regan*,[17] the state of New York had enacted a law mandating a variety of student testing including pupil evaluation, achievement and college qualifications tests. Church-operated schools were required to administer the state mandated tests. All schools were entitled to reimbursement from the state for the costs incurred in complying with the state's testing mandate. This reimbursement scheme was challenged as an unconstitutional establishment of religion. The Court, however, rejected the challenge, holding that church-operated schools were entitled to reimbursement for the costs of state mandated testing. The Court held that this type of aid did not violate *Lemon*.

The problem in *Committee for Public Education & Religious Liberty v. Regan* was that the church school had let itself become dependent upon the state. New York's funding scheme is the educational cousin of Virginia's *Bill Establishing A Provision For Teachers of the Christian Religion*.[18] That bill permitted each of the approved religious sects to enjoy a certain degree of financial support from the civil government. It allowed the civil government to bring all major religious sects under its roof. The government would collect a special property tax that otherwise would have gone to the original state-established church and distribute it to churches newly approved by the government, as long as that recipient was approved in its doctrine by the civil government.

New York did the same thing in enacting a law mandating student testing. It assumed jurisdiction over church schools. New York offered the schools a bribe for externally conforming to its aspirations in educational testing. In reviewing the law, the Supreme Court did not defend the rights of parents (or the school as the parent's agent) to direct the education and testing of their own children free from New York's control. The Court did not inquire whether New York had any jurisdiction to measure the knowledge of a child with or without the consent of the parent or whether the mandatory testing posed some problem for intellectual freedom. The Court did not rule on these matters. The likelihood that these matters were even raised by the parties or their lawyers is remote.

Equal Access and Unalienable Rights

Several other cases have also presented a slightly different conflict between religion and education. These cases involve either denial of equal treatment and involve discrimination against individuals because of their religion. It is well worthy of investigation to consider how the rule of equality impacts these education and religion disputes.

In *Westside Community Schools v. Mergens,*[18] the Court held that public high schools which make their facilities available to student organizations, must also allow equal access to school facilities for student-led Bible studies. The school was prohibited from closing its open forum to religious students. Neither the school's policy nor the Equal Access Act[19] violated the establishment clause although the Court was not able to agree upon a common rationale.

In *Widmar v. Vincent,*[20] the Court ruled that a public university must grant equal access to university facilities for student-led Bible studies. The University of Missouri at Kansas City had made its facilities available for the activities of student groups, but denied the use of the facilities to religious student groups. The Court focused their rationale on the free speech clause which required content-neutrality by the University.

In both cases "matters of religion" diminished or affected the equal civil capacities of students.[21] Religious students were not free to use the facilities like other students, because of their religious belief. This contravenes the idea of equality articulated so clearly by Virginia that, "all men [including students] shall be free to profess, and by argument to maintain, their opinions in matters of religion, and that the same shall in no wise diminish, enlarge, or affect their civil capacities." The apparent success in these cases, however, does nothing to advance the unalienable rights of parents, or in the context of higher education, the idea that no person should be compelled to contribute his money to institutions that advocate ideas which he would not otherwise desire to freely support.

Summary and Admonition

This Chapter began with an excerpt about true religion. It declared that pure religion before God is to look after the fatherless and widows in their affliction, and to keep oneself unspotted from the world. It emphasized the need for religious organizations to regard both admonitions and to establish and heed certain priorities in education. These priorities begin with the recognition of religion's obligation to practice true religion in the context of education by assisting families who legitimately and truly need assistance with the exercise of their parental rights.

These priorities also include recognition that religious organizations should endeavor to keep themselves and their litigation "unspotted" from the modern legal world. The modern approach to litigating religion/education cases, however, has rejected the law of nature and the Declaration's legal principles. The law and its principles are simply too embarrassing for lawyers and teachers of the law. The excerpt at the beginning of this Chapter, however, pleads for adoption of a legal strategy which is not at odds with the unalienable rights which God has given to all parents. The challenge is for religious legal organizations to litigate whenever possible on behalf of the unalienable rights of parents and intellectual freedom under state constitutions or statutes. It demands the practice of true religion, by refusing to embrace a litigation strategy which is alien to the laws of nature's God. Will religious leaders, their lobbying organizations and their attorneys realize that loving their neighbor as themselves, means they must defend the unalienable rights of all? Or will the salt of the earth continue to be trampled under judicial foot because it has lost its jurisprudential savor?[22]

✓ Key Idea:

☞ A RELIGIOUS ORGANIZATION'S PLEA FOR FINANCIAL CONTRIBUTIONS AFTER A CASE IS "WON" ON FALSE PRINCIPLES, IS A REQUEST TO SUPPORT THE ONGOING WORK OF REJECTING THE LAWS OF NATURE'S GOD.

The challenge for religious individuals and institutions is to first lay the constitutional and legislative foundation for the unalienable rights of parents to direct the education of their own children. Other unalienable rights involving property, contract and association will follow. Unalienable rights must be embraced not simply for the benefit of a religious individual or organization, but because the security of unalienable rights is the only security of any man's liberty, religious or otherwise. If indeed, it is true that all men and women are created equal, that they are endowed by their Creator with certain unalienable rights, that governments are instituted in order to secure those rights, then no more transcendent a mandate lies ahead than to secure those rights for all.

The present fight is between two visions of law, government and rights. Unalienable rights can either be regarded as "endowed by [the] Creator" or simply a primal "power, privilege, faculty, or demand, inherent in one person." They can either be viewed as conforming to the "laws of Nature's God" or "grounded in personality." But until trained advocates, lawyers and people of goodwill, recognize these differences, the legislative, executive and judicial branches will continue to apply the principles of unequal treatment. Such principles characterize a People who perish because they have neither vision nor knowledge. Adherence to unalienable rights and intellectual freedom, however, will ensure that those who profess true religion, practice true religion. Such adherence will also ensure that religious organizations remain unspotted by litigation strategies which may win occasional cases, but suppress unalienable God-given rights in the process.

★ **HYPOTHETICALLY SPEAKING . . . .**

Problem: **A wicked judge oppressed the people of Brownacre by declaring his own opinions equal to and above the law. The people hired a religious lawyer to get justice in the judge's court. The lawyer argued to the Court,**

"Why do you deny the people justice by declaring your own opinions equal to or above the law?" The wicked judge replied, "And how is it that you deceive your client by concealing your belief that your views are also equal to the law? You say you are defending the rule of law, but yet you refuse to admit the certainty of the law of nature of your God." The wicked Judge continued, "We are two of a kind. Neither of us believes the law is anything except what we say it is."

The lawyer agreed in private but argued that, "At least my opinions are just." The wicked judge laughed and replied, "There is no justice where a man's will is the standard of justice."

The lawyer comes to you and asks you to contribute money to his political campaign in order to unseat the wicked judge in Brownacre's next local election. He promises better results. Will you contribute?

Notes

1. James 1:27 (KJV).

2. ERNEST T. THOMPSON, PRESBYTERIANS IN THE SOUTH, VOL. 1: 1607-1861 (John Knox Press: Richmond, Virginia 1963) 237.

3. *Id.* at 238.

4. *Id.* at 235-50 and 471-87.

5. *Id.* at 475 (emphasis added).

6. *Id.*

7. An unsuccessful attempt to break free from this trend was Mozert v. Hawkins County Board of Education, 827 F.2d 1058 (6th Cir. 1987), *cert. denied* 484 U.S. 1066 (1989).

8. 473 U.S. 373 (1985). The "Shared Time" portion of Ball has since been overruled in Agostini v. Felton, No. 96-552, June 23, 1997.

9. 473 U.S. 402 (1985). Aguilar has since been overruled in Agostini v. Felton, No. 96-552, June 23, 1997.

10. The First Amendment was enacted as a limitation on Congress and not the power of state governments such as New York. The Supreme Court, however, has judicially extended the religious prohibitions of the First Amendment to the states through its construction of the Fourteenth Amendment. Under the Constitution as written and amended, however, state constitutions would control in matters of religion, not the federal Constitution. This view was commonly assumed and held before the Court's radical alterations. *See* 12 CORPUS JURIS (New York: The American Law Book Company, 1917) 955. ("The First Amendment to the constitution of the United States prohibiting congress from abridging the right to assemble and petition was not intended to limit the action of the state governments in respect to their own citizens, but to operate on the federal government alone, guaranteeing the continuance of the right only against congressional interference.") Of course, the state constitutions are required to conform to the principles of the Declaration of Independence as best as the people of the state understand that document.

The Supreme Court's incorporation doctrine flatly contradicts the original doctrine of federalism, though some district court judges have shown a willingness to reconsider the constitutionality of incorporation. *See* Jaffree v. Board of School Comm'rs of Mobile

County, 554 F. Supp. 1104, 1128 (S.D. Ala. 1983) *rev'd*, 705 F.2d 1526 (11th Cir. 1983) *aff'd*, 466 U.S. 924 (1984).

11. 403 U.S. 602 (1971). *Lemon* held that A legislative enactment does not contravene the Establishment Clause if it has a secular legislative purpose, if its principle or primary effect neither advances or inhibits religion, and if it does not foster an excessive entanglement with religion. Each component of this test was intended to secure the purpose of the no-establishment clause--to maintain a jurisdictional separation between the legitimate objects of religion and those of the civil government. The test, however, falls well short of this goal. As applied, it is not well informed by the laws of nature and of nature's God or the principles of the Declaration of Independence.

The central problem is an old one we have seen before--the Court is of the mistaken view that God has no legitimate function in the civil realm. Never mind the fact that the Declaration itself, which created the legal entity known as the "united States," asserts that God gives the law by which nations are established, that God defines the purpose of governments instituted under that law, and that God gives all human beings certain rights which that civil government is established to secure. The *Lemon* test asks us to also turn a blind pair of eyes to the framer's call upon God to act as the judge of their civil actions and superintend their civil progress. *But see* Church of the Holy Trinity v. United States, 143 U.S. 457, 467 (1882)(quoting the Declaration of Independence to the effect that an appeal to God as the Supreme Judge of the world is a valid civil appeal and not an establishment of religion).

Under the *Lemon* test, The Declaration itself would fail. Virginia's religious disestablishment statute would also surely be a candidate for offending the federal establishment clause since its very "unsecular purpose" was to secure that freedom of the mind which "Almighty God hath created" and which the "holy author of our religion, who, being lord both of body and mind, yet chose not to propagate it by coercions on either, as was in his Almighty power to do." VA. CODE ANN. § 57-1 (1950).

What is needed is not a simple rearrangement of the *Lemon* test with a scaled down view of religion, but rather a reorientation about the nature of law, the principles of unalienable rights, the equal security of those rights by the civil government and an understanding of the distinctions between the Constitutionally permissible inter-relationship between God the Creator and civil government, and the jurisdictionally separate and therefore constitutionally impermissible interrelationship between religion and civil government.

12. 472 U.S. 38 (1985).

13. 482 U.S. 578 (1987).

14. 449 U.S. 39 (1980).

15. ___U.S.___, No. 96-552, June 23, 1997.

16. The Virginia General Assembly was also concerned about the proper use of taxes to fund State propagation of ideas. It observed "that to compel a man to furnish contributions of money for the propagation of opinions which he disbelieves, is sinful and tyrannical." And "that even the forcing [of] him to support this or that teacher of his own religious persuasion, is depriving him of the comfortable liberty of giving his contributions to the particular pastor whose morals he would make his pattern, and whose powers he feels most persuasive to righteousness." ROBERT L. CORD, SEPARATION OF CHURCH AND STATE (New York: Lambeth Press, 1982) 249-50. *See also* An Act for Religious Freedom, VA. CODE ANN. § 57-1 (1950).

17. 444 U.S. 646 (1980).

18. CORD *supra* note 16 at 242-43.

19. 496 U.S. 226 (1990).

20. *See* 20 U.S.C.A. §§ 4071-4074 (1995 West Supp).

21. 454 U.S. 263 (1981).

22. *See also* CORD *supra* note 16 at 250.

23. The litigating and lobbying philosophy of securing preferential treatment for religious clients has brought First Amendment jurisprudence to an impasse. Special exemptions from generally applicable laws ought to be avoided and those laws examined in the bright light of the laws of nature and of nature's God, the unalienable rights God has given to every human being, and the expression of those rights in state and federal constitutional and legislative provisions.

Part II

Secondary Principles of Choice and Freedom

Part II

Part II

Secondary Principles of Choice and Freedom

Part I examined the foundational principles of choice and freedom. These principles include the following:

1) American law is based on the laws of nature and of nature's God;

2) The principles of the American Declaration of Independence are expressly based on this law;

3) The Declaration recognizes, in principle, that the Creator endows parents with the unalienable right to direct the education and upbringing of their children free from governmental interference, regulation or control;

4) The Declaration recognizes, in principle, that the Creator endows every person with the right to intellectual liberty--that is to say, it acknowledges freedom from governmental compulsion or coercion in things of the mind.

Part I indicated that these principles necessitated several results:
• Parents are not to be interfered with by the civil government in the exercise of their unalienable right to direct the education of their children;
• The civil government may not forcibly expose a child to any state-approved curriculum or idea, or certify or license teachers or parents, or compel attendance; and
• The civil government is barred from levying a tax of any type on the people or their property, in order to fund any government established school or provide education-related grants to any government established or private institution.

In Part II, the focus shifts to the United States Constitution and the United States federal government. This Part will examine the principles of choice and freedom in the context of constitutional law and limitations, rather than the law of nature. These principles include the following ideas:

1) The Constitutional convention rejected federal funding of, and intervention into education;

2) Many Presidents and Congresses recognized that an honest observance of the Constitution left the federal government and Congress wholly without jurisdiction to enter the field of education;

3) The Bureau of Education established in 1867 was rationalized as an extension of the census power of Congress, contrary to the Constitution;

4) The Department of Education established in 1979 was, contrary to the Constitution, rationalized as a means of promoting the general welfare.

5) The federal government's *National Education Strategy* to make America competitive in a global economy by the year 2000 and beyond, is contrary to the Constitution, and prefers the demands of business over that of parents.

6) The federal government's disastrous education of Native American Indians and incompetent oversight of education in the District of Columbia, are clear examples of why the federal government should never be permitted to influence or direct the education of any child, anywhere, at anytime.

Focus on the Constitution does not require neglect of the principles and limitations of the laws of nature and of nature's God or the principles of the Declaration. Such matters apply to the federal government since it is no less a civil government than a state government. The laws of nature prohibit the federal government from forcibly exposing a child to any government-approved idea or curriculum. The federal government is barred from levying a tax of any type, in order to fund government schools for minors, or provide education-related grants to any state or private institution. Thus, the law and its principles prohibit virtually all of the federal government's non-military educational research and funding activities.

What is of significance, however, is that the *Constitution* also requires these same results. The Constitution contains the secondary principles necessary to free American education from *federal* control. This Part examines how respect for the laws of nature and its principles were embedded in the Constitution. It examines how great a departure from the Constitution's plain meaning is required in order to justify federal jurisdiction over education. Finally, this part chronicles the federal government's systematic disapproval of the Constitution's limitations until Congress finally rejected the very Constitution itself.

Chapter 10

A Constitution to Rule Congress

That power which is not given by the Constitution, which the Convention refused to give, and which has been taken or recommended to be taken in contempt of it, is the offspring of rank usurpation.[1]

The ABC's of Governing the Federal Government

Certain legal and Constitutional principles bound the federal government and Congress of 1791 and continue to bind today.[2] These principles were examined in Part I and are clearly stated in the Declaration of Independence. Governments are instituted to secure the God-given unalienable rights of its citizens. When the civil government in some way impairs unalienable rights, then the people have the right and the duty to alter or abolish that government. Continued federal intervention into education deprecates the laws of nature and of nature's God, unalienable rights and intellectual freedom. It also distorts the Constitutionally enumerated limits on the federal and Congressional power of the United States.

✓ Key Idea:
☞ THE WHOLE AIM OF THE FEDERAL CONSTITUTION IS TO DEFINE AND LIMIT THE POWER OF THE FEDERAL GOVERNMENT.

When it comes to controlling Congress, the whole aim of the federal Constitution is to limit Congress to the exercise of only those powers enumerated in the Constitution. Since the Civil War, however, interpretation of the Constitution, especially relating to the power extended to Congress, has tended to

145

allow an expansion of that power despite the Constitution's plain limitations. This activist interpretive approach has infected all branches of the national government.[3] As far as the executive branch is concerned, the Constitution's significance tends to rise and fall with popularity polls on any given subject, at any given time and for any given Administration.

✓ Key Idea:

☞   FEDERAL INDIFFERENCE TO THE CONSTITUTION, BELITTLES THE AMERICAN PEOPLE WHO ESTABLISHED IT.

At its root, Constitutional distortion grows up where there is a failure to understand that the Constitution defines and institutes the *form and objects* of a civil government. Recall the view of President John Quincy Adams who said it cannot be denied that the framers "presuppose[d] the existence of a God, the moral ruler of the universe, and a rule of right and wrong, of just and unjust, binding upon man, preceding all institutions of human society and government."[4] Remember John Taylor's observation at the beginning of Chapter 3: "If the declaration of independence is not obligatory, our intire political fabrick has lost its magna charta, and is without any solid foundation. But if it is the basis of our form of government, it is the true expositor of the principles and terms we have adopted."[5]

Failure to consider the Constitution's meaning in the context of the principles of the Declaration of Independence would leave us without any "solid foundation."   With the Declaration's foundation in mind, basic rules of interpretation will generally result in clear and logical application of Constitutional meaning.

Limited and Enumerated Powers

The purpose of interpreting "a provision of the Constitution, is to discover the meaning, to ascertain and give effect to the intent of its framers and the people who adopted it."[6] Without this purpose,

> The Constitution would cease to be the Supreme Law of the Land, binding equally upon governments and [the] governed at all times and under all circumstances, and become a mere collection of political maxims to be adhered to or disregarded according to the prevailing sentiment or the legislative and judicial opinion in respect of the supposed necessities of the hour.[7]

A review of the Constitution indicates Congress is only delegated certain enumerated powers. The Constitution defines these limited powers. When power is exercised by the federal government, that power must be enumerated in the Constitution as understood in light of its text and context.

Constitutionally, the federal government is a government of limited and enumerated power. Power not delegated to the federal government by the written Constitution is reserved to the states or to the people respectively.[8] This is the clear meaning of the text and historical context. Only an amendment can change this meaning. Congress cannot change this meaning by passing a Statute. The President cannot change this meaning by an Executive Order. The Courts cannot change this meaning by a judicial opinion. And the people cannot change this meaning by a public opinion poll.

✓ Key Idea:

☞ THE CONSTITUTION'S MEANING CANNOT BE
CHANGED BY A PUBLIC OPINION POLL.

Applying these principles to the subject of education is straightforward. When the Constitution is examined, education is not found listed among the enumerated powers of Congress.[9] Article I does not authorize Congress to establish a Department of Education nor does it grant jurisdiction to encourage the education of the people in the several states. Furthermore, federal involvement in education is not an appropriate means plainly adapted to carry out an object contemplated by an enumerated power. Congress may, however, maintain educational facilities and academies if those means are plainly adapted to raising and supporting the military.

Though Congress is prohibited from entangling itself with the education of the people in the several states, it may concern itself with those objects enumerated in Article I, section 8, clause 17.[10] This clause grants Congress exclusive *legislative* authority over the District of Columbia. With respect to the District of Columbia, Congress has legislative authority *pro-tanto*. In other words, it has legislative power, as far as legislative power goes and no farther. It may act as a state legislature, but may not abridge any natural, unalienable or Constitutionally retained rights of the people over education. Its power does not extend to repealing the laws of nature, impairing intellectual freedom, regulating unalienable parental rights or ransacking the principles of the Declaration.

The Constitution also extends Congress's *proprietary* authority over federal territories and property under Article IV, section 3, clause 2.[11] This Clause grants Congress power to dispose of and make all needful rules and regulations respecting the territories or other property belonging to the United States. This grant of power is proprietary. It empowers Congress to be a good steward of their land. This proprietary function differs from the legislative function Congress exercises over the District of Columbia. Though both clauses constitute grants of power, neither extend Congress any general power over education.

The extent of express Congressional power with respect to education beyond military academies, is limited to the promotion of science and arts, and is provided for by Article I, section 8, clause 8.[12] This clause focuses upon patents and copyrights. It does not constitute a general warrant to promote science and the arts. The promotion of these ends is strictly controlled by the indicated means. The text is very clear and plain. The means Congress may employ in the promotion of these enumerated objects is Constitutionally declared. Congress may only promote science and art "by securing for limited Times to Authors and Inventors the exclusive Right to their respective Writings and Discoveries."

✓ Key Idea:

☞   THE CONSTITUTION RECOGNIZES NO GENERAL
       JURISDICTION OVER EDUCATION, AND EXTENDS
       NO GENERAL POWER TO CONGRESS TO FURTHER
       OR FUND EDUCATION.

Congress may not appropriate monies for the support of science or art, directly or indirectly. Congress may not Constitutionally award educational grants to fund research for the promotion of knowledge or discoveries.[13] If Congress exercises any power other than that Constitutionally enumerated to them, it would be pernicious both to the states and the people, and contrary to the Constitution as the Supreme Law of the Land. In the words of Thomas Cooper who was quoted at the beginning of this Chapter, the exercise of such power would be the "offspring of rank usurpation."

Thus, a brief overview of the plain terms of the Constitution indicates only two provisions that could be interpreted to legitimate Congressional power in the area of education. The first involves military training and academies, and the second involves the patent and copyright clause. Both clauses are specific in their scope of power and the means by which that power is to be exercised. Neither extends to Congress any general power to promote education, assist the states or strengthen parental education.

The Constitutional analysis, however, must go deeper than a facial analysis. The history and all important context pertaining to the adoption of these clauses must be considered. The remainder of this Chapter, therefore, will trace key educational and legal developments chronologically, beginning with the pre-Constitutional relationship that existed between Congress and education, and will be followed by a discussion of the Constitutional Convention.

A pattern will be seen indicating that the intent of the framers of the Constitution was to exclude Congress from educational matters. It will also be seen that, with some well-defined exceptions, Congress initially respected that intention. Subsequent Chapters will show that over time, however, Congress began to reject the limitations which the Constitution placed upon it to restrain its power until the Congress ultimately dismissed the Constitution itself.

Pre-Constitutional Educational Interests

When the Congress met in November of 1777, none of the present Constitutional limitations were yet in place. The Congress was then operating under the Articles of Confederation which they used as a guide even though all the States did not approve that form of government until 1781. Acting to reduce the Revolutionary War deficit, Congress undertook many measures. In 1780 Congress requested New York and Virginia in particular, to surrender their claims over certain lands. Virginia in particular claimed its lands were held by virtue of its charter from the King. Now Congress asked that these lands be conveyed to the national government of the united States (that is to say, to themselves). The national government hoped to dispose of these lands by sale. The money it obtained from the sale would help pay the war debt.

There was a problem, however, with Maryland who refused to endorse the Articles of Confederation until other states, especially Virginia, conveyed to the new government its claims on these northwestern lands. Fears and jealousies over land were not uncommon. It was thought that a large land state would dominate a smaller land state economically and politically. Thus, Maryland being small in terms of land mass, objected to Virginia which was correspondingly large. Maryland's objections effectively blocked the formation of the Confederation until 1781 around the time Virginia conveyed its claim.[14]

There was also another major barrier to the national government's scheme to sell territorial property. The land was still a wilderness and would not be easily settled. In order to induce settlement and sale of these frontier territories (now conveyed by Virginia to the national government), Congress passed an ordinance determining the best mode of disposing of this land. Among other provisions, this ordinance (adopted on May 20, 1785) reserved a section of every township for schools. Every section of the territory would have land designated for education. It was hoped that this provision would induce families to buy the land. This trend would in turn, aid in extinguishing the war debt. It would also help to settle the land, as well as increase territorial population. The net result of this activity was *eventually* to designate the territory as a state.

These aspirations (to buy, settle and populate the land) were reflected in another land ordinance passed on July 13, 1787 providing for local government of the territory of the United States northwest of the Ohio river. This 1787 law became known as the "Northwest Ordinance." The Northwest Ordinance (or law) not only reserved lands for educational purposes as did its predecessor, but contained an agreement that Congress would make states out of the territories and admit them into the union (and after the Constitution, into the "more perfect Union") on equal footing with the other states.[15]

The legality of Congressional action pursuant to the Articles of Confederation, in selling territories with designated tracts for "educational purposes," is no proof, however, that Congress under the Constitution, possessed any similar power with respect to state land. In other words, pre-Constitutional congressional enactments setting aside tracts of land in *its own territories* or other federal lands for settlement purposes, do not set an educational precedent for federal power over populated *land within the states*. The ordinances of 1785 and 1787 only served to demonstrate that the situation called for the expedited settlement and sale of territorial lands.

✓ Key Idea:
☞ THE NORTHWEST ORDINANCE EXTENDED CONGRESS NO JURISDICTION TO ENCOURAGE EDUCATION IN THE STATES.

With respect to its own territories, the national government legitimately exercised its proprietary authority. It observed the covenants that ran with the land according to the terms of its *possession* under the Northwest Ordinance. It acted as a good steward by designating a parcel of the property for educational purposes. This designation augmented the value of the whole and thereby encouraged its settlement. Education was not the object of the Confederation Congress's concern. The promotion of education was simply a means unto another end--to reduce the debt, settle the land and bring the territory to statehood. The 1785 and 1787 ordinances were established to induce sale of land and to settle those territories that had been voluntarily ceded to the national government by the state governments. After a territory was admitted as a state into the Union, however, any continuing federal "promotion" of education terminated along with the federal government's proprietary rights.

President James Buchanan was later to note in 1859 that numerous Congressional land grants for education "have been chiefly, if not exclusively, made to the new states as they successively entered the Union" (citing the language of the Ordinances of the Confederate Congress of 1785 and 1787). He resolved that "[i]t can not be pretended that an agricultural college in New York or Virginia would aid the settlement or facilitate the sale of public lands in Minnesota or California."[16]

Buchanan recognized that the original rationale for a land designation provision was to induce settlement of territories as a proprietary function. Any Congressional deviation from that rationale would be by pretext and therefore unconstitutional. Thus, when Congress reaffirmed the principles of the Northwest Ordinance during its first Session, it did so with respect to its Constitutional authority over its own territories, not over states.

The Constitutional Convention

Though no general Congressional authority over education has ever been a part of the Constitution, several attempts were made during the Constitutional Convention of 1787 to give Congress limited means to enhance education. On May 29th, Mr. Charles Pinckney presented his draft organizing a federal government. It provided, in part that the legislature of the United States shall have the power "to establish and provide for a national university at the seat of government of the United States." When the committee that considered the matter reported their Constitutional draft on August 6, they completely excluded this particular provision from its text.[17]

During the Convention on August 18, James Madison and others proposed several items to be included within the legislative power of the United States, including the power:

• To secure to literary authors their copyrights for a limited time.
• To establish a university.
• To encourage by proper premiums and provisions, the advancement of useful knowledge and discoveries.
• To establish seminaries for the promotion of literature, and the arts and sciences.
• To grant patents for useful inventions.
• To establish public institutions, rewards, and immunities, for the promotion of agriculture, commerce, trades and manufactures.

Madison drew a distinction between a national university, seminaries for the promotion of literature, arts and sciences, and other public educational institutions. A national university implied a university that taught all branches of learning, owned and/or operated by the federal government. Seminaries referred to any school, academy, college, or university, in which young persons were instructed in several disciplines, including theology. It did not merely connote a school of theology.

After considering these provisions, Congress rejected all but two. Only the patent and copyright provisions were found among the national legislature's authority when the matter was reported out of Committee. Although you would never know it today, the power to make grants (premiums and provisions) was excluded from Congressional power.[18]

On September 12, 1787, the "Committee of Stile and Arrangement" presented a Constitution that, apart from a few changes, became the present Constitution less amendments. That version contained no specific, enumerated, or expressed power in Congress to legislate concerning education, nor did it provide for Congressional encouragement or establishment of education or the advancement of useful knowledge and discoveries, directly or indirectly.[19]

On September 14, Mr. Madison and Mr. Pinckney, during debates on the submitted draft, moved once again to vest Congress with power "to establish [a] University, in which no preferences or distinctions should be allowed on account of Religion."[20] The proposal was again rejected by the Convention as a whole. On September 17 the Constitution, void of Congressional power over education, was ratified. Almost a year later on June 21, 1788, the ninth state ratified the Constitution giving it legal effect.[21] On April 30, 1789, General George Washington was inaugurated as the first President of the United States under the new form of government.

✓ Key Idea:

☞ THE CONSTITUTIONAL CONVENTION DENIED ANY GENERAL JURISDICTION OVER EDUCATION TO CONGRESS, ALLOWING ONLY FOR PATENT AND COPYRIGHT PROTECTION AND MILITARY TRAINING.

In retrospect, it is certain that Congress was denied the power to establish a national university. Congress was also denied the power to establish seminaries promoting literature, arts and sciences as well as establishment of other educational institutions. Congress was explicitly denied power to advance knowledge and science by funding and grant-making.

The only encouragement and advancement of useful knowledge and discoveries granted to Congress was the exception of the patent and copyright provisions of Article I, section 8, clause 8. It was wisely considered that the federal government should have no greater Constitutional power to encourage education among the several states beyond this particular enumerated object.[22]

Thus, when President George Washington came to his office, the only remaining question regarding education was whether Congress (acting like a state) pursuant to its Article I, section 8, clause 17 powers over the District of Columbia alone, could establish a national university within the exclusive geographical confines of the District of Columbia, and whether Congress could Constitutionally appropriate monies from the federal treasury for such a limited purpose.[23] This was the question which President Washington put to the Congress early in the life of the Republic.

★ HYPOTHETICALLY SPEAKING . . . .

Problem: **Thirty years ago you took out a mortgage on your house. The interest on your loan was fixed at 7 percent. Today your final payment is due and the house will be yours. You are about to take the final payment out to the mail box when the doorbell rings. You have received a federal express**

letter from the Savings and Loan you negotiated the loan from 30 years ago. The letter begins:

Dear Satisfied Consumer:

Thank you for your mortgage payments of the previously agreed upon principal and interest over the last thirty years. We appreciate your business. As you are aware conditions have changed greatly since your loan was negotiated 30 years ago. Many of these changes have adversely affected the Savings and Loan industry in general. While our institution has experienced sustained growth, we have re-examined many of our loan policies. General fluctuation of interest rates over the past 30 years has caused our institution to lose money when interest rates rise and our loans are locked in for 30 years at low rates.

In order to serve your mortgage and financial needs in a prompt and professional manner, the Board of Directors has authorized the re-computation of all fixed rate 30 year loans. These loans will be re-computed at a variable rate indexed to government indicators.

Your loan has been re-computed under this new method. Simply continue to make payments in the same amount as you have. We are unable at this time to provide an indication of how many more years payments are to be made due to the variable interest rates. We hope that our effort to maintain your monthly payments at their present levels will not cause you any financial inconvenience. In light of our present fiscal situation I trust you will find the modification of our original agreement entirely reasonable.

Thank you very much. We appreciate your business.

Sincerely yours,
Mr. Ni C. Guy

P.S. We are now offering a complimentary toaster for all new loan applicants! Have your friends apply today.

Assume that the re-computation of interest is financially reasonable in light of the changed circumstances over the past 30 years. Does the fact that re-computation is reasonable make it lawful?

Answer: No. It is not lawful for the S&L to change the terms of the loan agreement without the consent of the homeowner. This is true whether times have changed or whether the changes are reasonable or not.

Likewise, it is not lawful for the government to change the terms of the Constitutional agreement without the consent of the people. This is true whether times have changed or whether the changes are "reasonable" or not. The consent of the people must be expressed through the means articulated in the Constitution, Article V. That Article alone defines how the Constitution can be amended. It is not permissible for the Court or Congress to mail a "letter" to the people in the form of an opinion or law which changes the Constitution.

A free people should not let the government show contempt for unalienable rights and the Constitution, and offer us the legal equivalent of a toaster, *i.e.*, pork barrel, in exchange for liberty. Nor should they let public opinion polls supersede public opinion expressed in the supreme law of the land.

Notes

1. THOMAS COOPER, TWO ESSAYS: ON THE FOUNDATION OF CIVIL GOVERNMENT AND ON THE CONSTITUTION OF THE UNITED STATES (Columbia: D & J. M. Faust, 1826; reprint ed., New York: Da Capo Press, 1970) 32.

2. Changes in technology and science or economic conditions which suggest an adjustment of federal power, do not permit the federal government to *assume power* to correct the suspected defect. Should a change in technology or society require an alteration of the Constitution, then Article V provides the authorized means of realignment through the amendment process. When the early leaders of the country, such as Thomas Jefferson, believed that the Constitution was in need of change, they advocated amending it according to this means. They sought refuge, not in arguments of expediency which would tend to suspend the supremacy of the Constitution as the Supreme Law of the Land, but in the written terms of the Constitution itself. This was expressed and understood by the framers and founders of the Constitution and was a vital means of protecting the rights and freedoms of the people from tyranny (being ruled without their consent).

3. Despite recent emphasis on construing the Constitution according to the original intention of its framers and the founders, the judiciary by and large has not taken that intention seriously. The judiciary, however, is not the proper branch to find, define and implement the laws of nature. A court may only consider the laws of nature in its deliberations and opinions, where an organic or constitutional document, or legislative statute has given that law legal expression. For a general discussion of the conflict over Constitutional adjudication *see generally* ROBERT H. BORK, THE TEMPTING OF AMERICA: THE POLITICAL SEDUCTION OF THE LAW (New York: The Free Press, 1990). Former Judge Bork does not rule out the existence of "natural law." He simply indicates that federal judges are not empowered under the Constitution to "define it," for defining the law is the object of the elected legislature.

The Court may have begun to pay more attention to the Constitution if its opinion in Lopez v. United States, ___ U.S. ___, 115 S.Ct. 1624, 1313 L.Ed.2d 626 (1995) is to be followed. In *Lopez*, the Court struck down as unconstitutional a federal statute which made it a federal crime to possess a firearm within a 1000 feet of a school. The Court reasoned that Congress lacked the Constitutional power to enact such a law and that its claim to have such power under the federal Constitution's commerce clause, was purely pretextual. *Lopez* was the first case in over sixty years to overturn a federal statute on the basis that Congress has exceeded its commerce clause power.

    4. *See John Quincy Adams, The Jubilee of the Constitution, a Discourse delivered at the request of the New York Historical Society, on Tuesday, the 30th of April, 1839,* in J. OF CHRISTIAN JURIS. 6 (1986).

    5. JOHN TAYLOR [OF CAROLINE], NEW VIEWS OF THE CONSTITUTION OF THE UNITED STATES (Washington City: Way and Gideon, 1823; reprint ed., New York: Da Capo Press, 1971) 2.

    6. Home Building and Loan Assn. v. Blaisdell, 290 U.S. 398, 453 (1934) (Sutherland, J., dissenting) (citation omitted). Mr. Justice Sutherland also noted: "A provision of the Constitution, it is hardly necessary to say, does not admit of two distinctly opposite interpretations. It does not mean one thing at one time and an entirely different thing at another time." *Id.* at 448-49.

    The Court in Ex parte Milligan, 71 U.S. (4 Wall.) 2, 120-21 (1866) also stated: The Constitution of the United States is a law for rulers and people, equally in war and in peace, and covers with the shield of its protection all classes of men, at all times, and under all circumstances. No doctrine, involving more pernicious consequences, was ever invented by the wit of man than that any of its provisions can be suspended during any of the great exigencies of government. Such a doctrine leads directly to anarchy or despotism; but the theory of necessity on which it is based is false; for the government, within the Constitution, has all the powers granted to it, which are necessary to preserve its existence.

    The view that law was relative to time and circumstance and rooted in the evolutionary dogma of the times, was expressed by Oliver Wendell Holmes, Jr. in an essay entitled *Natural Law.* Holmes stated: "The jurists who believe in natural law seem to me to be in that naive state of mind that accepts what has been familiar and accepted by them and their neighbors as something that must be accepted by all men everywhere." OLIVER W. HOLMES, JR., COLLECTED LEGAL PAPERS, CONTAINED IN THE COMMON LAW & OTHER WRITINGS, [NATURAL LAW], (New York, Harcort, Brace and Company, 1920; reprint ed., Birmingham, Alabama: The Legal Classics Library, 1982), 312. If acceptability was the test, then that which is familiar today would become equally suspect tomorrow according to Holmes' analysis, the application of which philosophy would render Holmes' state of mind "naive."

    Critical of the duties and rights which flow from natural law, Holmes substituted his own view, declaring: "For legal purposes a right is only the hypostasis of a prophecy - the imagination of a substance supporting the fact that the public force will be brought to bear upon those who do things said to contravene it." *Id.* at 313. Such a position is completely contrary, however, to the immutable rights guaranteed to free men and women and embodied in such landmark charters as the Magna Carta or the Declaration of Independence. *See also* ALEKSANDR I. SOLZHENITSYN, A WORLD SPLIT APART (New York: Harper & Row, 1978). Solzhenitsyn states: [W]e have lost the concept of a Supreme Complete Entity which used to restrain our passions and our irresponsibility." *Id.* at 57.

    7. 290 U.S. at 449-50 (quotation marks omitted).

    8. U.S. CONST. amend. X states: "The powers not delegated to the United States by the Constitution, nor prohibited by it to the States, are reserved to the States respectively, or to the people."

    9. U.S. CONST., art. I, § 8, states: The Congress shall have power
       (1) To lay and collect taxes, duties, imposts and excises, to pay the debts and

provide for the common defence and general welfare of the United States; but all duties, imposts and excises shall be uniform throughout the United States;

(2) To borrow money on the credit of the United States;

(3) To regulate commerce with foreign nations, and among the several states, and with the Indian tribes;

(4) To establish an uniform rule of naturalization, and uniform laws on the subject of bankruptcies throughout the United States;

(5) To coin money, regulate the value thereof, and of foreign coin, and fix the standard of weights and measures;

(6) To provide for the punishment of counterfeiting the securities and current coin of the United States;

(7) To establish post offices and post roads;

(8) To promote the progress of science and useful arts, by securing for limited times to authors and inventors the exclusive right to their respective writings and discoveries;

(9) To constitute tribunals inferior to the supreme court;

(10) To define and punish piracies and felonies committed on the high seas, and offences against the law of nations;

(11) To declare war, grant letters of marque and reprisal, and make rules concerning captures on land and water;

(12) To raise and support armies, but no appropriation of money to that use shall be for a longer term than two years;

(13) To provide and maintain a navy;

(14) To make rules for the government and regulation of the land and naval forces;

(15) To provide for calling forth the militia to execute the laws of the union, suppress insurrections and repel invasions;

(16) To provide for organizing, arming, and disciplining, the militia, and for governing such part of them as may be employed in the service of the United States, reserving to the States respectively, the appointment of the officers, and the authority of training the militia according to the discipline prescribed by Congress;

(17) To exercise exclusive legislation in all cases whatsoever, over such district (not exceeding ten miles square) as may, by cession of particular States, and the acceptance of Congress, become the seat of the government of the United States, and to exercise like authority over all places purchased by the consent of the legislature of the state in which the same shall be, for the erection of forts, magazines, arsenals, dockyards, and other needful buildings; - And

(18) To make all laws which shall be necessary and proper for carrying into execution the foregoing powers, and all other powers vested by this constitution in the government of the United States, or in any department or officer thereof.

U.S., CONST. art. 4, § 3, cl. 2 states: "The Congress shall have Power to dispose of and make all needful Rules and Regulations respecting the Territory or other Property belonging to the United States."

See also McCulloch v. Maryland, 17 U.S. (4 Wheat) 316 (1819). "Let the end be legitimate, let it be within the scope of the Constitution, and all means which are appropriate, which are plainly adapted to that end, which are not prohibited, but consist with the letter and spirit of the constitution, are constitutional." (Marshall, C.J.) *Id.* at 421.

10. The Congress shall have power . . . to exercise exclusive Legislation in all Cases whatsoever, over such District (not exceeding ten miles square) as may, by Cession of particular States, and Acceptance of Congress, become the Seat of the Government of the

United States, and to exercise like authority over all Places purchased by the Consent of the Legislature of the State in which the Same shall be, for the Erection of Forts, Magazines, Arsenals, dock-Yards, and other needful Buildings . . . ."

11. "The Congress shall have Power to dispose of and make all needful Rules and Regulations respecting the Territory or other Property belonging to the United States."

12. "The Congress shall have Power . . . to promote the progress of science and useful arts, by securing for limited times to authors and inventors the exclusive right to their respective writings and discoveries."

13. DOCUMENTS ILLUSTRATIVE OF THE FORMATION OF THE UNION OF THE AMERICAN STATES, 69th Cong., 1st sess., House Document No. 398 (Washington, D.C.: Government Printing office, 1927) 563. The power to encourage by proper premium and provision the advancement of useful knowledge and discoveries was rejected by the Convention.

14. To gain an understanding of the proportions of the land at stake, Virginia's actual conveyance included the future states of Kentucky, Tennessee, Ohio, Indiana, Mississippi, Illinois, Alabama, Michigan, and Wisconsin. These states were eventually formed out of the territory Virginia ceded or were implicated in some way. *See* GEORGE B. GERMANN, NATIONAL LEGISLATION CONCERNING EDUCATION (New York: Columbia University, 1899, Library of American Civilization 15623) 13-14.

15. *Id.* at 17-20.

16. JAMES D. RICHARDSON, ED., COMPILATION OF THE MESSAGES AND PAPERS OF THE PRESIDENTS, 1789-1897 (Washington, D.C.: Government Printing Office, 1896) 5:549-50, Veto Message of James Buchanan, February 24, 1859. For a general discussion of state sovereignty *see* B. A. HINSDALE, COMP., U.S. OFFICE OF EDUCATION, DOCUMENTS ILLUSTRATIVE OF AMERICAN EDUCATIONAL HISTORY (Washington, D.C.: Government Printing Office, 1895) 2:1268-74.

Today there is no longer the vast expanse of *territory* which the federal government could feasibly sell to raise revenue. This is not to say that the federal government does not hold vast amounts of real estate. Including Alaska and sections of many western states, the federal government still owns nearly 740 million acres -- nearly a third of the United States! These lands are within states, not a territory. Federal retention of property in these states certainly violates the spirit of the Northwest Ordinance. That Ordinance contained an agreement between "the original States and the people and States in the said territory" that Congress should admit the territory into the Union on equal footing with all the other states when those areas became sufficiently populated. RICHARD PERRY, ED., SOURCES OF OUR LIBERTIES (American Bar Foundation: Chicago, Ill., 1978) 395. While the western states are not located in the geographic region defined by the Northwest Ordinance, the ordinance reflects the precise relationship that was to govern U.S., state and territorial relations. The controlling principle is this -- the purpose of federal ownership of land (excluding the District of Columbia, forts, etc.) is to bring it to sufficient maturity for statehood. Once statehood is established, the federal government must terminate its right, title and interest. This result is necessary whether western states are technically subject to the Northwest Ordinance or not, since to hold otherwise would put western and northwest ordinance states on un-equal footing in violation of Article IV, section 3.

17. DOCUMENTS ILLUSTRATIVE *supra* note 13 at 471-82. JONATHAN ELLIOT, COMP., THE DEBATES IN THE SEVERAL STATE CONVENTIONS ON THE ADOPTION OF THE CONSTITUTION, 5 vols. (Philadelphia: J.B. Lippincott Co., 1891) 1:147 & 226.

18. DOCUMENTS ILLUSTRATIVE *supra* note 13 at 563-64. ELLIOT, DEBATES *supra* note 17 at 1:247.

19. DOCUMENTS ILLUSTRATIVE *supra* note 13 at 702-12. ELLIOT, DEBATES *supra* note 17 at 1:297.

20. DOCUMENTS ILLUSTRATIVE *supra* note 13 at 725. Mr. Gov. Morris noted in response to Madison, that he was of the opinion that : "It is not necessary. The exclusive power at the Seat of Government, will reach the object." *Id.*

21. DOCUMENTS ILLUSTRATIVE *supra* note 13 at 1024.

22. If First Amendment establishment clause principles were applied to these educational "establishments," not one would survive. Furthermore, if the specific power was not enumerated in the Constitution, Congress failed to obtain it. The Tenth Amendment ratified in 1791 also reaffirmed this well known principle. For instance, when the Delegates of the people of Virginia ratified the Constitution, they did so with the understanding that "the powers granted under the Constitution being derived from the People of the United States may be resumed by them whensoever the same shall be perverted to their injury or oppression and that every power not granted thereby remains with them and at their will." DOCUMENTS ILLUSTRATIVE *supra* note 13 at 1027.

23. U.S. CONST. art. I, § 9, cl. 7 also states in part: "No Money shall be drawn from the Treasury, but in Consequences of Appropriations made by Law . . . ." *See also* HINSDALE *supra* note 16 at 2:1293-94.

Chapter 11

Presidential and Congressional Defense of Constitutional Government

When an honest observance of constitutional compacts can not be obtained from communities like ours, it need not be anticipated elsewhere . . . and the degrading truth that man is unfit for self-government admitted. And this will be the case if expediency be made a rule of construction in interpreting the Constitution.[1]

President George Washington and Congress

Not finding any power over education expressed in the text of the Constitution, it may be inquired whether or not the first several Congresses and Presidents understood this limitation on their Constitutional power. Beginning therefore with President George Washington, this Chapter will examine Presidential and Congressional pronouncements concerning the relationship between education and federal power under the Constitution--the supreme law of the land.

During his First Annual Address on January 8, 1790, President Washington advanced his goals for the young nation. He included a variety of proposals concerning such matters as naturalization, weights and measures, and foreign affairs. He also encouraged Congress to undertake certain projects and advance them by the proper Constitutional means. Noting the many advantages of knowledge and its desirability, he requested Congress to consider how this end may be properly encouraged. Washington stated: "Whether this desirable object will be best promoted by affording aids to seminaries of learning already established, by the institution of a national university, or by any other expedients will be well worthy of a place in the deliberations of the Legislature."[2]

Congress considered the President's petition. On May 3, Mr. Smith of South Carolina moved that the President's request, which specifically encouraged science and literature, be referred to a select House committee. This was objected to by Mr. Stone who (as shocking as it may seem to his modern contemporaries) "inquired what part of the Constitution authorized Congress to take any steps in a business of this kind? For his part, he knew of none."[3] An accurate scenario of what then took place has been preserved in the *Annals of Congress*. It notes that Mr. Stone continued:

> We have already done as much as we can with propriety; we have encouraged learning by giving to authors an exclusive privilege of vending their works; this is going as far as we have the power to go by the Constitution.
>
> Mr. Sherman said, that a proposition to vest Congress with power to establish a National University was made in the General Convention, but it was negatived. It was thought sufficient that this power should be exercised by the States in their separate capacity.
>
> Mr. Page observed, that he was in favor of the motion. He wished to have the matter determined, whether Congress has, or has not, a right to do any thing for the promotion of science and literature. He rather supposed that they had such a right; but if, on investigation of the subject, it shall appear they have not, he should consider the circumstance as a very essential defect in the Constitution, and should be for proposing an amendment.[4]

✓ Key Idea:

☞ EARLY CONGRESSES RECOGNIZED THAT THE CONSTITUTION PROHIBITED IT FROM PROMOTING EDUCATION.

In a nutshell, these debates acknowledged the Constitutional limitations preventing Congress from assuming jurisdiction over education, *i.e.*, the promotion of science and literature. They reflect three distinct points of view. Mr. Stone, Mr. Sherman and Mr. Page all understood that the Constitution did not authorize Congress to establish a National University or "do any thing for the promotion of science and literature." None of these Congressmen suggested that the Constitution was uncertain or unclear. None suggested that the intention of the framers was ambiguous. None implied that the ends of education justified an expansion of Congressional power.

Moreover, there was no Committee Report suggesting that the Constitution was an evolving document, one which must adapt to changing circumstances. These Congressman did not suggest a legal subterfuge to accommodate the will of a special interest. There was only the recognition that the Constitution did not provide for Congressional authority in this area and that if Congress wanted to proceed in that direction it had the power of proposing an amendment. No amendment, however, was proposed and Congress took no action whatsoever. This pattern of thought is a far cry from any business that has transpired in any Congress of recent years.

Seven years later near the end of his Presidency, in his Eighth Annual Address delivered December 7, 1796, Washington proposed a variation on his first suggestion since it was rejected. This time the President "proposed to the consideration of Congress the expediency of establishing a national university and also a military academy."[5] Washington understood that a military academy was a Constitutional option under Article I, section 8, clauses 12-16, which authorized Congress to govern and regulate the land and naval forces.

While this proposal was offered, another was presented on Monday, December 12, 1796 by Mr. Madison. Representative Madison moved to refer to the House of Representatives a Memorial drawn up by the Commissioners of the "Federal City" (the District of Columbia).[6] The Memorial, according to Madison, prayed "that Congress would take such measures as that they may be able to receive any donations which may be made to the institution."[7] The Commissioners wanted Congress to authorize them to receive money from private contributors in order to start a school.

During debate on Monday, December 26, the House took up both the President's request and the Commissioner's Memorial. With respect to the latter, Mr. Madison was of the opinion that "Congress has the sole jurisdiction over that District . . . . "[8] Since the Memorial specifically called for a university in the District of Columbia, he would vote for it. He was quick to note, however, that such a university was materially different than a national university since the former did not require any act of establishment by Congress whereas a national university would go beyond Congressional power. Nor did the Commissioner's request require any federal funds from the United States treasury,[9] whereas Washington's proposal would require both incorporation and funding.

As debate continued on the following day, Mr. Craik also expressed the same opinion:

> The Commissioners seemed to have anticipated the objections which have been made to a National University, and purposely avoided inserting it in their Memorial. They have cherished similar ideas which I have, of the eligibility of such an institution, but foreseeing that plan would not be approved they have relinquished that, and only requested incorporation to enable them to act in trust for the institution. They do not call upon this House to put their hand into the public Treasury.[10]

Mr. Craik recognized that establishment and federal funding of a national university was not a Constitutional option. All that he desired was that Congress enable the Commissioners to act in trust for the institution and receive private contributions of monies on its behalf. While the petition expressed the desirability of a university in the District of Columbia, the debate resulted in a vote to postpone the matter indefinitely.[11]

With respect to Washington's proposal, which was also postponed, the general tenor of Congress was that the President was perfectly entitled to take this last opportunity to recommend his proposal as a matter of his own conscience. With respect to both proposals, however, Mr. Nicholas said: "I would not be supposed to want a due respect either for those Commissioners or for the President; but, merely because recommended by them, we are not warrantable in adopting it."[12] In other words, just because the President asks Congress to consider a measure does not necessitate that Congress act.

Thus, at the conclusion of Washington's second term, the House was of the opinion that while Congress had been granted power over the District of Columbia, the establishment of a university in that District, even though privately endowed, was either a doubtful exercise of its authority[13] or not yet ripe for consideration.

President Thomas Jefferson and Constitutional Limitations

President Thomas Jefferson, also a friend to education, expressed his educational ideas in his Second Inaugural Address delivered on March 4, 1805. With pride, he first reiterated the ability of the United States of America to meet its fiscal obligations by inquiring: "it may be the pleasure and the pride of an American to ask, what farmer, what mechanic, what laborer ever sees a taxgatherer of the United States?"[14] Referring to revenue contributions on the conscription of foreign articles, he continued:

> These contributions enable us to support the current expenses of the government . . . and to apply such a surplus to our public debt . . . and that redemption, once effected, the revenue thereby liberated may, by a just repartition of it among the States and a corresponding amendment of the Constitution, be applied *in time of peace* to rivers, canals, roads, arts, manufacturers, education, and other great objects within each State.[15]

In other words, once the public debt was redeemed, the United States would have a surplus of money in the federal Treasury. The question, then became: "What will be done with the surplus money?" Jefferson suggested that these funds could be divided up among the states and the states could then apply the monies to education and other matters. This idea, however, was only viable if military and other Constitutional expenses were first met, and provided that the

Constitution was amended to extend Congressional authority to take money out of the federal Treasury for the purpose of partitioning it among the states.

The fact that the federal government could accomplish all this plus manage its Constitutional business at hand, without an internal tax on its citizens, should not be missed. It takes no exhaustive knowledge of current events to understand that each of these laudable aspects of Jefferson's administration are reversed today, point by point.[16] The Constitution has not been amended, but yet Congress takes billions of dollars from the federal Treasury and transfers it to the states. Congress increases the education budget and cuts military expenditures, citing the unconstitutional "needs" of the first against the constitutional demands of the second. Of course, all this transfer of money is based in a significant degree, upon a federal income tax that increases every few years entirely out of proportion to an increase in population. There are no surplus dollars. America has only debt, and yet the federal government regularly spends about 32-33 billion dollars a year through its Federal Department of Education.

So often proponents of governmental control of the mind and education erroneously idolize Jefferson as a champion of state-controlled secular education. To do so, they must ignore many of his official statements about the necessity of a Constitutional amendment. Perhaps adherence to the Constitution is not really what interests them?

✓ Key Idea:

☞ PRESIDENT JEFFERSON WAS HONEST ABOUT THE CONSTITUTION--IT AUTHORIZED NO FEDERAL JURISDICTION OVER EDUCATION.

Referring to federal intervention in education based on a surplus of federal revenues, President Jefferson initially stated:

> The subject is now proposed for consideration of Congress, because if approved by the time the State legislatures shall have deliberated on this extension of the Federal trust, and the laws shall be passed and other arrangements made for their execution, the necessary funds will be on hand and without employment.[17]

His reference to "this extension of the federal trust" means an extension of Constitutional power in accordance with Article V of the Constitution. He made this meaning clear when he concluded: "I suppose an amendment to the Constitution, by consent of the States, necessary, because the objects now recommended are not among those enumerated in the Constitution, and to which it permits the public moneys to be applied."[18] Without an amendment, Congress had no power to assist the states with education. Without an amendment,

Congress had no power to take money from the treasury in order to assist the states with education.

For Jefferson, federal involvement in state educational matters was not a matter of "how much" or the most "expedient means." It was an issue of Constitutional jurisdiction. Neither did he reason: "Well, I know the power isn't there, but let's just construe the general welfare clause or the commerce clause to fit our ends. After all, isn't education worth it?" No, Jefferson didn't stoop to debauching the Constitution's plain meaning or engage in some deceptive and manipulative construction of the law. An honest observance of the Constitution revealed that Congress simply had no Constitutionally delegated power to establish or encourage education and that it had no recourse to the federal treasury for any educational object as the Constitution stood. His Administration's priorities were in fulfilling the limited purposes of federal government.[19]

President James Madison and Constitutional Means

When James Madison became President, he was also keenly aware of the Constitutional limitations on the federal government and particularly Congress. Madison had been instrumental in presenting a measure at the Constitutional Convention to establish a national university, which was rejected on at least two separate occasions.[20] He had also transmitted to the House two items: Washington's request that Congress consider establishing a national university, and the Commissioners' Memorial to establish a local university in the District of Columbia. Both of these items were postponed indefinitely.[21] To say the least, Madison was also well acquainted with the Constitution.[22]

In his First Inaugural Address, delivered March 4, 1809, he reiterated certain Constitutional duties of his office. He pledged to support the Constitution. He said that the Constitution is "the cement of the Union" and should be respected in its limitations, as well as in its authority. He promised to respect the Ninth and Tenth Amendments by referring to the "rights and authorities reserved to the States and to the people as equally incorporated with and essential to the success of the general system."[23]

Madison was not parroting the language of expediency as is common in many political speeches today. He was not indicating that the same power was shared by the federal and state governments, and the people. He did not position himself as "the education president." Madison simply affirmed the Constitution as it was intended, not supposing that the federal government should act beyond the scope of its enumerated powers. Turning specifically to education, he expressed his desire that the federal government should observe proper Constitutional restraint. He encouraged Congress "to promote by *authorized means* [certain internal improvements]; to favor in like manner, the advancement of science and the diffusion of information as the best aliment [or nourishment] to true liberty."[24]

In 1815, he clarified what he meant by "authorized means" by calling for a Constitutional amendment, in order for the federal government to obtain "national jurisdiction and national means" to implement a series of internal improvements.[25] He then proceeded to urge Congress, "in like manner," to establish a "national seminary of learning within the District of Columbia, and with the means drawn from the property therein, subject to the authority of the General Government [over the District]."[26]

Madison arrived at this Constitutional solution in 1815, partly based on Congress' view of the subject expressed by them in 1811.[27] The House Committee notes are worth reviewing in detail, for they summarize much of what has been articulated:

> [I]t was necessary to consider whether Congress possessed the power to found and endow a national university.
>
> It is argued, from the total silence of the Constitution, that such a power has not been granted to Congress, inasmuch as the only means by which it is therein contemplated to promote the progress of science and the useful arts, is, by securing to authors and inventors the exclusive right to their respective writings and discoveries for limited times. The Constitution, therefore, does not warrant the creation of such a corporation by any express provision.
>
> But it immediately occurred that, under the right to legislate exclusively over the district wherein the United States have fixed their seat of Government, Congress may erect a university at any place within the ten miles square ceded by Maryland and Virginia. This cannot be doubted.
>
> Here, however, other considerations arise. Although there is no Constitutional impediment to the incorporation of trustees for such a purpose, at the City of Washington, serious doubts are entertained as to the right to appropriate the public property for its support. The endowment of a University is not ranked among the objects for which drafts ought to be made upon the Treasury. The money of the nation seems to be reserved for other uses.[28]

Can the matter be stated more clearly? Congress has no Constitutional basis for funding educational matters. Congress could incorporate trustees for a university in the District of Columbia, but "the endowment of a University is not ranked among the objects for which drafts ought to be made upon the Treasury." The Committee concluded with a show of restraint and judgment that is simply not conceived of today. It affirmed the specific objects to which the federal treasury was to be put and avoided Constitutional revisionism. The Committee concluded that:

The erection of a university, upon the enlarged and magnificent plan which would become the nation, is not within the powers confided by the Constitution to Congress . . . . If, nevertheless, at any time legislative aid should be asked to incorporate a district university, for the local benefit of the inhabitants of Columbia, and of funds of their own raising, there can be no doubt that it would be considered with kindness, as in other cases; but it must be remembered that this is a function totally distinct from the endowment of a national university, out of the treasury of the United States, destined, in its legitimate application, to other and very different purposes.[29]

What could be clearer? It is Constitutionally acceptable to "incorporate a district university for the local benefit of the inhabitants of Columbia, and of funds of their own raising." This is the outer limit of Congressional power. It is not acceptable for Congress to establish a "University of America" in the District of Columbia and then fund it out of the federal treasury.

✓ Key Idea:
☞   CONGRESS MAY NOT FUND EDUCATION IN THE
          DISTRICT OF COLUMBIA, BUT IT MAY *ENCOURAGE*
          EDUCATION OF THE DISTRICT'S INHABITANTS.

President James Monroe and the People as Sovereigns

During the Presidency of Madison's successor, James Monroe, the issue of a seminary for education was once again raised. Outlining his Constitutional perspective, he noted in the context of internal improvements that: "the result is a settled conviction in my mind that Congress do[es] not possess the right."[30] He also observed, however, that:

In cases of doubtful construction, especially of such vital interest, it comports with the nature and origin of our institutions, and will contribute much to preserve them, to apply to our constituents for an explicit grant of power. We may confidently rely that if it appears to their satisfaction that the power is necessary, it will always be granted.[31]

What is President Monroe saying? Is he saying that we cannot know the intention of the Constitution? Is he saying that since the intent may be unclear, that the best course of conduct is to do what we think is right, or worse yet just make up the interpretation as we go along? Monroe did not advance these deceptions. He said the right thing to do in such limited instances is "to apply to our constituents for an explicit grant." That means ask the people to amend the Constitution. How different such an approach seems when compared to the rule of political expediency presently relied upon by all branches of the federal government.

When it came to a seminary of learning, however, Monroe did not consider the Constitution to be unclear or uncertain. He believed that Congress did not have the power to intervene in educational affairs or fund educational ventures from the national treasury. The prior debate about a national university and seminaries of learning amply demonstrated that much. Referring to internal improvement measures he stated: "I think proper to suggest also, in case this measure is adopted, that it be recommended to the States to include in the amendment sought a right in Congress to institute likewise seminaries of learning."[32] This proposal was broader than the one calling for the establishment of a district university. This called upon Congress to establish more than one institution of learning without geographical limitation (or so it seems). When this matter was brought before the House, the proposition to consider the resolution was rejected.[33]

President John Quincy Adams and Delegated Power

The Presidency of John Quincy Adams illustrated a similar concern for the integrity of the Constitution. In his First Annual Message of 1825, he observed that "moral, political, [and] intellectual improvements are duties assigned by the Author of Our Existence to social no less than to individual man."[34] He strictly cautioned Congress as they undertook such improvements, to adhere to the powers that were delegated, warning; "the exercise of delegated powers is a duty as sacred and indispensable as the usurpation of powers not granted is criminal and odious."[35] What a statement! President Adams is saying that the exercise of power is *criminal* if it is not authorized by the Constitution. If this insight were applied to the federal government today, it would give new meaning to the term "habitual offender."

President Andrew Jackson and Honest Constitutional Interpretation

The principle of limited and enumerated Constitutional authority in Congress was also recognized by President Andrew Jackson. In the context of Congressional appropriations from the federal treasury for roads and canals without first resorting to an amendment,[36] Jackson stated:

> [i]f it be the wish of the people that the construction of roads and canals should be conducted by the Federal Government, it is not only highly expedient, but indispensably necessary, that a previous amendment of the Constitution, delegating the necessary power and defining and restricting its exercise with reference to the sovereignty of the States, should be made.[37]

There is little doubt that Jackson considered a Constitutional amendment as an essential prerequisite to granting the federal government jurisdiction over education as well as roads and canals. Even so, Jackson added a far more enduring principle which cautioned against Congress granting additional powers to itself. He warned that:

> When an honest observance of constitutional compacts cannot be obtained from communities like ours, it need not be anticipated elsewhere . . . and the degrading truth that man is unfit for self-government admitted. And this will be the case if *expediency* be made a rule of construction in interpreting the Constitution. Power in no government could desire a better shield for the insidious advances which it is ever ready to make upon the checks that are designed to restrain its action.[38]

President Jackson put his finger on one of the key issues of Constitutional construction--honesty. Many other Presidents touched upon other important points such as the intention of the framers and founders and the clarity of the text. Jackson, however, addresses one of the central points when he says: "When an honest observance of constitutional compacts cannot be obtained from communities like ours . . . ." What does he mean? He means that when the intention and meaning are clear and the text is plain and certain, then interpretation of the Constitution boils down to whether our leaders are going to be honest and trustworthy or whether they are going to be criminal and odious.

✓ Key Idea:
☞   FEDERAL INTERVENTION INTO EDUCATION IS
        CONSTITUTIONALLY DISHONEST.

Many modern American politicians, lawyers, judges, university administrators and school board members do not think that construing the Constitution against its clear intent or plain meaning is really corrupt and dishonorable, let alone criminal or odious. They are all too happy to pursue their "insidious advances . . . upon the checks that are designed to restrain" the government's power. Indeed, "insidious advances" tend to deliver the vote and keep politicians in office. The modern mind has perfected the "insidious advance" of raiding the Treasury and bestowing it upon new and larger special interest groups.[39] "Insidious advances" and not "honest observance" have become the stock-in-trade vote-getting calling card of Congressional and Presidential politics.

Moreover, these advances are almost always taken in the name of "educational excellence" or "the Children." Congress in particular, has made expediency its "rule of construction in interpreting the Constitution." The people have also become infected with this attitude. They have fulfilled the balance of

Jackson's prophesy, that honesty in construing the Constitution "need not be anticipated elsewhere . . . and the degrading truth that man is unfit for self-government admitted."

Sensing the self-serving disposition of their lawmakers, the people, however, in some states have embarked upon limiting their lawmaker's terms by prohibiting indefinite consecutive re-election to the same seat. This movement cannot, however, fail to stem the tide of governmental usurpation unless the people recognize that no legislator, irrespective of the *duration* of his or her term, should exercise undefined and unlimited power. The people themselves must reject the notion that the public treasury is a convenient point of transfer to special interests, especially themselves, in order to make any difference.

The American mind has become government-financed and consequently, unfit for self-government. The purported rationale for government funding of education is to prepare the people for self-government. But federal involvement has instead assisted in rendering the people unfit for that end.

President James Buchanan and Land-Grant Legislation

In 1859 President James Buchanan vetoed an Act originally introduced by Justin Morrill that would have granted public land for the maintenance of agricultural colleges within the several states *already admitted* to the Union. This was something new. Previous proposals that had been rejected only suggested that Congress set aside land in federal territories before that territory became a state. Now Congress was proposing to give land to states *already admitted to the Union*. This proposal is no different than reaching into the Treasury and giving money to the states for educational purposes.

Buchanan's veto was based upon the fact that the Act was "both inexpedient and unconstitutional."[40] It was inexpedient because it was "passed at a period when we can with great difficulty raise sufficient revenue to sustain the expenses of the Government."[41] Buchanan said that Congress shouldn't be taking money from the Treasury for education when the other expenses could not be met.

He then addressed the unconstitutionality of the matter. He explained to Congress that the "Constitution is a grant to Congress of a few enumerated but most important powers. . . . All other powers are reserved to the States and to the people." He reiterated for Congress that the "several spheres of action should be kept distinct from each other."[42] He also knew that the "[f]ederal Government, which makes the donation [of money], has confessedly no Constitutional power to follow it into the States and enforce the application of the fund to the intended objects. As donors we shall possess no control over our own gift after it shall have passed from our hands."[43] If this lacked clarity, he concluded in no uncertain terms:

I presume the general proposition is undeniable that Congress does not possess the power to appropriate money in the Treasury, raised by taxes on the people of the United States, for the purpose of educating the people of the respective States. It will not be pretended that any such power is to be found among the specific powers granted to Congress nor that "it is necessary and proper for carrying into execution" any one of these powers.[44]

Thus, President Buchanan vetoed the Land Grant Act in 1859, adding a warning to the people and the governments of the United States. He charged that should the federal government open its treasury to every special interest group, then the integrity of every government and the people would dwindle to a new low. Government would become nothing more than a means of feeding the vice of covetousness. He cautioned:

Should the time ever arrive when the State governments shall look to the Federal Treasury for the means of supporting themselves and maintaining their systems of education and internal policy, the character of both Governments will be greatly deteriorated. The representatives of the States and of the people, feeling a more immediate interest in obtaining money to lighten the burdens of their constituents than for the promotion of the more distant objects intrusted to the Federal Government, will naturally incline to obtain means from the Federal Government for State purposes. If a question shall arise between an appropriation of land or money to carry into effect the objects of the Federal Government and those of the States, their feelings will be enlisted in favor of the latter. This is human nature; and hence the necessity of keeping the two Governments entirely distinct. The preponderance of this home feeling has been manifested by the passage of the present bill. The establishment of these colleges has prevailed over the pressing wants of the common Treasury.[45]

Buchanan's words ought to be cut into stone and mounted in both houses of Congress so that all the members can see it when they speak. But soon Buchanan was out of office and Abraham Lincoln became President. Three years later, President Lincoln signed into law an almost identical Act from the one Buchanan had vetoed. Lincoln favored internal improvements and to that extent appears to have accepted the notion that at least granting of *land* to the *states* was permissible. The approved Act had been re-introduced by Justin Morrill and after signed by Lincoln, became known as the Morrill Land Grant Act of 1862.[46] It was hotly debated in both Houses of Congress and has been characterized as the "first real Federal role in education, the first divergence from Constitutional intent."[47]

Morrill himself envisioned a broader federal presence than the Constitution permitted or the Land Grant Act suggested. He later declared in 1888 that "I have attempted . . . not wholly unsuccessfully to bring forward a measure that would reinforce the Land-Grant Colleges with a supplementary national fund."[48]

✓ Key Idea:

☟   FEDERAL LAND GRANT LEGISLATION EXPANDED THE UNCONSTITUTIONAL IDEA THAT THE FEDERAL TREASURY SHOULD UNDERWRITE EVERY STATES'S EDUCATIONAL SELF-INTEREST.

Buchanan had rejected this type of Congressional intervention on the grounds of Constitutionality. Buchanan had accepted prior Congressional grants of federal territories and lands made to new states as they successively entered the Union, but rejected the outright donation of lands (suggested by Morrill) to all states for the erection of colleges. The former, if it rested on any Congressional power, was contained in Congress' Constitutional authority to dispose of territories belonging to the United States.[49] The advocates of the Land Grant bill, however, sustained their position by construing the Constitutional phrase "to dispose of" so as to embrace objects not contemplated by an enumerated power in the Constitution. Congress was beginning to enjoy "insidious advances" on its limited power. An honest observance of the Constitution was just too confining.

Buchanan had pointed all of this out very clearly in his Veto Message of February 24, 1859, but by 1862 the exigencies of the circumstances, the ongoing Civil War and the *absence of substantial southern representation in Congress*, proved detrimental to Constitutional limitations.[50] Buchanan's warning that Land Grant legislation would "confer upon Congress a vast and irresponsible authority, utterly at war with the well-known jealousy of Federal power which prevailed at the formation of the Constitution,"[51] was not heeded.

Thus between 1787 and 1861, an honest consideration of the Constitution was demonstrated. Constitutional limitations on the authority of the federal government were duly observed. Though a variety of factual rationales for federal intervention into education were asserted, they were always rejected in light of the Constitution's limited powers and the Ninth and Tenth Amendments. Not until 1862 did the first wedge of federal jurisdiction into education become manifested. As we will see, however, the most definitive Congressional usurpation outside the Article IV, section 3, clause 2 land grant debate, came in 1867 with the formation of the Federal Bureau of Education.

★ HYPOTHETICALLY SPEAKING . . . .

Problem: You are a first term member of the City-Council in Middle America. Middle America is an all American town. Middle America's Mayor says the town's main streets need to be re-paved. Middle America names their streets after famous Presidents. Jackson and Buchanan Streets in particular, have been ignored and neglected for years. He presents you and the rest of the City Council the following options to finance the repaving measure to "honor our Presidents."

1).   Raise local income, sales and property taxes; or

2).   Lobby the federal government to pay for all or most of the paving and not raise local taxes.

The Mayor reminds you that local council elections are coming up and its time to "produce." He assures you that Middle Americans don't like local tax increases and that its representatives in Congress "can deliver the pork!"

He solicits your support for the federal treasury handout. Should you vote for the local tax increase or for the federal "pork barrel" paving project? You have read your Constitution and can find nothing about federal power to pave local roads, but every city seems to accept federal money for that purpose.

What will you do?

Answer: You will have to answer some questions about what kind of person you are. Has the time arrived in Middle America when it shall look to the federal treasury for the means of supporting itself and maintaining its systems of education, roads and internal policy? If so, then the character of both governments, the city council and the federal government will be deteriorated. A vote for federal aid to pave Middle America's Buchanan Street will be a vote for the deterioration of council government, not merely the deterioration of a road.

Clearly the mayor and federal representatives feel a more immediate interest in obtaining money to lighten the burden on their constituents than for the promotion of the more distant matters Constitutionally entrusted to the federal government. Do you share their approach?

Has the time arrived in Middle America when an honest observance of the Constitution cannot be found among its City Council? If so, then a vote for federal aid to pave Middle America's Jackson street will constitute a vote recognizing the degrading truth that the City Council is unfit for self-government. This is always the case where expediency is made a rule of construction in interpreting the Constitution.

Notes

1. JAMES D. RICHARDSON, ED., COMPILATION OF THE MESSAGES AND PAPERS OF THE PRESIDENTS, 1789-1897 (Washington, D.C.: Government Printing Office, 1896) 2:491. Veto Messages of Andrew Jackson, May 27, 1830. Jackson also noted: "In no government are appeals to the source of power in cases of real doubt more suitable than in ours. No good motive can be assigned for the exercise of power by the constituted authorities, while those for whose benefit it is to be exercised have not conferred it and may not be willing to confer it." *Id.* at 2:492.

2. *Id.* at 1:66, First Annual Address of George Washington, January 8, 1790.

3. U.S., Congress, House, Representative Stone noted the unconstitutionality of the President's proposal regarding the promotion of science and literature, 1st Cong., 3 May 1790, THE ANNALS OF THE CONGRESS OF THE UNITED STATES, contained in JOSEPH GALES, COMP., THE DEBATES AND PROCEEDINGS OF THE CONGRESS OF THE UNITED STATES, 42 vols., (Washington: Gales and Seaton, 1834) at 2:1550-51. (Library of American Civilization 21604)

4. *Id.* at 2:1551.

5. RICHARDSON, PRESIDENTS *supra* note 1 at 1:202, Eighth Annual Address of George Washington, December 7, 1796.

6. U.S., Congress, House, Representative Madison noted the advantages of building a national university at the permanent seat of government, 4th Cong., 2nd sess., 12 December 1796, THE ANNALS OF THE CONGRESS OF THE UNITED STATES, contained in JOSEPH GALES, COMP., THE DEBATES AND PROCEEDINGS OF THE CONGRESS OF THE UNITED STATES, 42 vols., (Washington: Gales and Seaton, 1834) at 6:1600-01 (Library of American Civilization 21608).

7. *Id.* at 6:1600.

8. *Id.* at 6:1702.

9. *Id.*

10. *Id.* at 6:1706. Referring to the Memorial, Representative Harper stated:
> There was nothing in it that contemplated pledging the United States to find funds for its support; nor was it the object of the report to establish a National University . . . the object of the Commissioners was not to establish a National University or obtain money from the United States, but their direct object was, to be incorporated, so as to be enabled to receive such legacies and donations as may be presented to the institution . . . .

Id. at 6:1698. Mr. Baldwin continued that "nothing can prove it improper, since no pecuniary aid is required, no grant of money is asked. If it was, I should . . . disapprove of it . . . ." *Id.* Representative Livingston, who stated that though the proposition appeared straightforward, nevertheless voiced some reservations by inquiring, "If nothing was intended but a mere incorporation, why not apply to the State that could incorporate such a body? Something further seemed to be intended: public patronage was wanted to support this institution." *Id.* at 6:1701. Representative Lyman cautioned: "As far as I can understand, the land which is now to be appropriated for this University, is the property of the United States. Does not this look as though the United States are to patronize and support the establishment? If we take this step, I shall very much wonder if our next is not to be called upon to produce money." *Id.* at 6:1699. *See also* GEORGE B. GERMANN, NATIONAL LEGISLATION CONCERNING EDUCATION (New York: Columbia University, 1899, Library of American Civilization 15623) 23-25, and B. A. HINSDALE, COMP., U.S. OFFICE OF EDUCATION, DOCUMENTS ILLUSTRATIVE OF AMERICAN EDUCATIONAL HISTORY (Washington, D.C.: Government Printing Office, 1895) 2:1298-1305.

11. ANNALS OF CONGRESS *supra* note 6 at 6:1711. Compare this approach of incorporating a privately funded university in the District of Columbia with the present funding of special educational institutions incorporated in the District. The 1991 federal budget, for instance, appropriated about 291 million dollars to fund Howard University, Gallaudet University, The National Technical Institute for the Deaf and The American Printing House for the Blind. While aid to a District University, and to those who live with a speech, hearing and visual impairment is a worthy object, it is not a federal object.

12. ANNALS OF CONGRESS *supra* note 6 at 6:1709.

13. Article I, section 8, clause 17 provides that:
> The Congress shall have power . . . to exercise exclusive Legislation in all Cases whatsoever, over such District (not exceeding ten miles square) as may, by Cession of particular States, and Acceptance of Congress, become the Seat of the Government of the United States, and to exercise like authority over all Places purchased by the Consent of the Legislature of the State in which the Same shall be, for the Erection of Forts, Magazines, Arsenals, dock-Yards, and other needful Buildings . . . ."

14. RICHARDSON, PRESIDENTS *supra* note 1 at 1:379, Second Inaugural Address of Thomas Jefferson, March 4, 1805. Jefferson also notes that "the suppression of unnecessary offices, of useless establishments and expenses, enabled us to discontinue our internal taxes." *Id.* He added that the government should only increase revenue in proportion to increased population and warned that the government should "meet within the year, all the expenses of the year without encroaching on the rights of future generations by burthening them with the debts of the past." *Id.* If Congress were to observe this simple rule of thumb, the United States would not be running a deficit of hundreds of billions of dollars.

15. RICHARDSON, PRESIDENTS *supra* note 1 at 1:379 (emphasis in original), Second Inaugural Address of Thomas Jefferson, March 4, 1805. Jefferson stated: "[T]here will still ere long be an accumulation of moneys in the Treasury beyond the installments of public debt which we are permitted by contract to pay. . . . Nor, if our peace continues, will they be wanting for any other existing purpose. The question therefore now comes forward, To what other objects shall these surpluses be appropriated . . . during those intervals when the purposes of war shall not call for them?" *Id.* at 1:409. Sixth Annual Message of Thomas Jefferson, December 2, 1806.

16. Noting the fact of surplus revenues, the condition of peace and the satisfaction of military purposes, Jefferson also stated: "Education is here placed among the articles of public care, not that it would be proposed to take its ordinary branches out of the hands of private enterprise, which manages so much better all the concerns to which it is equal." RICHARDSON, PRESIDENTS *supra* note 1 at 1:409. Sixth Annual Message of Thomas Jefferson, December 2, 1806.

17. RICHARDSON, PRESIDENTS *supra* note 1 at 1:409-10, Sixth Annual Message of Thomas Jefferson, December 2, 1806.

18. RICHARDSON, PRESIDENTS *supra* note 1 at 1:410, Sixth Annual Message of Thomas Jefferson, December 2, 1806. Jefferson also added "that if Congress, approving the proposition, shall yet think it more eligible to found (a national establishment for education) on a donation of lands, they have it now in their power . . . ." *Id.*

19. His loyalty to the Constitution as a fixed and uniform document was made evident by the fact that Jefferson took no opportunity as President to utilize improperly and unconstitutionally the power of the federal Government to achieve these educational objectives for the sake of political popularity.

In 1779 he proposed a Bill for the More General Diffusion of Knowledge which was rejected. In 1816 he again proposed to establish a university within Virginia's exclusive jurisdiction, by upgrading "The Central College" already in existence at Charlottesville, Virginia. The 1816 proposal was accepted and the University of Virginia eventually began operation in 1822.

Thus, Jefferson's educational objective, having been rejected by the Commonwealth in 1779 could have easily influenced him to misuse his office of President from 1801-1809, in order to establish a university of greater magnitude and with greater resources than any state government could bring to bear. He resisted, however, this political appeal to undermine the Constitution, preferring instead to preserve, protect and defend that document. HENRY S. RANDALL, THE LIFE OF THOMAS JEFFERSON, 3 vols. (New York: Derby & Jackson, 1858, Library of American Civilization 20279-80) 3:461-71.

20. *See* Chapter 10 text accompanying notes 17-18.

21. *See supra* text accompanying notes 6-11.

22. *See generally* GAILLARD HUNT, ED., THE JOURNAL OF THE DEBATES IN THE CONVENTION WHICH FRAMED THE CONSTITUTION OF THE UNITED STATES AS RECORDED BY JAMES MADISON, 2 vols. (New York: G.P. Putnam's Sons, 1908)(Library of American Civilization 23016).

23. RICHARDSON, PRESIDENTS *supra* note 1 at 1:467, First Inaugural Address of James Madison, March 4, 1809.

24. RICHARDSON, PRESIDENTS *supra* note 1 at 1:468, First Inaugural Address of James Madison, March 4, 1809 (emphasis added).

25. RICHARDSON, PRESIDENTS *supra* note 1 at 1:567-68, Seventh Annual Message of James Madison, December 5, 1815.

26. RICHARDSON, PRESIDENTS *supra* note 1 at 1:568, Seventh Annual Message of James Madison, December 5, 1815. Five years earlier, Madison had proposed to add to the means of education provided by the several states, a seminary of learning instituted by the National Legislature within the limits of its exclusive jurisdiction, the expense of which might be defrayed or reimbursed out of the [sale of] vacant grounds which had accrued to the nation within those limits. RICHARDSON, PRESIDENTS *supra* note 1 at 1:485, Second Annual Address of James Madison, December 5, 1810.

In 1796, Madison noted that the constitutionality of a university at the seat of government would hinge on "whether Congress will encourage an establishment which is to be supported entirely independent of them." He made it clear that it would not "ask a single farthing from [Congress], nor that it would pledge Congress to endow the establishment with any support," and believed that sale of federal lands within the District might properly support such a local university. THE ANNALS OF THE CONGRESS *supra* note 6 at 6:1702.

Therefore, when Madison proposed a national seminary of learning, he meant that Congress may act pursuant to its exclusive jurisdiction over the District of Columbia granted in Article I, section 8, clause 17. This plan in no way involved education of the people in the several states as in the earlier "national university" plan. As it turned out, this later proposal drew no attention from the House whatsoever.

27. U.S., Congress, House, Representative Mitchill delivered the report on President Madison's March 4, 1809 proposal for the establishment of a seminary of learning, 11th Cong., 3rd sess., 18 February 1811, THE ANNALS OF THE CONGRESS OF THE UNITED STATES, contained in JOSEPH GALES, COMP., THE DEBATES AND PROCEEDINGS OF THE CONGRESS OF THE UNITED STATES, 42 vols., (Washington: Gales and Seaton, 1834) at 22:976-77 (Library of American Civilization 21624).

U.S., Congress, House, Representative Wilde delivered the report on President Madison's September 1 and December 5, 1815 proposal which related to the subject of a national seminary of learning, 14th Cong., 2nd sess., 11 December 1816, THE ANNALS OF THE CONGRESS OF THE UNITED STATES, contained in JOSEPH GALES, COMP., THE DEBATES AND PROCEEDINGS OF THE CONGRESS OF THE UNITED STATES, 42 vols., (Washington: Gales and Seaton, 1834) at 30:257-60 (Library of American Civilization 21633).

See also U.S., Congress, House, Representative Atherton, offered for consideration an amendment to the Constitution granting Congress power to establish a national university which was rejected, 12 December 1816. *Id.* at 30:268; U.S., Congress, House, Representative Wilde moved successfully to discharge indefinitely the Committee considering the bill for establishing a national university on the basis that such a bill was not intended for Congress but only for the people, 3 March 1817. *Id.* at 30:1063-64.

28. ANNALS OF CONGRESS *supra* note 27 at 22:976 (Library of American Civilization 21624).

29. ANNALS OF CONGRESS *supra* note 27 at 22:977 (Library of American Civilization 21624).

30. RICHARDSON, PRESIDENTS *supra* note 1 at 2:18, First Annual Message of James Monroe, December 2, 1817.

31. RICHARDSON, PRESIDENTS *supra* note 1 at 2:18, First Annual Message of James Monroe, December 2, 1817. For an overview of the Constitution's Article V, *see* Scott M. Robe, *The Objects, Authority and Limits of an Article V Constitutional Convention*, (Masters Thesis, Regent University, 1986).

32. RICHARDSON, PRESIDENTS *supra* note 1 at 2:18, First Annual Message of James Monroe, December 7, 1817.

33. U.S., Congress, House, Representative Hill submitted for consideration a resolution (which was rejected) to establish a national university within the District of Columbia, but if that was thought objectionable, to then apply to the people to be constitutionally vested with said authority, 16th Cong., 1st sess., 23 December 1819, THE ANNALS OF THE CONGRESS OF THE UNITED STATES, contained in JOSEPH GALES, COMP., THE DEBATES AND PROCEEDINGS OF THE CONGRESS OF THE UNITED STATES, 42 vols., (Washington: Gales and Seaton, 1834) at 35:780-81 (Library of American Civilization 21638).

34. RICHARDSON, PRESIDENTS *supra* note 1 at 2:311, First Annual Message of John Quincy Adams, December 6, 1825.

35. RICHARDSON, PRESIDENTS *supra* note 1 at 2:311, First Annual Message of John Quincy Adams, December 6, 1825. President John Quincy Adams approached the establishment of a university on a somewhat different basis. He noted that the "establishment of a uniform standard of weights and measures was one of the specific objects contemplated in the formation of our Constitution, and to fix that standard was one of the powers delegated by express terms in that instrument to Congress." From this he reasoned, that connected "with the establishment of an university, or separate from it, might be undertaken the erection of an astronomical observatory, with provision for the support of an astronomer, to be in constant attendance of observations upon the phenomena of heavens, and for the periodical publication of his observations." *Id.* at 2:313. It may be that "the cause of science" was so closely allied in his mind with a university and astronomical observatory that he considered them proper objects pursuant to Congress' authority to fix the standard of weights and measures, once scientifically ascertained. A national observatory, however, is a far constitutional cry from a national university or funding education in every state in the union.

36. President Madison had vetoed a similar bill pledging certain funds for internal improvements such as construction of roads and canals, as unconstitutional and beyond the power of Congress to regulate commerce among the several States, or provide for the common defense and general welfare. RICHARDSON, PRESIDENTS *supra* note 1 at 1:584-85, Veto Messages of James Madison, March 3, 1817.

37. RICHARDSON, PRESIDENTS *supra* note 1 at 2:491-92. Veto Message of Andrew Jackson, May 27, 1830. President Monroe's objections were also noted by Jackson in his Veto Message. *Id.* at 2:486.

38. RICHARDSON, PRESIDENTS *supra* note 1 at 2:491. Veto Messages of Andrew Jackson, May 27, 1830 (emphasis in original). Jackson also noted: "In no government are appeals to the source of power in cases of real doubt more suitable than in ours. No good motive can be assigned for the exercise of power by the constituted authorities, while those for whose benefit it is to be exercised have not conferred it *and may not be willing to confer it.*" *Id.* at 2:492 (emphasis added).

39. The state governments are, by far the biggest special interest groups. This has been true historically. A Report issued by the Commissioner of Education recalled quite correctly that "by the year 1836 a considerable surplus over and above the wants of the Government had accumulated in the National Treasury, the disposal of which became a political question." HINSDALE *supra* note 10 at 2:1286-87.

The surplus as of January 1, 1837 was $41,468,859. The eventual distribution of this money found its way to the states on a pro-rata basis. The states in turn executed various instruments promising repayment "whenever they should be required by the Secretary of the Treasury for the purpose of defraying any wants of the public Treasury." *Id.* at 2:1287. The Commissioner of Education observed that as of 1895, "the States receiving the deposits have never repaid them, and have never been called upon to do so." *Id.* Congress acknowledged it could not control the purpose to which the disposition of these funds would be applied. As it turned out, many states applied them to their own educational programs.

Former President Jackson considered distribution of national surpluses (what are now called block grants) to be prohibited by the Constitution. Originally Jackson had suggested an amendment to the Constitution to permit such a distribution from the federal treasury. *See* RICHARDSON, PRESIDENTS *supra* note 1 at 2:484. Veto Message of Andrew Jackson, May 27, 1830. He later opposed this suggestion, noting that such a distribution would be ruinous to the Union, constitutional provision and all. *See* EDWARD G. BOURNE, THE HISTORY OF THE SURPLUS REVENUE OF 1837 (New York: G. P. Putnam's Sons, 1885) 20 (Library of American Civilization 10050). The figure of $41,468,859.97 was quoted by Bourne. *Id.* at 16. Bourne also notes that Jackson was opposed to the whole matter of distribution on grounds of constitutionality and common sense. *Id.* at 20.

40. RICHARDSON, PRESIDENTS *supra* note 1 at 5:544, Veto Messages of James Buchanan, February 24, 1859.

41. RICHARDSON, PRESIDENTS *supra* note 1 at 5:544, Veto Messages of James Buchanan, February 24, 1859.

42. RICHARDSON, PRESIDENTS *supra* note 1 at 5:545, Veto Messages of James Buchanan, February 24, 1859.

43. RICHARDSON, PRESIDENTS *supra* note 1 at 5:546, Veto Messages of James Buchanan, February 24, 1859.

44. RICHARDSON, PRESIDENTS *supra* note 1 at 5:547, Veto Messages of James Buchanan, February 24, 1859. The President added: "Should Congress exercise such a power, this would be to break down the barriers which have been so carefully constructed in the Constitution to separate Federal from State authority." *Id.*

45. RICHARDSON, PRESIDENTS *supra* note 1 at 5:545, Veto Messages of James Buchanan, February 24, 1859.   Buchanan correctly articulated the tendency to unconstitutionally balance federal funds between that which was enumerated and that which was expedient. A present day application is clearly visible as defense purposes are played off against the Department of Education "needs."

46. An Act donating Public Lands to the Several States and Territories which may provide Colleges for the Benefit of Agriculture and the Mechanical Arts, 12 Stat. L. 503 (1862). President Lincoln signed this Act into law on July 2, 1862.

47. HARRY KURSH, THE UNITED STATES OFFICE OF EDUCATION (Philadelphia: Chilton Company, 1965) 27. Even the limited purpose of the Act, to provide funds for colleges and universities from the sale of federal lands, has been expanded beyond its original purpose. By 1965, every state had "at least one college or university which received direct cash grants from the Federal Government, *in lieu of land sales." Id.* (emphasis added).

48. Justin Morrill, *An Address in Behalf of the University of Vermont and State Agricultural College,* at Montpelier, October 10, 1888 (Montpelier: Argus and Patriot Printing House, 1888) at 1 (Library of American Civilization 40011).

49. "The Congress shall have Power to dispose of and make all needful Rules and Regulations respecting the Territory or other Property belonging to the United States." U.S. CONST. art. 4, § 3, cl. 2.

50. RICHARDSON, PRESIDENTS *supra* note 1 at 5:543-50, Veto Message of James Buchanan, February 24, 1859.

51. RICHARDSON, PRESIDENTS *supra* note 1 at 5:548, Veto Messages of James Buchanan, February 24, 1859. *See also* HINSDALE *supra* note 10 at 2:1275-87.

Chapter 12

The Bureau Of Education - 1867

Then what is this bureau to do? Simply to collect information: nothing more than that. It will be but an extension of the census of the people . . . . Therefore the [Bureau of education] bill in that regard is not amenable to the objection of centralization: if it were I would not press it.[1]

Rebellion Against The Constitution

Before the Civil War, President James Buchanan had warned that inventing federal jurisdiction over educational matters would confer upon Congress a vast and irresponsible authority. After the Civil War, Congress began to exercise that vast and unconstitutional power in may ways. For instance, Congress refused the admission of Senators and Representatives from eleven of the 36 states in the Union.[2] This left 25 states to govern 36 states. Rather than obeying their Constitutional duty to preserve the Constitution, an incomplete Congress chose to take advantage of this disenfranchisement and enacted a Federal Bureau of Education into being in 1867. This Act was a clear Congressional usurpation of jurisdiction with respect to educational matters. It was an insidious advance upon the Constitution's restraint of Congressional power.

A major force agitating for the federal promotion of education and the suppression of Constitutional limits after the Civil War, was The National Association of State and City School Superintendents. It had petitioned Congress to establish a Bureau of Education. Its memorial noted that the object of this Bureau was to "render needed assistance in the establishment of school systems where they do not now exist" as well as improve and vitalize existing systems.[3] And where was it believed that such *systems did not now exist*? The answer was to be found in the southern states of course--the states of the "Rebellion;" the states denied representation in Congress. Of course, the South had schools and education, but it did not have the sort of *system* of education found in the northern states. It did not have the sort of system which the National Association thought would be good for the South and southern children. The "assistance" requested was to be for six purposes:

1)   Secure greater uniformity and accuracy in school statistics.
2)   Bring together the results of school systems in order to determine their comparative value.
3)   Assemble the different methods of school instruction and management for distribution.
4)   Collect and diffuse information generated by school districts respecting state school laws, teacher qualifications, modes of heating and ventilation, and the management of such institutions;
5)   Help communities in the organization of their school systems.
6)   Encourage education as a valuable object and shield of civil liberty.[4]

In essence, the Association petitioned the federal government to serve as a "national channel of communication between the school officers of different States . . . without its being invested with any official control of the school authorities therein."[5] Translated into the realities of the reconstruction South: the federal government would use the experience of Northern states in centralizing their systems of education as a model for the south. There was, however, no mention of utilizing the federal treasury to fund any educational programs. The Bureau was to be a "bully pulpit" and educational statistical service located in Washington, D.C. Though the educational sphere of action was seemingly small, the bill requested Congress to assert jurisdiction over the sphere of education itself.

When debate opened in the House on June 5, 1866, James Garfield of Ohio (later to be elected the twentieth President) presented the bill as modified by himself, which was then read. It provided in part that:

There shall be established, at the City of Washington, a Department of Education for the purpose of collecting such statistics and facts as shall show the condition and progress of education in the several States and Territories, and of diffusing such information respecting the organization and management of schools and school systems and methods of teaching as shall aid the people of the United States in the establishment and maintenance of efficient school systems, *and otherwise promote* the cause of education throughout the country.[6]

Garfield himself, had expanded the original object of the bill. He was not only interested in statistics, but now sought to "promote the cause of education throughout the country." This was a grand assertion of power. The bill also provided that a Commissioner of Education report to Congress annually "the results of his investigations and labors, together with a statement of such facts and recommendations as will in his judgment subserve the purpose for which this department is established."[7] Thus, Congress would use the proposed Department to keep itself abreast of the educational developments throughout the country. But what of the laws of nature, the reserved power of the states and the people, the unalienable rights of parents and the Constitutional limitations of federal power? What of the Constitutional convention and the messages of past Presidents? What happened to this legacy? How was an honest observance of the Constitution overcome?

Debating Degrees of Usurpation

When debate on Garfield's bill began, the first speaker was Mr. Donnelly of Minnesota. After demeaning the southern states and the recent War, he suggested that "[w]e have found that the hitherto governing populations of those States could not be trusted to uphold the national Government, . . . [t]he responsibility for all this has been properly charged to slavery. Slavery has been swept away, but the ignorance, the degradation, which were its consequences remain . . . ."[8] After a rigorous sermon on the evils of ignorance and the illiterate conditions of the southern states which were equated to conditions in Mexico, he declared: "Pass this Bill and you give education a mouthpiece and a rallying point. While it will have no power to enter into the States and interfere with their systems, it will be able to collect facts and report the same to Congress, to be thence spread over the entire country."[9]

✓ Key Idea:

☞   CONGRESS USED THE SOUTH AND THE CIVIL WAR
     TO   JUSTIFY   FEDERAL   USURPATION   OVER
     EDUCATION.

The import of Mr. Donnelly's address was that Southern education only produced ignorance and illiteracy and had contributed to the War and threatened the very Republic. The remedy to prevent further evil of this nature was to control education in order "to make every man who votes an intelligent, conscious, reasoning, reflecting being. Then the true Republic will be realized."[10] Mr. Donnelly's concern was not merely to remedy ignorance. It was broader than that. By tying his remedy to voting, he effectively declared that loyalty to the federal government could be secured by indirectly controlling education from Washington. He neglected in his analysis, however, to demonstrate exactly how the availability of statistics would eradicate disloyalty and illiteracy without a related form of direct control.

But what is important to note is that this Congressman understood that federal involvement in education could serve a vital propagandistic and political purpose. The South and the War could be made the scapegoat to justify federal usurpation of education power. The War was especially used to tightly knit together federal influence over education on the one hand, with patriotism, liberty and the very Republic itself on the other hand. These ideas were joined within the American mind and became an integral part of the American mind. Federal education and perpetuation of the Country's very existence have remained tied together ever since, fed and nourished by the federal government's quest for unlimited power.

It is erroneous, however, to believe as did Mr. Donnelly, that the southern states did not know how to educate their children. Strategically, Donnelly had reduced education to an issue of loyalty and literacy. He had neglected other dimensions of education prevalent in states where parental rights were more consistently observed. Instead, he drew heavily upon the claims of anti-parental state *systems* of education that made literacy the sole bench-mark of education and the state the primary provider.[11] Mr. Donnelly did not quote any of the Presidents or their construction of the Constitution. He did not discuss the intention of the framers. He saw what he wanted and went for it. He was pragmatic. The Constitution was good, but his opinions were better.

The following speaker, Mr. Rogers of New Jersey, however, did not choose the broad path of expediency which Mr. Garfield and Donnelly took. He stated: "I had reason to believe that . . . no more Federal bureaus would be attempted to be established for the purpose of carrying out any particular ideas of philanthropy of any set of men whatever."[12] He observed that it was unheard of to establish a centralized "bureau for the purpose of giving the principles by which the children of the different states shall be educated." He understood that indirect control of education was behind this statistics bill. The Congress was now discussing indirect influence of the American mind.

Turning to the Constitution, he stated: "[T]here is no authority under the Constitution of the United States to authorize Congress to interfere with education of children of the different States in any manner, *directly or indirectly.*"[13]

✓ Key Idea:

☞ CONGRESS IGNORED WARNINGS NOT TO ASSUME
JURISDICTION OR INTERFERE WITH EDUCATION IN
ANY MANNER, *DIRECTLY OR INDIRECTLY.*

Congressman Rogers pointed out the inherent flaw in the bill. It purported to give Congress jurisdiction over education. Once jurisdiction over education was asserted, Congress could subsequently expand its power over education according to its own will. For Congress, to encourage education was no different than influencing or controlling it, if jurisdiction were once obtained. Mr. Rogers declared that the bill

> proposes to put under the supervision of a bureau established at Washington all the schools and educational institutions of the different States of the Union by collecting such facts and statistics as will warrant them by amendments hereafter to the law now attempted to be passed, to control and regulate the educational system of the whole country.[14]

Have truer words ever been spoken about Congress? This was a prophesy on the order of President Jackson's warning about honesty in observing the Constitution. Congressman Rogers correctly noted that the bill opened wide the power of Congress. The bill opened the door for control either directly or indirectly through funding or other means, at any time in the future when conditions proved that expediency could be made the rule of Constitutional construction. To assert that the degree of federal intrusion was small and limited to statistics, in no way impaired the jurisdictional claim; for once federal jurisdiction was established over the object of education, the federal government could assert complete sovereignty within that sphere whenever it wished.[15]

Mr. Rogers also focused on the enormity of the expense of the project and its open-ended nature, the false characterization of southern states as ignorant and illiterate, and the natural right of parents to educate their children.[16] He reiterated that:

> [N]o man can find anywhere in the letter or spirit of the Constitution one word that will authorize the Congress of the United States to establish an Education Bureau. If Congress has the right to establish an Educational Bureau . . . for the purpose of collecting statistics and controlling the schools of the country, then, by the same parity of reason, *a fortiori*, Congress has the right to establish a bureau to supervise the education of all the children that are to be found in . . . this country. You will not stop at simply establishing a bureau for the purpose of paying officers to collect and diffuse statistics in reference to education.[17]

Reread and mark those words well! If you like, pen them in a letter to your favorite compromising cosmetic conservative or coercive utopian liberal in Congress. What a perceptive, frank and honest Congressman was Mr. Rogers! Indeed, Mr. Rogers correctly observed that power with respect to education was not to be found among those enumerated to Congress. He recognized the threat of unbridled power. "You will not stop," he said, "at simply establishing a bureau for the purpose of paying officers to collect and diffuse statistics in reference to educations." An examination of the present Department of Education reveals that

Mr. Rogers was right. Congress has not stopped, will not stop and is moving toward supervising "all the children that are to be found" in this country.

The Department of Education's budget has averaged between 31-33 billion dollars a year during the 1990s. Congress is all too happy to pursue its insidious advances upon the checks that are designed to restrain its power. An "insidious advance" upon the Constitution and not an "honest observance" has become standard and routine. Congress has made expediency its rule of construction in interpreting the Constitution.

On June 8, 1866, the measure was considered for a second time. Mr. Moulton of Illinois, began the discussion, "Now, sir, what is the scope and object of this bill? What does it propose to do? It is simply a measure for the benefit of universal education."[18] After expressing personal veneration of educational thinkers for universal education, Mr. Moulton continued by asking: "Now, Mr. Speaker, what is the true, genuine spirit of our institutions? Upon what are they founded? The two great pillars of our American Republic, upon which it rests, are universal liberty and universal education."[19]

Suggesting the former had been achieved by passage of the Civil Rights Act of 1866, he then asserted in his usual rhetorical way:

> Now, sir, in order to make education universal, what do we want? What is the crying necessity of this nation today? Why, sir, we want a head. We want a pure fountain from which a pure stream can be poured upon all the States. We want a controlling head by which the various conflicting systems in the different States can be harmonized, by which there can be uniformity, by which all mischievous errors that have crept in may be pointed out and eradicated. We want a head to this great system for the purpose of giving direction and vitalizing the whole educational interest of the country.[20]

Mark well the words of belligerent nationalism, of rank usurpation, of expediency, of centralization, and of the arrogant claim of superior knowledge. See how easily these words all rolled off his tongue? But in case his fellow Congressmen were not sure what the proponents of the bill intended once Congress assumed jurisdiction, Mr. Moulton took great pains to point out the plan: "The very object of establishing a Bureau of Education is that these different systems may be brought together. We want all these school systems all over the land brought under one head, so that they may be *nationalized, vitalized, and made uniform and harmonious* as far as possible."[21]

No Caesar could have been clearer, nor Constitutional rebellion more certain. This is a call for control over the minds of children, the abridgement of parental rights, and annihilation of the Constitution's federal design. It also reflects a naive assumption that parents and states would eagerly accept this "pure fountain" of federal information and willingly fall in line with the "pure stream" of educational wisdom annually proclaimed by the Commissioner of Education (or any modern Secretary of Education).

✓ Key Idea:

   ☞   CONGRESS BECAME ENAMORED WITH THE POWER
        TO NATIONALIZE, VITALIZE, AND STANDARDIZE
        THE EDUCATION OF ALL CHILDREN.

Not only was Mr. Moulton lacking in a basic understanding of human nature, the laws of nature, parental rights and state power, but he demonstrated ample irresponsibility with the Constitution as well. The power and fervor of the Reconstruction Congress apparently dulled his Constitutional faculties, for he then remarked on the Constitutional issues raised by Mr. Rogers three days previous: "Let us look at this for a moment. Let us see whether we have constitutional power."[22] So finally the Constitutional question is addressed. Will the framer's intention be discussed? Perhaps it will be argued that the Constitution's text is ambiguous? Or perchance Mr. Moulton will just argue the Constitution is defective and call for an amendment. After all, he presents himself as an educated man. He is a man who knows a pure fountain and a pure stream when he sees one. He is a man who speak of the great pillars of our American Republic and the foundations upon which they rest.

    As it turned out, none of these approaches were taken. He simply misquotes the Constitution, declaring: "The Constitution provides that it shall be the duty of Congress to pass all laws which shall be necessary for the common good and welfare."[23] The provision (which does not grant Congress power over education directly or indirectly), which the Representative tried to quote is Article I, section 8, which states: "The Congress shall have Power to lay and collect Taxes, Duties, Imposts and Excises, to pay the Debts and provide for the common Defence and general Welfare of the United States . . . ." This clause imposes no duty on Congress. It grants Congress no educational authority.

    Adding parental insult to Constitutional injury, Mr. Moulton also appended to his ruse about the bureau being a legitimate function of the census power, a perverse argument that children had a natural right to be educated by the federal government for the faithful discharge of the duties of American Citizenship! He proclaimed that: "I take the high ground that every child of this land is, by natural right, entitled to an education at the hands of somebody, and that this ought not to be left to the caprice of individuals or of States so far as we have any power to regulate it. At least, every child in the land should receive a sufficient education to qualify him to discharge all the duties that may devolve upon him as an American citizen."[24]

    Mr. Moulton does not even refer to parents, but prefers to call them "somebody" and "individuals," thus diminishing the natural relationship from which this natural right springs. Moreover, the laws of nature, the unalienable rights of parents, intellectual freedom--all these are suppressed--and instead, the basis of his "natural right" to be instructed by the federal government on how to be a good little citizen of the new regime, is simple recourse to raw unbridled Congressional power, or as he threatens; "so far as we have any power to regulate it." The thoughtful reader cannot help but recognize the weary use of "good citizenship" as a pretext for bad government.[25]

✓ Key Idea:

☞   CONGRESS USED THE FRAUD OF PROMOTING "GOOD CITIZENSHIP" AS A PRETEXT FOR ABUSE OF A PARENT'S NATURAL RIGHT.

The federal government can never be a "pure stream" of educational insight. It possesses no monopoly on the best system of education despite its many Congressional devotees. Congress is made of human beings, not gods. They have no inherent wisdom that is not also found among the people from which they come. To view the matter otherwise, recalls to mind Thomas Jefferson's condemnation of the "impious presumption" of legislators who lord their views over the people they claim to serve. The relationship between collecting statistics and nationalizing, vitalizing, and harmonizing education, indicates that Congress sought to control American education indirectly through statistical standards and, eventually, to directly control education by money and force.[26] Control of education, however, is not consistent with any Constitutional power, including the power of the census or the general welfare clause.

Mr. Randall of Pennsylvania also spoke. He introduced an amendment in an effort to satisfy the proponents and opponents of the bill. His was the compromise measure. It proposed to establish a Bureau of Education for the sole purpose of collecting statistics. Since, he argued, this purpose was properly within the authority of the Department of the Interior (if any department), he considered it sufficient to placate the fears of the opponents. He gives his reasons plainly: "The systems of education throughout the country have been left to State authority. The raising of the revenue for educational purposes, the method of its expenditure, and the system of instruction have all been left entirely with the States."[27]

Clarifying the object of the amendment, he proposed that the federal government "leave this question of statistics in reference to the State educational systems to the Secretary of the Interior, where it properly belongs, if it belongs to any Department of the Government. It is . . . a part of the system, or should be part of the system, of taking the census."[28] The Constitutional purpose of a census is to number the people of the states so that their states may be represented (in the House of Representatives) in proportion to their population relative to every other state. The census has nothing to do with collection of educational statistics *per se* for any reason, especially statistics to determine the people's level of formal education. Moreover, it is clear that the original objects of the bill--diffusing organizational and school management methods as well as teaching methods--are no part of the work of a census, nor does Congressional power to conduct a census permit promotion of the cause of education throughout the country.

✓ Key Idea:

☞ CONGRESS DISHONESTLY RATIONALIZED INTERVENTION INTO EDUCATION AS AN EXERCISE OF ITS CENSUS POWER.

When the final vote on the bill to establish the Bureau of Education was taken, the measure was defeated 59 to 61, the Democrats voting solidly *against* it. Later in the day, Congressman Upton of Michigan moved for reconsideration of the matter.[29] On June 19, 1866, his motion came to a vote. Garfield, who had introduced the original bill, argued strenuously on its behalf. He claimed that education was an interest that had no lobby to press its claim and urged that the House reconsider "this liberal and progressive measure."[30]

Upon reconsideration, a number of representatives abstained from voting and the bill passed. The change in the vote was directly tied to the abstentions, "the persistent zeal with which [Garfield] urged the measure in private,"[31] and the obvious fact that in a post Civil War Congress, southern representatives were not readmitted to their Congressional seats. Others suggested that Garfield had "bamboozled" the House into passing the bill.[32] Garfield, however, maintained that the bill disclaimed any control over the educational systems of the states, though jurisdiction had been asserted by the national government.[33] In the end, the bill was passed in both houses and signed into law by President Andrew Johnson on March 2, 1867.

Decline of Constitutional Restraint

In 1806 President Thomas Jefferson considered federal presence in education to be unconstitutional. In 1862 the first Morrill Act was successfully passed, donating federal lands for higher education. By 1867 Representative Garfield, Congress and President Johnson bypassed the United States Constitution altogether. As a result, the Department of Education (thereafter downgraded to federal Bureau status) was created.[34]

After 1867, the jurisdictional issue, having been waylaid, Congress steadily expanded its unconstitutional reach into education. Every subsequent law need not be examined to understand this trend. A few laws will do. In 1890 a second Morrill Act, which provided federal *funds* for land-grant colleges and universities, was approved. In 1907 the Nelson Amendment to the Morrill Acts increased aid to land grant institutions. In 1917 the Smith-Hughes Act provided federal aid to states for vocational education. The Bankhead-Jones Act of 1935 increased federal funds for land-grant institutions.

In 1954 Congress authorized the appointment of a National Advisory Committee on Education charged with the responsibility of advising the Secretary of Health, Education and Welfare on problems of national concern in education. Having outlived its utility, the Department of Interior census ruse was abandoned. The National Defense Education Act of 1958 authorized federal aid to all levels and several categories of education. In 1963 Congress authorized financial assistance for construction and rehabilitation of facilities in higher education (which was completely contrary to the House Committee Report of 1811).[35]

Congress had come full circle in education by unilaterally suspending the Constitutional limitations imposed upon its power. The expansion of federal jurisdiction beyond its Constitutional boundaries, once sustained, provided ready justification for a variety of Congressional abridgements with respect to education.

✓ Key Idea:

☞   CONGRESS HAS PERSISTENTLY INFLATED ITS POWER OVER EDUCATION SINCE LAND GRANT LEGISLATION IN 1862 AND THE ORGANIZATION OF THE BUREAU OF EDUCATION IN 1867.

The period from 1862 to 1979 was not a transition period as much as it reflected the consistent expansion of unlawful federal jurisdiction over education. The Federal Department of Education Act of 1979 was not the apex of these events, but rather another development in a series of accelerated rejections of limited and Constitutional government.

Thus, by the 1990s, the jurisdictional claim of Congress over education had grown to include over 300 separate federal education programs. This expansion of jurisdiction is sustained without so much as a Constitutional whimper from either liberals or conservatives. Strict constructionists and judicial activists alike say nothing about the Constitution. Federal expenditures reaching near 33 billion dollars a year, spread out over 40 federal departments and agencies are not a problem--they are rather considered a good reason for being elected. Making educational grants, providing services and issuing regulations is business as usual. Republicans and Democrats act as though the Constitution is non-existent. Only Libertarians currently show any Constitutional awareness. Presidents Carter, Bush and Clinton have described themselves as "Education Presidents" as if it is a natural federal object.

The prediction of Congressman Rogers in 1866, however, was correct: "You will not stop at simply establishing a bureau for the purpose of paying officers to collect and diffuse statistics in reference to education."[36]   Our Representatives and Senators will not stop.   Our executive officials will not stop.[37]   Education Secretaries William Bennett and Lamar Alexander, Jr., did not stop and Secretary Richard Riley will not stop.   The 1990s National Education Strategy and federal involvement of every kind is ample proof that the government will not stop.   The federal government now influences or funds:

  -grants for the disadvantaged including migrant education,
  -merit school funding,
  -maintenance and operation of schools,
  -disaster assistance, and construction,
  -block grants to the states,
  -strengthening teaching and administration,
  -magnet school assistance,
  -bilingual, immigrant and refugee education,
  -school to work,
  -education for the handicapped,
  -rehabilitation services and research,
  -vocational and adult education,
  -student financial assistance,
  -college housing and academic facilities loans,
  -education research and statistics,
  -libraries,
  -early childhood programs and job training,
  -Indian education, and
  -national science foundation funding.[38]

What began as a modest departure from the Constitution, has become a wholesale renunciation.   Congress has perfected the lessons of Reading, 'Riting and Constitutional Revisionism taught so well by the Reconstructionist Congress and reflected in its spirit of expediency and criminal usurpation in Constitutional construction.

★ HYPOTHETICALLY SPEAKING . . . .

Problem: The Ni C. Guy Savings and Loan was "shocked and dismayed" at your recent letter. They suggest you are "unreasonable" in rejecting their decision to re-compute your mortgage payments on a variable interest schedule.   They inform you that Mr. Moulton, the President of their institution still wants to help you.   Consequently they have proceeded to unilaterally change the terms of your loan.   But you refuse to pay and now they threaten foreclosure in a lawsuit.

**   Your day in court arrives. The S&L argues:**

1) the original intent of the contract is unclear. The S&L's lawyer introduces the opinion of a former Supreme Court justice that the term "fixed interest rate" could also legally mean "variable interest rate;" and

2) in the alternative, even if the term is clear, the law must keep up with the times. Changing the terms of the loan is financially reasonable in light of the changed circumstances over the past 30 years.

Your turn comes. You argue that a deal is a deal. Everybody knew the terms of the loan and the fixed interest rate. You point out that even the S&L never doubted what was intended since they took your monthly payments for 30 years. As a matter of fact the S&L wrote the agreement, so they should know what it means. It's not your fault that they are losing money, no one forced them to loan money for thirty years. In closing, you say that the court should protect and enforce the original loan agreement.

Your argument sounds pretty good. Just as the judge is about to issue his ruling, the S&L's lawyer brings in a last minute surprise witness. The witness is an expert pollster. He testifies that what is lawful should not be contrary to what is reasonable. He testifies that a poll shows that almost 70 percent of the people polled say that changing the loan agreement is reasonable in light of the financial circumstances. Consequently the lawyer argues that it is reasonable for the S&L to change your loan. The judge is convinced and rules against you. He says that while the terms of the loan are pretty clear--fixed interest only, justice must necessarily control the outcome of the case. The judge says that since 70 percent of the people think changing the agreement is reasonable, then changing the interest is therefore lawful. You have to pay up or be foreclosed. Did the judge rule correctly?

Answer: No. It is not lawful for the S&L to change the terms of the loan agreement without your consent. This is true whether times have changed or whether the changes are reasonable or not, or what the general public may or may not think. Likewise, the Constitution does not contain any terms that authorize the Congress of the United States to establish an Education Bureau. Congress, however, construed the census and general welfare clause out of context to reach a constitutionally impermissible result. They said, like the S&L, the original intent of the Constitution's census and general welfare powers cannot be defined so narrowly. Congress also argued that the law must keep up with the times. They cite to ignorance and illiteracy, the world economy, technology and competition in the next century, as the modern circumstantial basis upon which to justify federal corruption of law.

The Constitution, however, does not give Congress power to expand its own power. It is not lawful for the government to change the terms of the Constitutional agreement without the legal consent of the people. Public opinion polls do not supersede or qualify as legal consent of the people. This is true whether or not times have changed or those changes are reasonable.

Notes

1. U.S., Congress, House, Representative Moulton commenting on the Bureau of Education, 39th Cong., 2nd sess., 8 June 1866, THE CONGRESSIONAL GLOBE at 3046.

2. JAMES D. RICHARDSON, ED., COMPILATION OF THE MESSAGES AND PAPERS OF THE PRESIDENTS, 1789-1897, (Washington, D.C.: Government Printing Office, 1896) at 6:391-92, Special Session Message of Andrew Johnson, June 22, 1866.

3. B. A. HINSDALE, COMP., U.S. OFFICE OF EDUCATION, DOCUMENTS ILLUSTRATIVE OF AMERICAN EDUCATIONAL HISTORY (Washington, D.C.: Government Printing Office, 1895) 2:1290.

4. *Id.* at 2:1290.

5. *Id.* at 2:1290-91. The Association argued that it is "a law of educational progress that its impulse and stimulus comes from *without*. Hence it is that Adam Smith and other writers on political economy expressly excepted education from the operation of the general law of supply and demand . . . [and] that demand for education must be awakened by external influences and agencies." *Id.* at 1290. Even if (for the sake of argument) the "law of educational progress" is "excepted" with respect to education, it is not the "external influences and agencies" of the federal government which are authorized to awaken the child to education. The law of nature, which supersedes any other law of educational progress testifies that the child is to be awakened to the ideas chosen by his parents, and not the state or a bureau of education.

6. U.S., Congress, House, Representative Garfield urged the passage of the bill to establish the Federal Department of Education, 5 June 1866, CONGRESSIONAL GLOBE *supra* note 1 at 2966 (emphasis added).

7. 5 June 1866, CONGRESSIONAL GLOBE *supra* note 1 at 2966.

8. U.S., Congress, House, Representative Donnelly noted the results of the census literacy figures and recent war, concluding that the lack of compulsory education was to blame, 5 June 1866, CONGRESSIONAL GLOBE *supra* note 1 at 2966-67.

9. 5 June 1866, CONGRESSIONAL GLOBE *supra* note 1 at 2968. "How far" asked the Congressman, "were the dirty, unkempt hordes of ignorant men who flocked under the standards of Lee and Johnston fitted for self government, fitted to hold up the polished pillars of the great temple of law, order, and civilization?" *Id.* at 2968. It is more likely, however, that the "dirty hordes" had a better understanding of self-government than Congressman Donnelly, who now sought to expand federal power at their expense. It was President Jackson who properly characterized Mr. Donnelly's philosophy of "self government" when he said in 1830 that:

> When an honest observance of constitutional compacts cannot be obtained from communities like ours, it need not be anticipated elsewhere . . . and the degrading truth that man is unfit for self-government admitted. And this will be the case if *expediency* be made a rule of construction in interpreting the Constitution. Power in no government could desire a better shield for the insidious advances which it is ever ready to make upon the checks that are designed to restrain its action.

According to the standard articulated by President Jackson, Mr. Donnelly and those of his expedient persuasion were more likely ignorant men unfitted to hold up the polished pillars of the great temple of law, order, and civilization.

10. 5 June 1866, CONGRESSIONAL GLOBE *supra* note 1 at 2968.

11. The facts he pointed out supporting his proposition were derived from the United States census figures of 1850 and 1860. Mr. Donnelly relished pointing out the antithetical educational philosophies of a northern state, Massachusetts, and its southern

counterpart, Virginia. Noting that Massachusetts required compulsory state education as early as 1642, while Virginia had left education to parents, he turns to the census figures and concludes that as a result of this development, a very small percent of Massachusetts citizens could not read or write but nearly three quarters of white Virginians were illiterate.

He draws the same inferences with respect to dollars spent on education within the states. He concluded the discussion by requesting Congress to pass the bill on the basis of these statistics, suggesting that compulsory attendance and dollars spent on education are significantly related to literacy and loyalty. 5 June 1866, CONGRESSIONAL GLOBE *supra* note 1 at 2967-68.

Fifteen years later, however, Mr. Montgomery, an Assistant Attorney General with the United States also reviewed these very same statistics in the context of education. He noted that illiteracy rates in Massachusetts and other compulsory attendance states were indeed low, approximately one illiterate to every 312 white inhabitants, while Virginia, for example, stood at one illiterate for every 12 white inhabitants. He did not stop there, however. If compulsory state education was the cornerstone of the civilized American Republic as it was (and is) commonly believed, then its greatness should be reflected in *all* the statistics of the census. Mr. Montgomery's findings are as follows:

> Those educated under the New England [compulsory] system had one native-born white criminal to every 1,084 native white inhabitants, while those who had generally rejected that system had but one prisoner to every 6,670, being a disproportion, according to the whole number of native whites, of more than six criminals in New England to one in the other community. A glance at the same table will show that the natives educated under the New England system [compulsory] had one pauper to every 178, while those who managed to live without that luxury had one pauper to every 345.
>
> Of those who in one year died by suicide, New England had one to every 13,285 of the entire population, while Virginia and her five sister [states] had but one suicide to every 56,584, and of those who perished, the victims of their criminal lusts, New England had one to every 84,737, while her neighbors, that had never enjoyed her educational advantages, had but one such victim to every 128,729.

ZACH MONTGOMERY, COMP., THE SCHOOL QUESTION FROM A PARENTAL AND NON-SECTARIAN STAND POINT, 4th ed. (Washington: Gibson Bros., 1889; reprint ed.; New York: Arno Press, 1972) 12.

Mr. Montgomery was not so brash as to set up a cause and effect relationship as did Mr. Donnelly. He merely concluded that the loss of parental authority and home influence over children, by a state-controlled system of education, alongside the public neglect of moral and religious education and training, contributed to the decline of the Republic, even though its citizens may be literate. *Id*. at 30.

Modern nationwide, suicide, crime and illiteracy rates should cause significant reconsideration of the present effects of today's public education if such statistics are in fact related, as Mr. Donnelly (and modern contemporaries) constantly (though selectively) argue.

12.   U.S., Congress, House, Representative Rogers, noted the historical and constitutional impediments precluding direct and indirect federal involvement in education, 5 June 1866, CONGRESSIONAL GLOBE *supra* note 1 at 2968.

13.   5 June 1866, CONGRESSIONAL GLOBE *supra* note 1 at 2968 (emphasis added).

14.   5 June 1866, CONGRESSIONAL GLOBE *supra* note 1 at 2968.

15. When challenged on the grounds that Congress had established a Bureau of Agriculture to collect statistics and this was not objected to, Mr. Rogers replied that the "object for which the Agricultural Bureau was established is one almost coeval with the formation of the Government itself." He then observed: "It is one which is necessary in order to hold complete and intimate connection with foreign countries and get the necessary information for the Federal Government. It is necessary for the diffusion of knowledge of a national character all over the country, and has no analogy to this interference with the simple right of the States in regard to the education of their own people." U.S., Congress, House, Representative Rogers' reply to Mr. Grinnell's inquiry regarding the constitutionality of the statistical function of the Department of Agriculture as it pertained to commerce with foreign nations, 5 June 1866, CONGRESSIONAL GLOBE *supra* note 1 at 2969.

Abraham Lincoln, however, noted that he had more than this in mind when he created the Department.

To carry out the provisions of the Act of Congress of the 15th of May last, I have caused the Department of Agriculture of the United States to be organized.

The Commissioner informs me that within the period of a few months this Department has established an extensive system of correspondence and exchanges, both at home and abroad, which promises to effect highly beneficial results in the development of a correct knowledge of recent improvements in agriculture, in the introduction of new products, and in the collection of the agricultural statistics of the different States.

Also, that it will soon be prepared to distribute largely seeds, cereals, plants, and cuttings, and has already published and liberally diffused much valuable information in anticipation of a more elaborate report, which will in due time be furnished, embracing some valuable tests in chemical science now in progress in the laboratory.

The creation of this Department was for the more immediate benefit of a large class of our most valuable citizens, and I trust that the liberal basis upon which it has been organized will not only meet your approbation, but that it will realize at no distant day all the fondest anticipations of its most sanguine friends and become the fruitful source of advantage to all our people.

RICHARDSON, PRESIDENTS *supra* note 2 at 6:133. Second Annual Message of Abraham Lincoln, December 1, 1862.

16. 5 June 1866, CONGRESSIONAL GLOBE *supra* note 1 at 2969.

17. 5 June 1866, CONGRESSIONAL GLOBE *supra* note 1 at 2969.

18. U.S., Congress, House, Representative Moulton extolled the virtues of a centralized, government-controlled educational system under the head of the federal government, 8 June 1866, THE CONGRESSIONAL GLOBE *supra* note 1 at 3044.

19. *Id.* at 3044. He did not attempt to explain how universal education was rejected by the framers of the Constitution as worthy of federal control.

20. *Id.* at 3044.

21. *Id.* at 3045 (emphasis added). Moreover, Mr. Moulton declared that "If we decide that [a bureau of education] is necessary to promote the general welfare, no other branch of this government can question our power." *Id.* Apparently, in his mind, Congressional Acts were not subject to judicial review in federal court.

22. *Id.* at 3045.

23. *Id.* at 3045.

24. *Id.* at 3045. Congress has power under Article I, section 2 to number the people every ten years after 1790. The context and intent of this enumeration is to determine the number of people in the several states so that the people of the state can be represented in proportion to the people of the other states. The 1990 census has gone beyond this Constitutional object by making inquiries regarding matters of race, color, national origin, housing accommodations, whether you rent or own your own home, level of formal education, occupation of yourself and your spouse, and so forth. Such inquiries bear no relation to the legitimate Constitutional purposes of an enumeration or census of the people and constitute an abuse of power.

25. How similar are such statements to Adolf Hitler's later claim: "Your child belongs to me already. A people lives forever. What are you? You will pass on. Your descendants however now stand in the new camp. In a short time they will know nothing else but this new community." He noted that the "new Reich will give its youth to no one, but will itself take youth and give to youth its own education and its own upbringing." NAZI CONSPIRACY AND AGGRESSION, OFFICE OF THE UNITED STATES CHIEF OF COUNSEL FOR PROSECUTION OF AXIS CRIMINALITY (United States Government Printing Office: Washington 1946) 1:312.

26. Direct federal control over education has been achieved to a certain significant extent through the Department of Justice and the Department of Education's civil rights enforcement efforts against schools that receive federal funds under Title VI of the Civil Rights Act of 1964. *See* 42 U.S.C. § 2000d *et seq.* Title IV prohibits recipients of federal funds from discriminating in institutional programs or policies on the basis of race, color, and national origin. *See also* 20 U.S.C. § 1681 *et seq.*, popularly known as Title IX of Education Amendments of 1972. Title IX prohibits recipients of federal funds from discriminating in institutional programs or policies on the basis of sex.

For an example of how far the federal government is willing to go to regulate the details and climate of education in pursuit of an ideological end, see 62 Fed. Reg. 12033, March 13, 1997, Office of Civil Rights; Sexual Harassment Guidance: Harassment of Students by School Employees, Other Students, or Third Parties. The Office of Civil Rights goes so dangerously far as to affirm that where an educational institution determines that certain speech *may* be derogatory on the basis of sex, that "the school can take steps to denounce those opinions and ensure that competing views are heard." See 62 Fed. Reg. at 12046.

This means that the government now encourages school officials to *denounce* certain views or ideas. Denounce ideas? It is one thing to state a general institutional policy. It is quite another to denounce individuals and their views. One can only imagine the school board meeting as the Board defends itself:

We [the Board] must establish a network of informants. But this is only the beginning comrades. And can we be responsible for what others may do--for mob violence that may break out against an individual after our public denunciation? We lament violence brothers, but is not a hostile environment yet more dangerous to the new Campus? We stand on principle. This has nothing to do with federal money!

27. U.S., Congress, House, Representative Randall proposed an amendment to the education Bill to place it within the Department of Interior as an appendage of the national census as far as consistent with its purpose and constitutional limitations, 8 June 1866, CONGRESSIONAL GLOBE *supra* note 1 at 3047.

28. 8 June 1866, CONGRESSIONAL GLOBE *supra* note 1 at 3047.

29. 19 June 1866, CONGRESSIONAL GLOBE supra note 1 at 3269.

30. U.S., Congress, House, Representative Upton of Michigan moved for reconsideration of the Bill previously defeated respecting the educational involvement of the federal government, 19 June 1866, THE CONGRESSIONAL GLOBE *supra* note 1 at 3270.

31. B. A. HINSDALE, PRESIDENT GARFIELD AND EDUCATION (Boston: Osgood & Co., 1882) 165 (Library of American Civilization 15659).

32. THEODORE C. SMITH, THE LIFE AND LETTERS OF JAMES ABRAM GARFIELD, 2 vols. (New Haven: Yale Univ. Press, 1925) 2:781 (Library of American Civilization 23799-800).

33. *Id.* at 2:781. The bill's history carried overtones of a European-styled centralized education under a general, rather than a national government. Garfield for instance cited approvingly M. Guizot, then Minister of Public Instruction in France. *See* HINSDALE, GARFIELD *supra* note 31 at 204. Garfield noted that the "learned and brilliant Guizot, . . . regarded his work in the Office of Minister of Public Instruction, in the government of France, the noblest and most valuable work in his life . . . ." *Id.* Guizot declared: "Napoleon felt that the educational department . . . should hold closely to the [French] State government, receive its powers from that source, and exercise them under its general control. Napoleon created the University, adapting it to the new state of society." CHARLES BROOKS, SOME REASONS FOR THE IMMEDIATE ESTABLISHMENT OF A NATIONAL SYSTEM OF EDUCATION FOR THE UNITED STATES, 2ND ED. (Boston: John Wilson & Sons, 1869) 19-22 (Library of American Civilization 40011).

34. An Act to Create a Department of Education, 14 Stat. L. 434, March 2, 1867.

35. U.S., Congress, House, Representative Mitchill delivered the report on President Madison's March 4, 1809 proposal for the establishment of a seminary of learning, 11th Cong., 3rd sess., 18 February 1811, THE ANNALS OF THE CONGRESS OF THE UNITED STATES, contained in JOSEPH GALES, COMP., THE DEBATES AND PROCEEDINGS OF THE CONGRESS OF THE UNITED STATES, 42 vols., (Washington: Gales and Seaton, 1834) at 22:976-77 (Library of American Civilization 21624).

For a listing of various Congressional Acts, *see* HARRY KURSH, THE UNITED STATES OFFICE OF EDUCATION (Philadelphia: Chilton Company, 1965), Appendix A & B. For an inside look at the Office of Education within the Department of Health, Education and Welfare and the same predictable rationales of expediency utilized by the federal government to set the educational policy and agendas of the people and states, *see*, FRANCIS KEPPEL, THE NECESSARY REVOLUTION IN AMERICAN EDUCATION (New York: Harper & Row, 1966); RUFUS E. MILES, JR., THE DEPARTMENT OF HEALTH, EDUCATION AND WELFARE (New York: Praeger, 1974).

Joseph Califano exhibited greater awareness of the dangers of federal control than did Francis Keppel, though both failed to clearly understand any substantive jurisdictional claims. Califano warned that "in its most extreme form, national control of curriculum is a form of national control of ideas." JOSEPH A. CALIFANO, JR., GOVERNING AMERICA (New York: Simon & Schuster, 1981) 297. Compared to Presidents Bush and Clinton, Califano's statement during the Carter Administration "that proposals for federal testing programs, however, well intentioned, are misguided; that even a wholly voluntary national test or set of standards would be a step in precisely the wrong direction" now appear radically conservative.

36. 5 June 1866, CONGRESSIONAL GLOBE *supra* note 1 at 2969.

37. *See* Senate, Committee on Governmental Affairs, Legislative History of Public Law, 96-98, Department of Education Organization Act, pts. 1-2, 96th Cong., 2d sess. (Washington, D.C.: Government Printing Office, 1980) at 1:3.

38. *Education Week*, Vol IX, Number 20, Feb. 7, 1990, pp. 1, 22 & 23.

Chapter 13

The Department Of Education - 1979

[T]he United States, will help ensure that education issues receive proper treatment at the Federal level, and will enable the Federal Government to coordinate its education activities more effectively.[1]

Introduction

The key focus of this Chapter will be on the erroneous Constitutional basis upon which the Department of Education Act is wholly structured, the pseudo-legal conception of federalism which "shares" power, the belligerent nationalism inherent in federal "protection" of state and parental duties, and the denigration of those parental duties from a Constitutionally reserved and unalienable status to mere "traditional functions."

It is not the purpose of this Chapter to examine the 1979 Federal Department of Education Act word for word. By its own terms, the Act flows from the belief that the federal government is vested with Constitutional jurisdiction over education in any degree that is expedient. Once jurisdiction was usurped in 1862 and 1867, Congressional intrusion gradually expanded to its present multi-billion dollar depletion of the federal treasury. Thus, to detail comprehensively the extent of present federal efforts on behalf of expediency, would be to dwell on secondary factors and ignore the controlling jurisdictional issue.

It need not be demonstrated that the legal and political experts who packaged this Act for a Constitutionally inexperienced Congress and President were themselves Constitutionally illiterate. Perhaps they had not yet fully imbibed from the "pure stream" of education wisdom emanating from the Department of Housing, Education and Welfare. Whatever their excuse, it will be evident that they neither understood nor acknowledged that the Constitution limited the jurisdiction and the power of Congress. In other words, they did not understand their own form of government. How could this have happened after a hundred years of federal involvement in education for the purpose of making good citizens? These specialists, so called experts, merely employed "the rule of expediency" in Constitutional construction, presuming that the American people were "unfit for self-government" and therefore in need of federal guidance over their minds and thoughts. Such is the creed of the bureaucratic state, the challenge of a more efficient tyranny, and the buffoonery of Constitutional pretenders.

From Census Power to General Welfare Power

As noted in the previous Chapter, the census power of Congress served as a pretext for early federal expansion of its power. Having outlived its usefulness, Congress turned to another clause of the Constitution to abuse for a while. The clause that seems destined for distortion in the hands of unfaithful public servants is the "general welfare" clause. To understand the concept of the general welfare, it is necessary to understand the significance of limiting the power of government. When considering the power of the federal government it is important to keep uppermost in mind that the federal government is a government of limited and enumerated powers. It is supreme within its own sphere of jurisdiction, but not with respect to state power, which is supreme within its separate and distinct sphere. It is a fundamental truism of federalism that power is not shared between the states and the federal government unless the Constitution specifically authorizes concurrent jurisdiction. It is also true that the general welfare of the United States is best ensured by Congressional adherence to the limited powers enumerated and no others.

There is one substantive provision of the Constitution that refers to the general welfare, though the term is also referred to in the preamble. The preamble states: "We the People of the United States, in Order to form a more perfect Union, establish Justice, insure domestic Tranquility, provide for the common defence, *promote the general Welfare*, . . . do ordain and establish this Constitution for the United States of America."[2]

The preamble outlines the broad purposes of the Constitution. It explains that the people are forming a national government in order to achieve some purpose. One such purpose is to promote the general welfare. The preamble is not a grant of power to Congress, nor a prohibition of power. The preamble states that the Constitution is established to accomplish certain purposes.

We have already examined the general object of civil government in previous Chapters. It was noted that the Declaration of Independence defines the source of unalienable rights that civil governments are instituted to protect. When these rights are protected and secured from interference, then and only then can it be said that the general welfare of the people is promoted. When these rights are denied and disparaged, then it can be said that the general welfare of the people is not promoted, but abridged. When the Constitution's limitations are observed, that is consistent with promoting the general welfare. When Congress exercises powers not granted, then it tramples on the people's unalienable right of government by consent and thereby undermines their general welfare.

The Constitution, therefore, is to be interpreted consistently with the promotion of the general welfare among the people of the United States. The phrase "promote the general welfare" is not a grant of power or a bottomless pit to be filled by the cleverest branch of government based on the rule of expediency. An authoritarian Congress exercising broad and undefined powers, acts contrary to promoting the general welfare of the people. It is inconsistent with the principle of self-government upon which the Republic has always stood and is adverse to our system of dual governments and liberty. A Congress that is given only limited and enumerated powers is the best safeguard against tyranny.

The Department of Education Organization Act of 1979 assumes exactly the opposite notions about the general welfare. It assumes that when Congress exercises power that the Constitution does not extend to it, then the general welfare is promoted. As a matter of fact, Congress thinks that by simply chanting the term "general welfare," it may then invoke the power to do whatever it likes. The Act accepts these false notions as true when it states:

> The Congress declares that the establishment of a Department of Education is in the public interest, will *promote the general welfare* of the United States, will help ensure that education issues receive proper treatment at the Federal level, and will enable the Federal Government to coordinate its education activities more effectively.[3]

Thus Congress, in declaring federal jurisdiction over education, pointed to and relied upon the *preamble* of the Constitution as the legal basis on which the statute and its consolidated functions rested. That is truly embarrassing. The establishment of a Constitution to, *inter alia*, promote the general welfare, however, cannot sanction an undefined grant of power to Congress. It cannot be construed to grant Congress power to "ensure that education issues receive proper treatment at the Federal level" or enable Congress to "coordinate its educational activities more effectively." Thus, by employing this language of "promoting the general welfare," either Congress acted mistakenly, negligently, or intentionally to usurp the Constitutionally retained jurisdiction of the people over education.[4]

If Congress were simply mistaken, they may have confused the preamble with Article I, section 8 which states: "The Congress shall have Power To lay and collect Taxes, Duties, Imposts and Excises, to pay the Debts and *provide for the common Defence and general Welfare* of the United States."[5] Confusion is likely when the instrument is unfamiliar to those who interpret it.

Confusion existing between "promoting" and "providing" for the general welfare as reflected in the preamble and Article I, section 8, has occurred on other occasions. For instance, in *Steward Machine Co. v. Davis*,[6] Justice Cardozo continually referred to the promotion of the general welfare. In that case, the Court found that Congress's Article I, section 8 spending power was broad enough to include the unemployment compensation scheme created by the Social Security Act of 1935.

While that Article clearly articulates Congressional power to provide for the general welfare, Cardozo stated that the general welfare of the nation could be Constitutionally promoted thereby.[7] Cardozo failed to acknowledge that the Preamble was not a grant of power to Congress and that Congressional authority to provide for the general welfare was not intended to be an open-ended authorization for social reform.

A review of the Constitutional Convention, however, indicates no similar confusion. Grants of power to the national legislature were intimately discussed in relationship to the states. A proposition had been put forward at the Convention for giving Congress "Legislative power in all cases to which the State Legislatures were individually incompetent."[8] But "Mr. Pinkney and Mr. Rutledge objected to the vagueness of the term *incompetent*." They preferred to "see an exact enumeration of the powers comprehended by this definition." In fact:

> Mr. Butler repeated his fears that we were running into an extreme in taking away the powers of the States, and called on Mr. Randolph for the extent of his meaning. Mr. Randolph disclaimed any intention to give indefinite powers to the national Legislature, declaring that he was entirely opposed to such an inroad on the State jurisdictions, and that he did not think any considerations whatever could ever change his determination. His opinion was fixed on this point.[9]

When the initial draft of these powers was subsequently reported on Monday, August 6 in Convention,[10] neither the preamble nor the Article VII (now Article I) contained any provision with respect to the general welfare of the people. When Article VII was taken up on August 16, in Convention,[11] it remained unaltered in this respect.

When the committee of eleven reported Article VII on Tuesday, September 4, 1787, it requested that the phrase "provide for the common defense & general welfare, of the U.S." be included. This was agreed to.[12] There was no raging debate that "general welfare" implied some new expansive power yet undefined. Precisely the opposite was true. It was added to authorize Congress "to provide for the common defence and general welfare, and for that purpose, among other express grants, they are authorized to lay and collect taxes . . . ."[13]

Just as the preamble noted the Constitution's purpose was to promote the general welfare by limiting the powers of the national legislature, so too, the Article I power, to provide for the general welfare was not a grant of wide and exhaustive power. It was a grant of specific power, limited in its application in its own right and limited in its application to the objects thereafter stated. The Constitution's Article I is not a delegation of powers inconsistent with: 1) the entire instrument, 2) the educational practices of the states, 3) the decision of the Convention affirmatively rejecting Congressional power over education, 4) the views of the Presidents, 5) the reports of the early Congressional committees, or 6) the Ninth and Tenth Amendments' reservation of educational rights and powers to the people.

✓ Key Idea:

☞ THE GENERAL WELFARE OF THE UNITED STATES IS BEST PROMOTED BY LIMITING CONGRESS TO THE EXERCISE OF THOSE FEW POWERS EXPRESSLY STATED IN THE CONSTITUTION.

Thus the Article I, section 8 "general welfare clause" includes no Congressional power over education. Such power was specifically rejected at the Convention and cannot be resurrected by the disparagement of that section through expediency.

No Concurrent Jurisdiction
The Act also suggests that the federal government "shares" jurisdiction with the states. The Constitution, however, has already established the only instances of mixed or concurrent jurisdiction. A simple review of the Constitution does not reveal any leeway for a "significant, but carefully restrained Federal role in education."[14] It does not provide that "education is and should be of concern to Federal, State and local governments."[15] It does not support other fictitious and self-serving propaganda such as, "[i]n all cases, Congress has been careful to stick to the Constitutionally-backed principle that the Federal role is limited to supplementing, not supplanting, State and local prerogatives and rights . . . ."[16]

These statements are gibberish and nonsense. They are by any other name, "insidious advances" designed to destroy the Constitutional limits on Congressional power. The jurisdictional outlines of the Constitution do not support any shared federal-state presence in education. The Constitution does not permit either "supplementing" or "supplanting." These words only describe degrees of unauthorized federal usurpation.[17]

Civil Government and Self-Government
Moreover, the Constitution does not vest in Congress an authoritarian power to protect the states and parents from their own educational choices. Article IV, section 4 affirms that each state shall be guaranteed a republican form of government, and prohibits the federal government from establishing a centralized or *general* government in which the states are merely administrative

organs of federal agencies. Article IV also confirms the controlling principle of government by consent, by entrusting the people with a republican government in which they participate, precisely because they can govern themselves.[18] Any unenumerated centralization of power in the hands of Congress is at odds with this principle.

Congress, however, cared nothing for the principles of limited government or self-government. For instance, Congress affirmed: "It is the intention of the Congress in the establishment of the Department to protect the *rights of States* and local governments and public and private educational institutions . . ."[19] While the Tenth Amendment reserves *power* to the state, it reserves no *rights* to the states whatsoever. The Ninth Amendment declares that the people alone retain rights, not the states. Thus, when Congress claims that it is protecting "the rights of the States" it claims a Constitutional impossibility to justify its own usurpation.

Moreover, to compound its error, Congress also introduced unconstitutional distinctions between private and public rights and primary and secondary responsibility. The Act stated that "parents have the primary responsibility for the education of their children, and States, localities, and private institutions have the primary responsibility for supporting that parental role." By making these distinctions, Congress limited the exercise of parental rights to the *private* sphere, and furthermore diminished the unalienable right to a "role" which anyone could assume.[20] Thus, within the private sphere the state and voluntary institutions are to support parents, but in the public sphere the unalienable rights of parents are diminished to a secondary role.

This abridgment is well demonstrated by the next Congressional declaration. "[I]n our Federal system, the primary *public* responsibility for education is reserved respectively to the States and the local school systems and other instrumentalities of the States."[21] Congress would have us believe that in the public sphere, the states, rather than parents, are awarded educational custody of children. In both instances, however, Congress made an intentional effort to share (by usurpation) educational jurisdiction alongside either the states and parents, or the state and its instrumentalities. Congress gets an "A" for manipulation and an "F" for Constitutional literacy.

The distinction between public and private, and primary and secondary is simply contrived to achieve expedient objectives. Moreover, concurrent power over a child's education is not given to the Congress and the states, and is repulsive to the unalienable and natural rights of parents to educate their children, publicly and privately, directly and indirectly. It is also repugnant to our form of Constitutional and limited government and runs contrary to the principles embodied in the Declaration of Independence.

If an honest observance of the Constitutional compact cannot be had by Congress, it need not be expected anywhere else. If Congress acknowledged its Constitutional limitations, it would provide a first step towards rekindling self-government of the people and return to parents power over local educational matters. It would decentralize control. It would eliminate (not merely reduce) the federal deficit. It would eliminate Constitutionally non-enumerated expenditures. It would also provide the necessary leadership for others to follow suit and improve education rather than strengthen federal oversight and influence. Parents on the whole are competent to educate their children even though they may have been willing past participants in the wrongful centralization of educational power in the federal government.

✓ Key Idea:

    ☞   GOD ENDOWS PARENTS, NOT THE STATE OR FEDERAL GOVERNMENT, WITH THE UNALIENABLE RIGHT AND DUTY TO EDUCATE CHILDREN.

The Strengthening of Centralized Power

Permit one historical example to illustrate the dangers of centralized power. Centralization of power in a national government on the basis of expediency is not new in this century. In Germany, under the "Weimar Constitution of the pre-Nazi regime, the states, provinces, and municipalities enjoyed considerable autonomy in the exercise of governmental functions --legislative, executive and judicial." This all changed, however, under national socialism.[22] In *Mein Kampf*, Adolf Hitler stated that:

> National Socialism, as a matter of principle, must claim the right to enforce its doctrines, without regard to present federal boundaries, upon the entire German nation and to educate it in its ideas and its thinking. The National Socialist doctrine is not the servant of political interests of individual federal states but shall become the ruler of the German nation.[23]

In other words, the ideas of the people must be centralized through the national government. Thus, the education of the people must be centralized without regard to "state" boundaries.[24]

The ghost of Congressman Moulton's 1866 speech on the floor of the United States House of Representatives is to similar effect. Moulton declared: "The very object of establishing a Bureau of Education is that these different systems may be brought together. We want all these school systems all over the land brought under one head, so that they may be *nationalized, vitalized, and made uniform and harmonious* as far as possible."[25]

Rejecting the notion that parents are competent public educators of their children, Adolf Hitler stated at Elbing, Germany: "Your child belongs to me already. A people lives forever. What are you? You will pass on. Your descendants however now stand in the new camp. In a short time they will know nothing else but this new community." He noted that the "new Reich will give its youth to no one, but will itself take youth and give to youth its own education and its own upbringing."[26]

Adolf Hitler's speech could have provided an additional authoritative footnote for the Court in *Ambach v. Norwick*,[27] wherein the Court, while not referring to the Fuhrer, approvingly added that "Other authorities have perceived public schools as an 'assimilative force' by which diverse and conflicting elements in our society are brought together on a broad but common ground."[28] The Court missed a fine footnote opportunity in neglecting the Fuhrer's speech.

✓ Key Idea:

    ☞   GERMAN NATIONAL SOCIALISM ASSERTED THE RIGHT TO EDUCATE GERMAN CHILDREN IN ITS IDEAS AND THINKING WITHOUT REGARD TO LOCAL BOUNDARIES OR PARENTAL RIGHTS.

Is the comparison which has been made between the Fuhrer's actual centralization of German education, and federal encroachment into American education, a claim that the federal government is controlled by Nazis? Of course not. It is to say, however, that the Reich, the Executive Branch, the Supreme Court and Congress have all adopted companion organizational and philosophical goals for education--centralize power over education in the national government and use public schools to assimilate the people into a common government-approved mass culture fitted for "good citizenship" and productive labor. Which government has had the greater success in achieving this philosophical goal would be worthy of discussion. Recall the fact that German education was itself centralized, and this action was later considered *by the United States* during the Nuremberg Trials, as evidence of an indictable conspiratorial offense of acquiring totalitarian control over the people in violation of international *and domestic law*.[29] As we judged others, the measure of judgment by which we judged, we shall be judged.

Does such an indictment await every new Congress? For each Congress must choose whether an "honest observance" of the Constitution will be its eternal guide, or whether it will continue to pursue its "insidious advances" upon that instrument by taking our youth and giving our youth its own education.

★ HYPOTHETICALLY SPEAKING . . . .

Problem: **You have survived your first term as a member of the City-Council in Middle America, but the Mayor is infuriated with you. First, you voted against his federally funded pork barrel road project. Second, Middle America's Council adopted your proposal to cut off its funding of**

pornographic, obscene and blasphemous "art" and use the money it saved for repaving Buchanan and Jackson Streets. Not exactly a stand for the Constitution but you are satisfied with the results.

The Council was also enamored by your expert witness on art. She testified that a well paved road was no less a work of art than other physical expressions. This testimony persuaded the Council to reject the mayor's arguments for federal funding. The citizens admire you because you didn't raise taxes and also got the roads paved.

Now Middle America is enjoying a national reputation for "road art"-- a new form of concrete expression in reaction to the abstract forms. Your political shrewdness divided the opposition against you and permitted you to survive their political assault in the last election. You are beginning to entertain notions of national political recognition. Friends encourage you to run for the House of Representatives.

The Mayor, however, has his eye on that seat. He is not to be outdone. He persuades Middle America's current representative in Congress to attach a rider on an appropriations bill that "recognizes art as the *joint responsibility* of federal and local governments." It recognizes the "pitiful shape of America's roads" and commends "the leadership of the Mayor in bringing Middle America to the forefront of funding road art and repairing roads." The rider also authorizes "the federal government to *promote the general welfare* by funding road art in the Nation's road art capital--Middle America!" The rider is passed by Congress. All that Middle America's City Council needs to do, is pass a unanimous resolution accepting the funds.

Your aspiration for a national political reputation is hanging in the balance. The Mayor has called your "road art" bluff. Your constitutional conscience is also starting to bother you. You again ask yourself: "Has the time arrived in Middle America when an honest observance of the Constitution cannot be found among my political principles?" "Is the degrading truth that I am unfit for self-government a reality?" "Will I make expediency the rule of construction in interpreting the Constitution?"

The big day arrives. The funding motion is now put before the City Council. One by one all Council members concur to accept federal funds *and* federal control. You are the last to vote. The national media are present. They have scheduled live coverage of the vote to air between a T.V. documentary on Adolf Hitler's centralization of German education, and a special report on the social maladjustment of home schooled children.

The time has come. The T.V. cameras zoom in on you as the Mayor smugly asks, "And what is your vote?" Your head is spinning. All you can think about are two phrases out of some book you read once: "honest observance" and "insidious advances." You don't remember what they mean exactly but you know somehow that you must choose one of them and then vote. Which do you mumble and how do you vote?

Notes

1. Senate, Committee on Governmental Affairs, Legislative History of Public Law 96-88, Department of Education Organization Act, pts. 1-2, 96th Cong., 2d sess. (Washington, D.C.: Government Printing Office, 1980) 1:3.

2. U.S. CONST. preamble (emphasis added).

3. LEGISLATIVE HISTORY *supra* note 1 at 1:3 (emphasis added).

4. The U.S. CONST. art. VI, § 3 states: "The Senators and Representatives . . . and all executive and judicial Officers, both of the United States and of the several States, shall be bound by Oath or Affirmation, to support this Constitution." To the extent that members of Congress act in defiance of the Constitution, they violate the oath of their office.

5. U.S. CONST. art. I, § 8, cl. 1 (emphasis added).

6. 301 U.S. 548 (1937).

7. 301 U.S. at 587, 589. *See also* United States v. Butler, 297 U.S. 1 (1936)(Article I, section 8, clause 1, case invalidating the Agricultural Adjustment Act of 1933).

8. DOCUMENTS ILLUSTRATIVE OF THE FORMATION OF THE UNION OF THE AMERICAN STATES, 69th Cong., 1st sess., House Document No. 398 (Washington, D.C.: Government Printing office, 1927) 129.

9. *Id.* at 129-30.

10. *Id.* at 471.

11. *Id.* at 552-57.

12. *Id.* at 659-60.

13. JAMES KENT, COMMENTARIES ON AMERICAN LAW (New York: O. Halsted, 1826; reprint ed., New York: Da Capo Press, 1971) 1:222. For an overview of the General Welfare Clause, *see* William C. Wood, Jr., *The General Welfare: A Constitutional Framework*, (Masters Thesis, Regent University, 1986).

14. LEGISLATIVE HISTORY *supra* note 1 at 1:518. (Report No. 96-49, Calendar No. 54, 96th Cong., 1st sess., p. 1).

15. LEGISLATIVE HISTORY *supra* note 1 at 1:519. (Report No. 96-49, Calendar No. 54 96th Cong., 1st sess., p. 2).

16. LEGISLATIVE HISTORY *supra* note 1 at 1:532. (Report No. 96-49, Calendar No. 54 96th Cong., 1st sess., p. 15).

17. *See generally*, U.S. CONST. art. I, § 8, cl. 16; art. IV, and art. V for examples of express mixed federal and state authority, and yet even these are not truly concurrent in the sense that both governments may exercise each other's power.

18. For more on the unalienable right of government by consent *see*, Kerry L. Morgan, *The Unalienable Right of Government by Consent and The Independent Federal Agency*, 8 J. CHRISTIAN JURIS. 33 (1990).

19. LEGISLATIVE HISTORY *supra* note 1 at 1:3 (emphasis added).

20. LEGISLATIVE HISTORY *supra* note 1 at 1:2.

21. LEGISLATIVE HISTORY *supra* note 1 at 1:2.

22. NAZI CONSPIRACY AND AGGRESSION, OFFICE OF THE UNITED STATES CHIEF OF COUNSEL FOR PROSECUTION OF AXIS CRIMINALITY (Washington, D.C.: United States Government Printing Office, 1946) 1:221.

23. *Id.*

24. In addition to the general centralization of power, "[t]he Nazi conspirators through Rosenberg's Office for Supervision of the Ideological Training and education of the NSDAP and the Office of the Deputy of the Fuhrer induced the substitution of National Socialist mottoes and services for religious prayers and services in the schools of Germany." *Id.* at 266. The federal courts have achieved substantially the same result in the United States through ruling unconstitutional religious acts in state schools and compelling state-approved curriculums to be taught.

25. U.S., Congress, House, Representative Moulton extolled the virtues of a centralized, government-controlled educational system under the head of the federal government, 39th Cong., 2nd sess., 8 June 1866, THE CONGRESSIONAL GLOBE at 3045 (emphasis added).

26. NAZI CONSPIRACY AND AGGRESSION *supra* note 22 at 1:312 (emphasis omitted). The German government's influence over the mind of "its" children was established and solidified through a variety of means. The most successful, however, involved the use of the educational system to direct the ideas to which the minds of the next generation were routinely exposed. As a matter of fact, the official instructor's manual for high school students was founded upon the premise that "the German school is a part of the National Socialist Educational order." *Id.* In terms of federal oversight and control, Congressional implementation of President Clinton's National Standards for what students should know and an accompanying system of voluntary national examinations is no different in kind from an indoctrination point of view. *See* U.S. Congress, House of Representatives, Conference Report 103-446, Goals 2000: Educate America Act, 103rd Cong., 2nd sess., March 21, 1994, (Washington D.C.: Government Printing Office, 1994).

27. 441 U.S. 68 (1978).

28. *Id.* at 77, citing JOHN DEWEY, DEMOCRACY AND EDUCATION, AN INTRODUCTION TO THE PHILOSOPHY OF EDUCATION, (New York: The MacMillan Company, 1916) 26. The full quotation is as follows:

> The assimilative force of the American public school is eloquent testimony to the efficacy of the common and balanced appeal.
>
> The school has the function also of coordinating within the disposition of each individual the diverse influences of the various social environments into which he enters. One code prevails in the family; another, on the street; a third, in the workshop or store; a fourth, in the religious association. As a person passes from one of the environments to another, he is subjected to antagonistic pulls, and is in danger of being split into a being having different standards of judgment and emotion for different occasions. This danger imposes upon the school a steadying and integrating office. *Id.*

29. NAZI CONSPIRACY AND AGGRESSION *supra* note 22 at 1:21. The formal indictment, Count One, begins on page 14 and 15 of volume 1.

Chapter 14

Standardizing the American Mind

[E]very school in America will ensure that all students learn to use their minds well, so they may be prepared for responsible citizenship, further learning, and productive employment in our Nation's modern economy.[1]

The German youth besides being reared within the family and school, shall be educated physically, intellectually, and morally in the spirit of National Socialism to serve the people and the community, through the Hitler Youth.[2]

Federal Influence--Now and Then

When President Andrew Johnson and Congress created a Bureau of Education in 1867, it was not simply a matter of creating an administrative organization and authorizing appropriations. Congressional debate reiterated what former Presidents including Jefferson, Monroe, and Buchanan had clearly articulated: that federal interference in educational matters was unconstitutional. In 1866 Congressman Rogers noted that the formation of a Bureau of Education was unconstitutional declaring that "there is no authority under the Constitution of the United States to authorize Congress to interfere with the education of the different States in any manner, directly or indirectly."[3]

In 1979, however, when President Jimmy Carter and Congress created a Cabinet-level Department of Education, Congressional debate was monopolized by bureaucratic wrangling, organizational and appropriations considerations. Absent during the proceedings were discussions of the crucial historical and Constitutional limitations that prevented continued assertion of federal jurisdiction over education.[4]

Following in the footsteps of President Carter, President George Bush announced in 1991 that his administration had launched a new national education strategy--America 2000. Its purpose was to "reinvent American Education--to design New American Schools for the year 2000 and beyond."[5] The President announced that he would seek federal funding for 535 New American Schools designed to meet newly instituted *national* educational goals including New World Standards.[6]

Proving that Constitutional pretenders are habitually to be found in the Democratic as well as the Republican party, President Bill Clinton set forth an educational agenda that took the final step in the federal prelude to direct control over American education. He not only furthered many of the national educational goals announced by President Bush, but President Clinton insisted that the federal government go beyond those goals and "create a set of *National Standards* for what students should know." The creation of national standards, however, means that "*a National Examination System*" must be established in order "to measure our students' and schools' progress in meeting the National Standards."[7] Congress agreed with the President and these goals and adopted the "Goals 2000: Educate America Act" in 1994.[8]

In heralding the deliverance of education from its downward spiral, however, President Clinton did not mention that parents had an unalienable right to direct the education of their children. He only said that parents should have a "choice" to send their child to any public school as long as racial, religious and *income* discrimination is prohibited.[9] Nor did the President recognize that the Constitution does not authorize the federal government to create national education "standards," "examinations" or "systems." Forgotten was the Constitutional rule that the federal government may not make schools accountable to itself, private business or new world standards even if he believes it all makes sense politically.

Examination of the Department of Education in the previous Chapter indicated that the federal government has continued to elbow its way into education. This Chapter examines that tendency in light of developments in both the Bush and Clinton Administrations. Though there are important differences between the two Administrations, indeed some irreconcilable differences between the desired *content* for students, both nevertheless are firmly agreed that the Constitution is of no consequence in limiting federal power to force that content on students.

Federal Education Goals

Presidents' Bush and Clinton mix federal and state jurisdiction in essentially the same way as President Carter. Each assume a "limited role" for the federal government and emphasize state and local control of education. All profess that federal "assistance" does not mean federal control, and that parents are included in the process of governmental education. None regard the limited role the Constitution assigns to the federal government--patent, copyright and military/militia training and none respect the unalienable rights of parents.[10]

This approach establishes *federal* educational goals. Federal goals are not the same as parental goals since federal interests differ from state and parental interest. Although the federal government wants the public to believe that federal interest in education is identical to parental interest, that is a belief against all reason. Federal (or state) interest in education can never escape the difficulties which Thomas Jefferson observed plagued state interest in religion. He noted that,

> [T]he impious presumption of legislators and rulers, civil as well as ecclesiastical, who, being themselves but fallible and uninspired men, have assumed dominion over the faith of others, setting up their own opinions and modes of thinking as the only true and infallible, and as such endeavoring to impose them on others, hath established and maintained false religions over the greatest part of the world and through all time.[11]

When federal goals are examined, bear in mind that we are really examining the arrogant presumptions of the fallible and uninspired Bush and Clinton Administrations as they propagate their own opinions and modes of thinking as the only true and infallible national standards. Respect for parental rights, however, requires abandonment of the federal strategy to mold the minds of America's children in the image of temporal humanistic federal standards. America does not need new schools for a new world or federal aid in "helping" parents prepare *their own* children. America needs respect for the Constitutional rule of law and parental rights.[12]

✓ Key Idea:
☞ THE BUSH AND CLINTON ADMINISTRATIONS HAVE SOUGHT TO PROPAGATE THEIR OWN OPINIONS AND MODES OF THINKING AS THE ONLY TRUE AND INFALLIBLE STANDARD.

Presumption 1. Parents Need the Federal Government

The first presumption embodied in the National Education Goals is that parents need the federal government to prepare their children to receive an education. This approach emphasizes the goal of preparing pre-school children to "start school ready to learn."[13] Congress has added that "children will receive the nutrition, physical activity experiences, and health care needed to arrive at school with healthy minds and bodies, and to maintain the mental alertness necessary to be prepared to learn."[14] (If only Congress could arrive every morning at the Capital in such a condition). This goal translates into greater federal interference with parental rights and family autonomy. It expands federal jurisdiction into the early stages of home education. Schools could be open to "children from three months to age eighteen."[15] The federal government falsely believes it can "close the knowledge gap" by exposing children to government authorized ideas and programs at the earliest possible age.[16]

President Clinton has also suggested that his administration may consider federalizing state truancy laws. While Governor of Arkansas he "[a]uthorized fines for parents who refuse to attend a parent-teacher conference or allow their children to be chronically truant."[17] His campaign promise to "put people first by dramatically improving the way parents prepare their children for school" assumes a sharp proportion in this light. Fines are dramatic. Setting up federal opinions and modes of thinking as the only true and infallible standard and imposing them on parents will be dramatic. Despite their dramatic feature, however, forcible suppression of parental rights, centralized influence of education and ideas, and belligerent nationalism are more properly attributes of fascism. Thus, under this National Education Goal, American youth, like their historic German counterpart, besides being reared within the family and school, shall be educated physically, intellectually, and morally in the spirit of National Standards to serve the people and the community.

Presumption 2. We Need National Standards

The federal approach also calls for emphasis on ensuring "demonstrated competency over challenging subject matter including English, mathematics, science, foreign languages, civics and government, economics, arts, history, and geography."[18] A system of national examinations will measure competency in these areas. Congress is slated to collect statistics to see how well the nation's children are conforming to the new standards.

In other words, the federal government is going to use its economic leverage to induce schools to adopt national curricular standards. Though the government denies that it is establishing a national curriculum, it is certainly establishing National Standards which it expects the schools to meet. When push comes to shove in federal funding and support, what school will not conform their curriculums to contain the information that the National Examinations will test? And what school will refuse the national exams if the federal government cajoles colleges to utilize them in their admissions process?

Moreover, federal emphasis on ensuring "demonstrated competency" really means compulsion, but even if this federal emphasis were truly voluntary, that which is "voluntary" today will inevitably be made mandatory tomorrow. It is only a matter of time before Congress will herald the statistics it has been collecting under the America 2000 "voluntary" plan, and then declare: "Based on these statistics, America will not reach its goal unless the federal system becomes fully mandatory!" This is how Congress works.[19] Total and forced inclusion is a fact of political life and in the nature of unbridled power.

Recall Thomas Jefferson's charge that the tendency of a subsidy or inducement is to "corrupt the principles" it is meant to encourage, "by bribing, with the monopoly of worldly honors and emoluments those who will externally express and conform to it." With respect to those who are so bribed, he notes "that though indeed these are criminal who do not withstand such temptation, yet neither are those innocent who lay the bait in their way . . . ."[20]

How might this charge apply to the Federal government? In fact, the federal education goals are also based on a system of giving and taking bribes. A Presidential Citation for Educational Excellence or a federal grant of money, is a classic "worldly honor" for those who will externally express and conform to the grant's conditions. Such bribes corrupt the principle of learning. They reward those who will conform to federal performance standards.

✓ Key Idea:

☞ FEDERAL GOALS ARE BASED ON A SYSTEM OF GIVING AND TAKING BRIBES FOR THOSE WHO WILL PROFESS AND THEN CONFORM A STUDENT'S MIND TO "NATIONAL STANDARDS."

Presumption 3. The Government Can Make Responsible Citizens

Federal emphasis in ensuring "that all students learn to use their minds well, so that they may be prepared for responsible citizenship, further learning, and productive employment in our Nation's modern economy" is another National Education Goal.[21] Notice that the usual justification for state or federal intervention into education--preparation for responsible citizenship--is markedly expanded.

Is the federal government competent to set or establish standards of knowledge for "responsible citizenship" when its very approach to government runs entirely contrary to the laws of nature and nature's God, the clear principles of the Declaration of Independence, the unalienable rights of parents, the right of intellectual freedom and the express Constitutional limitations on Congressional and federal power?

The federal government mistakenly believes that it has the power and capacity to prepare American students for responsible citizenship. It also claims to ensure "that all students learn to use their minds" and use them "well." Oh really? We have already seen how "well" Congress has used its mind in misconstruing the Constitution according to the rule of expediency and how Congress has engaged in "insidious advances" upon the written checks that were designed to restrain its power. We shall momentarily see how "well" the federal government has done with respect to its educational efforts to create responsible citizens out of Native-American Indians. We shall also see how education in the District of Columbia--a District under direct federal oversight--has fared.

Whatever the rhetoric of producing "responsible citizens" actually means in practice, it is obvious that it does not mean that children will be taught to use their minds to understand, question or challenge the unconstitutional exercise of federal jurisdiction.

The emphasis on education for productive employment is also noteworthy. The federal government, however, has no jurisdiction to conform the minds of students to fit Department of Labor workforce 2000 *predictions* pertaining to projected labor requirements in the next decade and beyond.[22] While ensuring productive employment in our modern economy is important, that objective is far more attainable through parental exercise of their unalienable rights to educate their children, than by federal imposition of standards through National Examinations.

✓ Key Idea:

☞   FEDERAL GOALS ARE PART OF AN EFFORT TO MOLD TODAY'S STUDENT INTO THE FEDERAL GOVERNMENT'S STATISTICAL NOTION OF TOMORROW'S NEW WORLD WORKFORCE.

Recall that James Kent reiterated the correct approach, both to making good citizens and to building the workforce of tomorrow. He said that parents are obliged by God to make "reasonable provision for their [child's] future usefulness and happiness in life, by a situation suited to their habits, and a competent provision for the exigencies of that situation."[23] A "reasonable provision for their [children's] future usefulness and happiness in life" means, *inter alia*, parental education of children for truly responsible citizenship and productive employment.

Zach Montgomery also recognized that:

The law of nature and nature's God, which ordains that it is both the right and duty of parents to educate their children "in such manner as they believe will be most for their future happiness" is utterly disregarded and set at naught by the State, which ordains that it is neither the right nor the duty of parents, but of the State, to say when, where, by whom, and in what manner our children shall be educated.[24]

National standards and every other federal plan or strategy by whatever name or promotional campaign, however, ordain that it is not the right or the duty of parents to say when, where, by whom, and in what manner their children shall be educated for citizenship or future productive employment. These standards or goals are political schemes which instead ordain that it is the right and duty of the federal government to set standards, contribute funds and push and prod our children so that they shall be educated for future productive employment in the government orchestrated workforce of tomorrow.

Presumption 4. Reform Means New Technology

The federal approach developed most significantly under the Bush Administration, emphasized "breaking the mold" in school reform efforts. It proposed to test the new theories of "high performance" education in a New Generation of American Schools.[25] This emphasis on breaking the mold is essentially an emphasis on rearranging instructional time, space and resources. For instance, "America 2000" suggests that some "schools may make extensive use of computers, distance learning, interactive video-discs and other modern tools." Other schools may "redesign the human relationship and organizational structures of the school."[26] In other words, breaking the mold does not mean breaking the mold of government regulation of education. But if there is any mold to break today, it is this very mold of state established schools.[27]

✓ Key Idea:

☞ THE STATE ESTABLISHED SCHOOL IS THE ONE MOLD THAT MUST BE BROKEN IF REFORM IN EDUCATION IS EVER TO SUCCEED.

The real solution to break the mold is to encourage the states to recognize the unalienable rights of parents. The fraudulent solution, however, actually proposed by the federal government, is to *give* parents the choice to carry some form of federal subsidy to a government approved school. President Bush would have *allowed* parents to select any school including private and religious institutions that are "supported by public funds, [and] answerable to public authorities and regulation."[28] Parents, however, could not exercise this choice unless state or local policy permits. President Clinton would *permit* parents to choose from among public schools only, provided they meet certain non-discrimination requirements including an income related criteria.[29]

If the federal government should *give, allow or permit* parents anything, it should assure them that the federal government will respect its constitutional limitations. Likewise, if the state governments should *give, allow or permit* parents anything, it should assure them that it will recognize and protect their unalienable rights to direct the education of their children free from governmental interference, regulation and control.[30]

Physician, Heal Thyself

But no matter how strong parental rights are argued against federal intervention, many legislators, attorneys and academics nevertheless remain firmly convinced that the federal government and only the federal government can really bring reform to education. To them, the thought of the federal government marching into the states in order to "help" causes no concern whatsoever. For those who profess confidence in the eventual success of the new federal education strategy, might it be prudent to consider past efforts of the federal government in leading America to higher standards of educational excellence? Certainly no one so confident in the ability of the federal government to create new schools for a new world, would object to examining the successes of *federally aided or operated schools* in the here and now.

A. Federal Indian Education

For instance, historically the federal government assumed charge of the American Indian and his or her education. Education was considered essential to fully assimilate the Indian into American society. By 1876 instruction in "industrial or manual training, as well as schooling in reading, writing, and arithmetic" constituted the basic federal curriculum.[31] The rationale for Indian education was "to make the Indians self-supporting . . . and to bring an end to the enormous governmental outlays needed to maintain large numbers of Indians . . . ."[32] This is not unlike the present federal emphasis on the core curriculum and ensuring "that all students learn to use their minds well, so they may be prepared for . . . productive employment in our Nation's modern economy." Same meaning, different language.

By 1889 the federal government standardized Indian Education under the leadership of Thomas J. Morgan, then Commissioner of Indian Affairs. The Commissioner "came to the Indian Office with firm opinions on the value of education as an essential means for the promotion of American Citizenship and on the necessity of a public school *system*" for Indians.[33] He declared that the education of the Indian "was a responsibility of the federal government that could not safely be shirked or delegated to another party." He envisioned a cultural transformation of the Indian at the prompting of the federal government.[34] The observant reader will recognize that this emphasis is virtually identical to the federal goal of ensuring "that all students . . . be prepared for responsible citizenship" and is constantly echoed by the Supreme Court as a legal rationale for governmental control of education (as discussed in prior Chapters).

The future of Native Americans and their children was therefore firmly in the hands of the federal government. By 1928 the "Indian Bureau's Education Division had been directing Indian schooling for almost fifty years." Forty years later, however, the Kennedy Report was issued by a special Subcommittee on Indian Education. The 1969 report was entitled "Indian Education: A National Tragedy--A National Challenge."[35] This report concluded that the "dominate policy of the federal government towards the American Indian has been one of coercive assimilation."[36] The federal government's honorable education effort resulted in "disastrous effects on the education of Indian children."[37]

Since the Kennedy Report, the trend in education of Native American Indians has been toward Indian controlled schools and decisively away from federal control. Federally inspired instruction and standards are not a model of "the enlightenment that a sound and well-rounded education provides."[38] Federally aided Indian institutions are not "mold buster" schools. They are what remains of belligerent nationalism, paternalism, coercion and assimilation--not a very flattering testimony.

✓ Key Idea:

    ☞   FEDERAL CONTROL OF INDIAN EDUCATION RESULTED IN WIDESPREAD STUDENT FAILURE AND DESTROYED THE INDIAN CHILD AS WELL AS THE INDIAN FAMILY.

Unfortunately for the federal propagandist, the federal education of Indian children has been soundly rejected by Indian parents, tribal leaders and most Americans. The federal government's approach to American Indian education as applied to the rest of the American people, however, has never been rejected by the federal government. The federal government's Indian educational objectives are resurrected in "Goals 2000" and "America 2000." The present federal emphasis on education for "responsible citizenship," development of productive employment skills and competency in basic subject matter including English, is essentially a Madison Avenue re-packaging of the failed Indian education policies of the past 100 years.

Moreover, the federal emphasis on preparing "children from three months to age eighteen" to "start school ready to learn," is essentially identical in principle to the Indian education strategy of enlightening the Indian through boarding schools and through the "outing system." These measures involved taking Indian children from their parents as early as practicable, educating them in boarding schools away from their culture and family influence. The children were also placed in the homes of others who would nuture and mature their development into western culture.[39] It boggles the mind to think that another federal strategy, intended to attract children from their parents at ever younger ages and assimilate their thinking into National Standards, can likewise achieve anything but disastrous results. Must our destiny also turn us toward Washington D.C. so that we too may benefit from the wisdom and consent of our Great White Father?

B. Federal Education and the District of Columbia

    The federal government's inability and failure to educate Native Americans throughout the United States is appalling. Perhaps a simpler test of its ability and competence to educate on a more localized scale would redeem the federal effort. Hope springs eternal for the disciples of federal power. If the federal government yearns to set a National Education Strategy for the entire United States, then it ought not be too much to ask it to first prove itself capable in the federal city--the District of Columbia.

In fact, the Constitution gives Congress the power to "exercise exclusive legislation in all cases whatsoever over such District."[40] Congress originally construed this power in the context of higher education to mean that:

> any time legislative aid should be asked to incorporate a district university, for the local benefit of the inhabitants of Columbia, and of funds of their own raising, there can be no doubt that it would be considered with kindness, as in other cases; but it must be remembered that this is a function totally distinct from the endowment of a national university, out of the treasure of the United States, destined, in its legitimate application, to other and very different purposes.[41]

If this view of Congressional power over the District of Columbia were applied to elementary and secondary school education, then it would be Constitutionally acceptable for the federal government to *incorporate* district schools "for the local benefit of the inhabitants of Columbia, and of funds of their own raising." This application, however, would constitute the outer limit of Congressional power. It would not be acceptable to *operate or fund* district schools out of the federal Treasury. Such activities would also impair the unalienable rights of District parents to direct the education and upbringing of their children free from civil government's influence, regulation or control.

In evaluating the success of Congress in educating the children of the District, one must recognize that Congress has adopted the principle of home rule. The Mayor and the District government oversee the operation of the city and its schools. They carry out their responsibilities, however, under the oversight, and ultimately control, of Congress. What outstanding educational results have been achieved under Congressional oversight of the District's education? How much money has been spent and who has benefitted? Has the District achieved the National Goals?

In 1988-89, the District of Columbia ranked sixth among the states in per pupil *revenue*. (The District is not a state, but is commonly compared to the states for many purposes). An average of $6,135 per year was received in revenue per student. The United States average was $4,812.[42] Per pupil *expenditures* of $6,724 elevated the District to a ranking of 4th among the States.[43] When the figures are adjusted for expenditures per pupil *in average daily attendance,* the District spends $7,850. This amount is significantly ahead of neighboring Maryland at $5,758 and Virginia at $4,539. The national average is $4,639.[44] When compared, however, for school district size the District is not as large as its neighbors which spend less.[45]

The Department of Education, National Center for Education Statistics reported that in the Fall of 1987, the District of Columbia enjoyed an enviable student-teacher ratio of 13.9 students for every 1 teacher. Only Connecticut (13.3 to 1), Vermont (13.4 to 1) and Massachusetts (13.9 to 1) enjoyed a superior or comparable ratio. When these ratios are factored for urbanicity (compared with similar statistically defined urban centers), the District achieved a number 1 ranking, superior to all States. The District's 13.9 to 1 ratio was better than the urban average of 15.4 to 1 for Middle Atlantic States and better than the national urban average of 17.6 students to 1 teacher.[46]

The Department of Education also ranks the average annual salary of elementary and secondary school teachers. The Department rated the District teacher compensation for the 1988-89 school year, fourth among the States. The average annual salary was $38,022, well above the national average of $30,981. The District's teachers were, on average, only paid less on a State by State basis, than Alaska ($43,746), Connecticut ($39,125) and New York ($38,403).[47] The Department of Education also publishes statistics on minimum teacher salary. This is the average starting salary that a beginning teacher could expect in a public elementary or secondary institution. The Department found the District's starting salary in 1989-90 was $22,983. This level of compensation ranks the District 4th among States.[48]

With excellent revenues, expectations, student-to-teacher ratios and well above average salaries one might expect corresponding high student achievement. Among students taking the 1989-90 Scholastic Aptitude Test (SAT), District of Columbia Public School students scored an average of 409 verbal and 441 mathematics, in comparison to national average scores of 424 and 476, respectively.[49] When compared to the States in SAT scores, the District's students ranked sixth from the bottom in verbal and third from the bottom in mathematics. Only South Carolina (397), North Carolina and Georgia (401), Hawaii (404), and Indiana (408) did more poorly in verbal, and North Carolina (440) and South Carolina (437) did worse in mathematics.[50]

✓ Key Idea:

☞ ONLY THE SIMPLETON, CONTINUES TO EXPECT THE FEDERAL GOVERNMENT TO DO FOR EDUCATION IN THE STATES, WHAT IT CANNOT DO FOR ITSELF IN THE DISTRICT OF COLUMBIA.

To summarize: When compared to states, the District is sixth in revenue and fourth in expenditures per-pupil. It is fourth in teacher compensation. The District is first in average daily student-teacher ratios. These high rankings have produced students that rank 45th in SAT verbal and 48th in SAT math. These results are scandalous. They illustrate that Presidential assurance about how the federal government is competent and qualified to improve American Education, is a massive fraud on the people. The District's pathetic scores should destroy confidence in any federal pledge that "Washington can help by setting standards" or by "empower[ing parents] with the knowledge they need to help their children enter school ready to learn."[51] This type of political rhetoric is shameless, blathering hogwash. The fact is, that Congress has a proven track record of incompetence and inefficiency in managing the District's educational affairs. The blind cannot lead the blind. The physician cannot heal others if he does not first heal himself.

The Past is Prologue

We would do well to heed Congressman Rogers' distrust of federal intervention. He observed in 1866 that the federal government's proposed education strategy would,

> put under the supervision of a bureau established at Washington all the schools and educational institutions of the different States of the Union by collecting such facts and statistics as will warrant them by amendments hereafter to the law now attempted to be passed to control and regulate the educational system of the whole country.[52]

America 2000 and its Clinton counterpart, Goals 2000: Educate America Act, are simply "amendments hereafter . . . to control and regulate the educational system of the whole country." Expediency has become the rule of Constitutional construction. The Congressman's warning continues to be ignored. He declared:

> If Congress has the right to establish an Educational Bureau, . . . for the purpose of collecting statistics and controlling the schools of the country, then by the same parity of reason, *a fortiori*, Congress has the right to establish a bureau to supervise the education of all the children that are to be found in . . . this country. You will not stop at simply establishing a bureau for the purpose of paying officers to collect and diffuse statistics in reference to education.[53]

Presidents Carter, Bush and Clinton have not stopped "at simply establishing a bureau." Carter proposed a Department of Education. Bush proposed New American Schools and New World Standards. Clinton proposed National Standards and a *voluntary* National Examination System. A future President will propose that voluntary standards must become mandatory. The federal government will not stop with these intrusions on our liberties. It has not stopped and will not stop unless the wise parent who understands the loathsome end that awaits their children, make it stop.

★ HYPOTHETICALLY SPEAKING . . . .

Problem: Your televised speech during the last City Council meeting has brought you to the attention of certain high ranking public officials including Republican Samuel Insider, the most powerful politician in the Country. You have so impressed Sam that you have resigned your County Council seat and have accepted an appointment to serve as Middle America's Chief Judge--an appointment that Sam pulled all the right strings to get for you.

You are excited to hear your first case. The facts are simple. Mr. Washington, the defendant, is charged with cheating several widows out of their life savings. Mr. Washington's method of operation is uncomplicated. He vigorously solicits women recently widowed, promising to improve their financial lot in life and provide a perpetual fund for the education of their children. He assures them that their future and their children's future usefulness and happiness can be guaranteed. All they need to do is give him a limited share of the inheritance left by their late husbands. He promises to invest it, nurture it and improve it. He guarantees a payback which will make them wealthy even beyond the year 2000. He also gives them a bumper sticker for their car that says: "Washington Knows Best."

In fact, however, Mr. Washington does not know best and does none of the things he promised. Instead, he takes the money and speculates in pork futures, an extremely high risk low yield investment which only benefits himself. Mr. Washington is actually a colossal failure in the investment field. Moreover, he has used the widow's inheritance to live in the lap of luxury on Capital Boulevard, the widest thoroughfare in Middle America.

Mr. Washington has converted the widows' money to his own use and has defrauded them and their children out of their future security through a pattern and practice of half-lies, pushing and prodding and Madison Avenue "feel good" marketing. He is certainly guilty of the charges against him. Washington's only defense was that he sincerely believed his approach would "make these widows and their children all that they should be in the year 2000 and beyond" although he admits no evidence supports his claim.

After hearing the evidence and arguments, you are about to find Mr. Washington guilty as charged when your clerk interrupts to say you have an important telephone call. You take a short recess to answer the call. Samuel Insider is on the phone. He says he has high hopes that you can move up in the Administration. He reminds you that he can pull all the right strings. He then informs you that Mr. Washington is his nephew. "I don't care about the facts" he says, "just don't go against Washington!" You exchange pleasantries and hang up. You know Washington is guilty of many offenses. You also know that his Uncle Sam is powerful. You know both are wrong. You know your political future and legal credibility are on the line.

Will you find Washington has put his own lust for money and power ahead of the widows and children of Middle America and declare him guilty as charged, or will you find that sincerity negates lawlessness (and also helps you politically) and declare him not guilty?

Notes

1. U.S. Congress, House of Representatives, Conference Report 103-446, Goals 2000: Educate America Act, 103rd Cong., 2nd sess., March 21, 1994, (Washington D.C.: Government Printing Office, 1994) 7.

2. NAZI CONSPIRACY AND AGGRESSION, OFFICE OF THE UNITED STATES CHIEF OF COUNSEL FOR PROSECUTION OF AXIS CRIMINALITY (United States Government Printing Office: Washington 1946) 1:316.

3. U.S., Congress, House, Representative Rogers noted the unconstitutionality of the proposed federal Bureau of Education, 39th Cong., 2nd sess., 5 June 1866, THE CONGRESSIONAL GLOBE at 2968. Opponents of the department also predicted that the original budget of $1,678.67 would eventually become expensive and unduly burdensome. Presidents' Bush and Clinton fiscal year budget request for the Department of Education averaged between 31-33 billion dollars.

4. See RUFUS E. MILES, JR., A CABINET DEPARTMENT OF EDUCATION (Washington, D.C.: American Council on Education, 1976) 38; U.S., Congress, Senate Committee on Governmental Affairs, Hearings-Department of Education Act of 1977, pts. 1-2, 95th Cong., 1st sess., (Washington, D.C.: Government Printing Office, 1977). These key sources are inordinately devoid of any jurisdictional understanding which is consistent with the Constitution or history.

5. White House Press Release, April 18, 1991, Remarks by the President at the presentation of his National Education Strategy.

6. See America 2000: An Education Strategy, U.S. Department of Education, April 18, 1991, 11-14.

7. Clinton-Gore on Education, Policy Paper on Education, (Clinton/Gore '92 Committee, Little Rock, AK.) [2] (emphasis in original).

8. See Goals 2000: Educate America Act *supra* note 1. The Act also provides that the examinations are voluntary, that the states are not compelled to operate their schools in any particular way unless federal funds are present (which they always are) and that parental assistance is desirable. *Id.* at 64-66. The controlling question, however, is "What Constitutional provision authorizes Congress to enter into the field of education in the first instance?"

9. *Id.*

10. In further elaborating on its self-defined "limited" role, [recall that if its "self defined", then by definition it is not limited], the Department of Education (DOE) employs Madison-Avenue use of "feel good" language. The DOE indicates that the:

> federal government's role in this strategy is limited as--wisely--its part in education has always been. But that role will be played vigorously. Washington can help by setting standards, highlighting examples, contributing some funds, providing flexibility in exchange for accountability, and pushing and prodding-- then pushing and prodding some more.

America 2000 *supra* note 6 at 2.

11. An Act for Religious Freedom, adopted by the Virginia General Assembly on January 16, 1786, VA. CODE ANN. § 57-1 (1950).

12. Withdrawal of federal jurisdiction would also:
1. Strengthen the people in the exercise of their preexisting unalienable rights and power over education acknowledged by the Ninth and Tenth Amendments;
2. Strengthen the federal government by redirecting its time, energy and resources toward those objects for which it bears express constitutional responsibility;
3. Strengthen the national economy by acknowledging the constitutional limitations on the purpose to which the federal treasury may be directed and by reducing federal deficits;
4. Strengthen education by encouraging educational diversity and by opposing continued expansion and centralization of educational policy.

13. Goals 2000: Educate America Act *supra* note 1 at 7.

14. *See* Goals 2000: Educate America Act *supra* note 1 at 7.

15. Remarks of Lamar Alexander, Kansas Governor's Educational Summit, Wichita, Kansas November 1-2, 1989 cited in the *Education Reporter*, Vol. 61, Feb. 1991, p. 1.

16. *See* text and accompanying notes 31-40 *infra* for a discussion of the destructive effects of federal education on young Native-American children.

17. Clinton-Gore on Education *supra* note 7 at p. [3].

18. Goals 2000: Educate America Act *supra* note 1 at 7.

19. The development of Social Security from a policy of voluntary inclusion to a mandatory one is but one example of this development.

20. An Act for Religious Freedom, adopted by the Virginia General Assembly on January 16, 1786, recited in VA. CODE ANN. § 57-1 (1950). *See also* ROBERT L. CORD, SEPARATION OF CHURCH AND STATE (New York: Lambeth Press, 1982) 250, quoting Thomas Jefferson's *A Bill for Establishing Religious Freedom.*

21. America 2000 *supra* note 6 at 9. *See* Clinton-Gore on Education *supra* note 7 at pp. [4-5], and Goals 2000: Educate America Act *supra* note 1 at 7.

22. *See generally,* Bureau of Labor Statistics, "Outlook 2000," U.S. Department of Labor (Bulletin 2352) April 1990; Bureau of Labor Statistics, "Projections 2000," U.S. Department of Labor (Bulletin 2302) March 1988; Employment Standards Administration, "Opportunity 2000: Creative Affirmative Action Strategies for a Changing Workforce," U.S. Department of Labor, September 1988.

23. JAMES KENT, COMMENTARIES ON AMERICAN LAW (New York: O. Halsted, 1826; reprint ed., New York: Da Capo Press, 1971) 2:159.

24. ZACH MONTGOMERY, COMP., THE SCHOOL QUESTION FROM A PARENTAL AND NON-SECTARIAN STAND POINT, 4TH ED. (Washington: Gibson Bros., 1889; reprint ed.; New York: Arno Press, 1972) 52.

25. America 2000 *supra* note 6 at 15.

26. America 2000 *supra* note 6 at 16.

27. Lamar Alexander has remarked that public education "ranks right up there at the top with the most coercive aspects of America Society." He compares compulsion in education with "land condemnation and the military draft." The former Secretary of Education concluded that, "I can't imagine how we ever drifted into requiring parents to send their children to particular schools." Alexander Redefines Public School, *The Washington Times,* March 19, 1991, A-5.

28. *Id.* Independent and private schools are unable to receive federal or state funds unless they submit to government regulation and control. Control is the reason neither political party wants to give up the race to dominate education. It is not excellence in education which is the true object of federal reform. Control is the true object. Independent and private schools have achieved the highest success in student

accomplishment. If an independent school is doing a superb job in education, however, it is not entitled to assistance unless it submits to governmental control and regulations. *Federal control, therefore, is more important than student achievement.* Ironically, independent schools which succumb to the temptation of accepting government funds, will then be subject to a myriad of regulations under which other schools have labored, tending to produce lesser student achievement.

29. *See* Real Differences on Education Between Clinton and Bush Come Down to Commitment, Money, *Wall Street Journal*, Aug. 6, 1992, A-14. *See also* Clinton-Gore on Education *supra* note 6 at p. [3].

30. Former Director of the Office of Personnel Management Donald Devine has recognized that control is the real issue. He writes, "the problem is the monopoly of government control itself: that those who manage public institutions can assume they have a captive student audience that must accept the results of the political bargaining taking place." Devine observes that, "the problem for Mr. Alexander, who apparently agrees with the critique, is that he knows the extremely powerful NEA and its allies in Congress will fight choice to death." As Governor of Tennessee, Mr. Alexander "dealt away choice to the educational establishment in a deal to establish merit pay." Devine concluded encouraging then Secretary Alexander to set a few priorities and confront the NEA in the style of Ronald Reagan. Education Reformer or Cheerleader?, *The Washington Times*, Feb. 19, 1991, D-3.

31. FRANCIS P. PRUCHA, AMERICAN INDIAN POLICY IN CRISIS (Norman, OK: University of Oklahoma Press, 1976) 269-70. President Clinton's support for a core curriculum is not exactly a novel federal innovation.

32. *Id.* at 270.

33. *Id.* at 296 (emphasis added).

34. *Id.* at 298-302. For the text of Commissioner Morgan's proposals *see* FRANCIS P. PRUCHA, ED., AMERICANIZING THE AMERICAN INDIANS, *Supplemental Report on Indian Education,* (Cambridge, MA: Harvard University Press, 1973) 221-38.

35. U.S. Senate, 1969 Report of the Committee on Labor and Public Welfare, Special Sub-committee on Indian Education, SEN. RES. 80, 91st Cong., 1st Sess. (Washington, D.C., 1969).

36. *Id.* at 21.

37. *Id.* This report concluded that the federal effort resulted in "absenteeism, dropouts, negative self-image, low achievement and ultimately, academic failure for many Indian children." This is no recipe for building "self-esteem."

38. Press Release *supra* note 5.

39. *See generally* PRUCHA *supra* note 30 at 299. *See also* STEVEN UNGER, ED., THE DESTRUCTION OF AMERICAN INDIAN FAMILIES (New York: Association of American Indian Affairs 1977) 14-17.

40. U.S. CONST. art. 1, § 8, cl. 17.

41. U.S., Congress, House, Representative Mitchill delivered the report on President Madison's March 4, 1809 proposal for the establishment of a seminary of learning, 11th Cong., 3rd sess., 18 February 1811, THE ANNALS OF THE CONGRESS OF THE UNITED STATES, contained in Joseph Gales, comp., THE DEBATES AND PROCEEDINGS OF THE CONGRESS OF THE UNITED STATES, 42 vols., (Washington: Gales and Seaton, 1834) at 22:977 (Library of American Civilization 21624).

42. U.S. Department of Commerce, Economic and Statistics Administration, Public Education Finances 1988-89, Table 18, States Ranked According to Selected Per-Pupil Elementary-Secondary Public School System Revenue Amounts, 1988-89 (GF89-10),

1989, p. 82. Alaska ranked the highest at $8,216 revenue per pupil and Utah the lowest at $2,818. The District's immediate neighbors Maryland and Virginia did not enjoy the revenue per pupil that the District enjoyed. Maryland was ranked 8th among the States at $5,654 per pupil and Virginia ranked 21st at $4,749.

43. *Id.* at Table 19, States Ranked According to Selected Per-Pupil Elementary-Secondary Public School System Expenditure Amounts, 1988-89, p. 83. Alaska was still rated first with an average expenditure of $7,866 per pupil. The United States average was $4,813. The District's neighbor Maryland was ranked 7th at $5,557, while Virginia was ranked 23rd at $4,767 dollars expended per pupil.

44. The Department of Education, National Center for Education Statistics, Digest of Education Statistics, Table 159, Current Expenditures Per-Pupil in Average Daily Attendance in Public Elementary-Secondary Schools, 1988-89, (NCES 91-697) November 1991, p. 156.

45. *Id.* at Table 89, Enrollment of the 130 Largest Public School Districts, Fall 1989, p. 100. The District ranked 28th in the Fall of 1989 with an official enrollment of 81,301 students, well behind neighboring Montgomery County, Maryland's 19th ranking and enrollment of 100,261, Prince Georges County, Maryland's 16th ranking and enrollment of 106,974, and Fairfax County, Virginia's 10th ranking and enrollment of 126,261.

46. The Department of Education, National Center for Education Statistics, Survey Report-December 1990, Table 11A, Student Teacher Ratios (NCES 91-074), p. 76.

47. Digest *supra* note 43 at Table 73, Estimated Average Annual Salary of Teachers in Public Elementary and Secondary Schools by State, 1969-70 to 1989-90, p. 82.

48. Digest *supra* note 43 at Table 74, Minimum Teacher Salary by State, 1989-90, p. 83. Again, only Alaska ($29,763), New York ($25,000) and this time Hawaii ($23,381) paid more on average to beginning teachers. When compared to its neighbors, the District is higher though comparable. Maryland's average was $22,172 and Virginia's $21,217. These figures place the District, Maryland and Virginia above the national average of $20,476.

49. Digest *supra* note 44 at Table 127, Scholastic Aptitude Score Averages by State, 1989-90, p. 126. A score between 200 and 800 is possible.

50. Digest *supra* note 44 at Table 127.

51. Clinton-Gore on Education, *supra* note 7 at p. [2].

52. U.S., Congress, House, 39th Cong., 2nd sess., 5 June 1866, THE CONGRESSIONAL GLOBE at 2968.

53. *Id.* at 2969.

Part III

Choosing Freedom In American Education

Part III

Choosing Freedom In American Education

Anyone familiar with the expanding scope of federal and state power over education in the United States should understand that with greater centralization also comes increased control and loss of freedom. Joseph Califano, former Secretary of the United States Department of Health, Education and Welfare exhibited an awareness of this danger. Secretary Califano warned that "in its most extreme form, national control of curriculum is a form of national control of ideas."[1]

The truth of this warning is a good place to begin Part III. Not only was this warning proven in Germany,[2] it is being daily proven in the United States. If the example of Germany sounds extreme, consider that it did not sound extreme to Germans in the late 1930s. It sounded no more extreme to them as "America 2000" or "Goals 2000: Educate America Act" sounds to us. Even so, extreme or not, the point is that centralized influence or control of education is to be avoided as harmful to liberty. Any government, especially our own, which knowingly ignores and suppresses the lawful and Constitutional limitations upon its express delegated powers, can also be expected to suppress the right of its people to self-government, parental liberty and intellectual freedom.

Part III, therefore, is concerned with political and legal action to deliver the American mind from captivity and defund institutions that suppress parental rights. It is concerned with disestablishing the unconstitutional Department of Education, and like the established church, the state established school will become a thing of the past.

Some will ignore these mandates and will defend the official government approved idea that the civil government must fund education in government-approved institutions, and that the federal government is well within its Constitutional power to compel taxpayers to support such an undertaking. Such

229

as these have accepted this government approved doctrine instilled by the government in them since their youth, and they refuse to know anything else but this approach.[3] They will never accept the laws of nature and of nature's God, by whatever name that law is called. They will not believe that God has given parents the unalienable right to direct the education of their own children despite the evidence for that proposition. The Declaration is simply too old to accept. Let each choose their beliefs as he or she will.[4]

Notes

1. JOSEPH A. CALIFANO, JR., GOVERNING AMERICA (New York: Simon & Schuster, 1981) 297.

2. The recent debacle of the East German government has resulted in some unanticipated education results. For many years, the East German government had required every college student to study four years of Communist ideology irrespective of his career path. But now, "[i]n Universities through[out] Eastern Europe, the rigid, Soviet inspired curriculum that made Marxism-Leninism . . . mandatory for all students is being eliminated. . . ." The sole purpose of such mandatory instruction, according to one student, was "to put the ideology of the country in the people's heads." *The Washington Post*, May 10, 1990, page A-41. Justice Blackmun acknowledged the same effect in America when he said: "The school is designed to, and inevitably will, inculcate ways of thought and outlooks." Board of Ed. v. Pico, 457 U.S. 853, 879 (1982) (Blackmun, J., concurring in part).

3. Predictably typical of this view are recipients of federal subsidies. *See* "Rethinking the Federal Role in Education," *Harvard Educational Review*, Volume 52, Number 4 (November 1982).

4. Judges 11:24.

Chapter 15

Real Freedom

The duties of parents to their children, as being their natural guardians, consist in maintaining and educating them during the season of infancy and youth, and in making reasonable provision for their future usefulness and happiness in life, by a situation suited to their habits, and a competent provision for the exigencies of that situation.[1]

Where to Start?

This Chapter is written for the legal and policy expert and is quite technical in a Constitutional sense. Any reader, however, may yet find the first eight or so pages valuable if interested in model state legislation to secure parental rights. Other readers may wish to skip over to Chapter 16 for basic questions and answers.

The place to begin for those interested in implementing change, is with the laws of nature and of nature's God as articulated in the Declaration of Independence. Do not think this point can be skipped over because the Declaration can be politically dangerous. *The entire subject of educational disestablishment is politically dangerous! Ask James Madison and Thomas Jefferson about their equivalent experience with religious disestablishment.* The laws of nature are actually the least of the difficulties. In this regard, it is better to simply realize that the government approved mind will always argue that reform should be approached as it always is approached--with reliance on expediency as a rule in drafting legislation.[2]

Having said this about the laws of nature and the Declaration, it must also be observed that neither the Declaration nor the various constitutions based thereon are self-implementing. There is abundant proof that "a mere demarcation on parchment of the constitutional limits of the several departments, is not a sufficient guard against those encroachments which lead to the tyrannical concentration of all the powers of government in the same hands."[3] The laws of nature and the Declaration need ordinary people who are persuaded by the evidence supporting its truth and relevance, to advance and defend its principles in a legislative setting.

The Unalienable Right of Parents to Educate

A short review of such principles is therefore in order. One would do well to remember and advance the principles of the laws of nature and of nature's God. We have already reviewed this law in detail and it need not be reiterated here except to point out its central features.   This law indicates that parents are endowed with certain unalienable rights; that parents have the superior legal right and duty to educate their children. The legal basis for a teacher's authority to educate is and must, therefore, be derived immediately from the child's parents by free consent.[4] Teachers have no right to teach unless they can demonstrate that a parent has *contractually* extended them specific authorization to do so. The authority of a teacher does not come from themselves, from teacher organizations or from the civil government for none of these has the power to give consent. A child's residence within a community will not suffice to give a local teacher or school the authority to teach that child. Only the free and voluntary consent of a child's parents will suffice. And if that consent is withheld, then that choice must not be disturbed by any person or civil government.[5]

Moreover, state laws that mandate certification of teachers, require approval of curriculum, set minimal qualifications or educational standards, or compel attendance or education, violate the unalienable right of parents. The state school must be disestablished and its facilities either sold to the private sector or converted to a legitimate civil governmental function.

The Unalienable Right of Intellectual Freedom

The trustworthy legislator, policy expert or parent must also remember to articulate the principle of intellectual liberty. Civil government wrongly assumes authority over the opinions and the minds of its people by forcing them to be exposed to government approved ideas, or by forcing them to finance the teaching of those ideas, or by forcing them to underwrite and support those who teach such ideas.

At the elementary, secondary and high school levels, the principle of intellectual freedom prohibits local, state and federal authorities from compelling attendance or education at schools. Compulsory attendance or education laws are the equivalent to forcing a child to be exposed to the government's view of life and the government's perspective on the world of ideas. The issue is not that children may disbelieve the ideas to which they are exposed. Certainly they may disbelieve them. The legal issue is, that children may not be compelled by the civil government to be exposed to ideas in the first instance. Thus, the civil government has no authority to direct the attention and thinking of children to those ideas, core curriculums or National Standards, which, in the civil government's judgment, are worthy of propagation, "outcomes" or "demonstrated competency."

No human law should coerce parents to send their children to be exposed to government approved ideas and opinions. These ideas may in one case, be contrary to parental desire and in another consistent therewith. But whether contrary or consistent, the coercive nature of the exposure breaches the liberty of parents to teach or choose their child's own instructor free from state compulsion or regulation.

If a state statute or teachers' union policy interferes with an instructor or teacher who educates according to the contractual arrangement existing between himself or herself and the child's parents, then such a law or policy is also harsh. Statutes and ordinances that in any way regulate or interfere with such education are contrary to the principle that God created the mind free. This is no less true in the context of the state church than it is in the context of the state school.

State statutes that compel government funding, erection and/or maintenance of a school building or financial support of teachers by taxation, are contrary to an individual's right to support only those ideas which he or she believes.[6] The issue is not that taxpayers may disbelieve the ideas they are taxed to support. The legal issue is that taxpayers are being compelled by the civil government to support ideas in the first instance.

Compulsory education and finance laws are no less a usurpation of the freedom of the mind today than similar laws with respect to religious ideas were in Thomas Jefferson's day. The legislative remedy for such abuse is to free education from civil oversight by, 1) repealing the present practices of compulsory influence, exposure and financial support, 2) enacting laws or adopting state constitutional provisions that protect parental rights and intellectual freedom, and 3) by providing statutory punishments and judicial remedies[7] for parents and their agents against any person who interferes with a parent's educational choice, and/or a parent and child's intellectual freedom.[8]

Model State Constitutional Amendments or Legislation

Central to disestablishment is the adoption of state constitutional provisions or the enactment of state legislation intended to protect unalienable rights. The following is a Model Act designed to incorporate many of the suggestions previously discussed. It is designed to present the general idea of intellectual freedom and of unalienable rights. Though its wording is not perfect, its object is certain. This measure or its legal equivalent should be considered by state legislatures who are serious about their obligation to secure the unalienable rights of the people and of parents.

If a state has already constitutionalized deprivation of parental rights or intellectual liberty through its educational establishment provisions, then those provisions will have to be repealed or amended and suitable constitutional provisions substituted before enabling legislation can be adopted. The language of Sections 3 and 8 below would be suitable for constitutional inclusion as stand alone amendments.

AN ACT to Further Secure Unalienable Rights: of Intellectual Freedom and of Parents

Section 1. [Authority and Construction]
This Act shall be liberally construed to secure intellectual freedom and the unalienable right of parents to direct the education and upbringing of their own children free from international, federal, state, county, municipal and private interference, regulation and control.

This Act is an appropriate legislative expression of the laws of nature and of nature's God as embodied in the Declaration of Independence, the principles of which are hereby expressly acknowledged as binding on this state as a member of the Union on equal footing with all other states. [Cite to admission statute or Declaration if original state.]

This Act implements and furthers the meaning of this state's constitutional section referring to unalienable or inherent rights [where applicable; indicate that this statute or Act is intended to further the meaning of the state's constitutional provision.]

This Act is a valid exercise of the power reserved to the States under the Tenth Amendment of the United States Constitution. Its object is to define and secure the unalienable rights of parents retained by the people as guaranteed in the Ninth Amendment of the United States Constitution.

Section 2. [Definitions and Exclusions]
a) For the purposes of this Act alone, the term "parent" includes a natural parent, legal guardian or any person acting *in loco parentis* pursuant to a contract for educational services, but shall not include any governmental entity.

b) The term "education" includes any instruction, propagation or discipline that is intended to enlighten or expose one to any idea, set of ideas or curriculum, whether formal or informal, directly or indirectly.

c) The terms "children," "child," or "minor" shall include any person under the age of [insert relevant state age of majority, *i.e.,* 16-21 years of age.]

d) Nothing herein shall be construed to prohibit the state legislature from establishing, funding and maintaining institutions to: 1) instruct any member of this state's Militia in military science; 2) provide instruction or education to persons lawfully incarcerated, provided participation is on a voluntary basis, except in the case of minors where the state acts in *parens patriae* pursuant to a lawful court order; or 3) preclude making available information or publications pertaining to the operation of any governmental entity or service.

e) Specific performance shall not be judicially ordered in cases or controversies arising *ex contractu* between parents and their educational agents, though other relief or damages, legal and equitable may be ordered.

Section 3. [Unalienable Rights of Parents]

a) Every parent has the unalienable right to direct the education and upbringing of his or her child, free from any civil governmental interference, regulation or control.

b) No law shall control, regulate or alienate this right, including any law relative to when, where, by whom or in what manner children are to be educated.

c) No parent shall be compelled to expose his or her own child to any education, curriculum or instruction, nor shall any parent be punished or fined for failure to instruct or expose their own children to same.

Section 4. [Limited Parental Liability]

a) No minor child shall be considered or declared abused or neglected or otherwise in need of services [refer to relevant governmental social services agencies or standards] solely on the basis that his or her parent has not attended to his or her education.

b) No parent shall be declared unfit [refer to relevant portion of the probate code where applicable] or be deprived of custody of his or her child solely on the basis that a parent has not attended to his or her child's education.

c) No child has any right to compel his or her parent to provide him or her with an education, the natural relationship between parent and child not being subject to regulation by any civil power. No governmental entity shall interfere with the parent-child relationship, absent demonstrable evidence indicating imminent endangerment of the physical health or physical safety of the child. No governmental entity shall interfere with the parent-child relationship on the basis of a psychological or mental condition arising from the child's education or lack thereof.

d) Whether or not a parent attends to the education of his or her child shall not control a judicial determination of whether or not the best interests of the child are legally met.

Section 5. [Financial Support]

a) No person shall be compelled to financially support by any means including taxation, fees, assessments or by any other means, any teacher, school, school district, education, instruction in any idea, set of ideas or any curriculum.

b) No person shall be compelled to financially support by any means including taxation, fees, assessments or by any other means, any commission or endowment for science, arts or humanities, or any school, trade, educational or teaching institution, community college, college or university whatsoever.

Section 6. [Compulsion in Attendance]
No minor child shall be compelled to attend any school, educational or teaching institution whatsoever. Nothing herein shall be construed to prohibit any parent from compelling his or her own minor child from attending any school, home school, or educational or teaching institution whatsoever.

Section 7. [Regulation of Parents and Teachers Prohibited]
a) No person shall be subject to any registration, licensure, certification, approval or review by any state, county, local or other governmental authority, or governmental agency as a condition or qualification to teach or instruct any child.

b) Nothing in this section shall be construed to prohibit any private authority or organization from establishing voluntary standards or regulating its own voluntary membership.

c) No civil government or its agents shall be eligible to enter into a contract for educational services except as permitted in Section 2(d).

Section 8. [Intellectual Freedom]
a) All persons shall be free to profess, and by argument to maintain, their opinions, and that the same shall in no wise diminish, enlarge, or affect their unalienable, civil or any constitutional rights. No person shall be restrained, harassed, or interfered with in his or her person or property by any state, county, local or other governmental authority, or governmental agency, nor shall otherwise suffer on account of his or her own opinions or beliefs nor on account of transmitting those beliefs to his or her child.

b) Nothing in this section shall be construed to affect the laws of this state pertaining to [refer to laws protecting minors from exposure to lewd or pornographic materials.]

Section 9. [Freedom of Contract]
Every parent shall be free to select or not select his or her own agent as tutor, instructor or teacher and no state, county, local or other governmental authority, or governmental agency, shall approve, license, register, certify or otherwise regulate or interfere with that freedom.

Section 10. [Judicial Relief]
Any parent, natural guardian or any of their lawful agents who are
interfered with by any person acting under state law, color of state law or
in a private capacity in any way prohibited by this Act, except as provided
in Section 2(e), has a right to seek legal and equitable relief including
double damages, costs and attorney fees in an appropriate court of
competent jurisdiction in this state. [Define the court(s) of competent
jurisdiction. Determine whether statutory attorney fee should be imposed
against defendant if plaintiff prevails on any of its merits.]

Section 11. [Nature of Rights and Freedom]
The rights and freedoms asserted herein are the natural and unalienable
rights of parents and of intellectual freedom. All restraint thereof is
against the laws of nature and is the hallmark of tyranny.

This is the essence of state legislation designed to secure unalienable rights
pertaining to education.[9] This legislative approach can also be used in concert
with a judicial approach. A state court has jurisdiction to strike down compulsory
or regulatory education laws, or accomplish disestablishment provided that the
state constitution or a statute expressly indicates that the people are guaranteed
certain unalienable, inherent or natural rights. This state constitutional or statutory
provision should declare that unalienable rights exist in an explicitly general, and
preferably in a specific, way. The reason that a legislative expression is
necessary, is because courts are not empowered to find and articulate unalienable
rights on their own accord (*sua sponte*).

What About Federal Jurisdiction?
Apart from the Constitutional provision encouraging science and literature
by the exclusive means of patent and copyright laws, the power to maintain a
military and provide for the militia, and the power to encourage learning in the
District of Columbia without drawing funds from the treasury, Congress is wholly
without delegated power in this sphere. Furthermore, the power to promote higher
education and research "by proper premiums and provisions," including grants,
was rejected at the Convention in 1787.

Adherence to the Constitution requires that Congress repeal as
unconstitutional, the Department of Education and all federal laws extending
premiums, provisions, funding, endowments and grants to public and private
recipients. If Congress fails to act, a federal court has jurisdiction to hold such
laws unconstitutional and enjoin their operation on the basis that they exceed the
limited powers extended by the federal Constitution to Congress, especially under
Article I, section 8.[10]

A federal court, however, may only entertain federal jurisdiction to strike
down compulsory or regulatory *state* education laws or accomplish state

disestablishment of education *provided* that the federal constitution or a federal statute secures unalienable, inherent or natural rights. This federal constitutional or statutory provision should cite to the right, and evidence should exist that the right is of the unalienable variety. A review of the present Constitution and federal statutes, however, indicates that neither the unalienable right of parents to educate or intellectual freedom is enumerated or expressed.[11] The next question then becomes, does Congress have any Constitutional jurisdiction to find and articulate these rights?

The only Constitutional power that Congress may possibly employ to articulate and statutorily protect presently un-enumerated unalienable rights is found in:

1) Article I, section 8, pertaining to the express powers of Congress,

2) Article IV, sections 3 and 4 pertaining to the admission of states into the Union on equal footing with other states and the Congressional guarantee of a republican form of government, or

3) the Fourteenth Amendment, section 1, pertaining to the privileges and immunities of federal citizenship, in combination with section 5 granting Congress power to enforce that section and clause.

The Federal Guarantee of Republican Government
A. Federal Jurisdiction and Unenumerated Unalienable Rights

We have already spent several Chapters demonstrating that option number 1 pertaining to Article I, section 8 and the express powers of Congress, does not grant Congress any power to statutorily protect either the unalienable right of parents or intellectual freedom.

Moreover, option number 2, Article IV, section 3 and 4 pertaining to the admission of states into the Union on equal footing with other states and the Congressional guarantee of a republican form of government has also been discussed in previous Chapters. It was pointed out that Congress relied upon these Constitutional provisions to enact federal statutes to admit each state (beyond the original thirteen) into the union. Some of these statutes contain provisions that incorporate by express references the principles of the Declaration, which include the general proposition that persons are endowed by their Creator with certain unalienable rights. In essence Congress has required that the state's constitution and laws made in pursuance thereof must conform to the "principles of the Declaration of Independence."[12]

Any state law that abridges the unalienable educational rights of parents or of intellectual freedom clearly does not conform to the "principles of the Declaration of Independence." So may one obtain a remedy in federal court under the federal admission statute relative to that state under Article IV, section 3 and section 4? No. Even though the argument is appealing, the clause cannot be made to stretch so far as to give the federal courts power to define or enumerate rights flowing from the laws of nature and nature's God as affirmed by the

Declaration. Unenumerated substantive unalienable rights such as parental educational rights and the like cannot be enacted by Congress *via* Article IV or a federal admission statute, or by the federal courts through interpretation thereof. The former would involve Congress in the exercise of a power not Constitutionally enumerated or extended to it, and the latter would involve the federal judiciary in the extra-constitutional process of identifying rights--a legislative function by its very nature (and a state legislative function by virtue of principles of federalism).[13]

B. Federal Jurisdiction and State Enumerated Unalienable Rights

If the federal Congress or courts are not empowered to protect or identify unalienable rights, then are they empowered to enforce previously enumerated state statutory or constitutional unalienable rights? If so, what is the actual federal jurisdictional basis to construe *state* enumerated unalienable rights? Does Article IV, section 4 of the United States Constitution provide a basis for federal jurisdiction? That Article as we have seen, empowers the United States to "guarantee to every state in this union a Republican form of government . . . ." If the reference to republican government could embody both the form *and* the object of state government, *i.e.,* -- the security of state constitutionally enumerated unalienable rights, then could federal jurisdiction exist?

But if reference to republican government embodies only a naked federal guarantee of a republican *form* of government and *not* federal security of the object of state government, *i.e.,*--the security of state constitutionally enumerated unalienable rights--then federal courts have no Article IV jurisdiction to adjudicate whether a specific state law contravenes a state constitutionally defined and enumerated unalienable right. The better argument appears to be that direct Article IV jurisdiction would improperly involve the federal courts in an extra-constitutional definition of a republican government beyond questions of its form. Since the text of Article IV refers only to the "form" of government, it appears that the exercise of any power beyond questions of the form, are not federal questions. Thus, neither the federal Congress nor federal courts are empowered to enforce previously enumerated state statutory or constitutionally enumerated unalienable rights under Article IV.

In other words, where the people or their state legislative representatives have identified and embodied unalienable rights in their state laws or constitution, federal courts *do not* have jurisdiction *via* Article IV *and* under that state's Congressional admission statute (the enabling Act), to decide whether state legislation alleged to deny or disparage an enumerated unalienable right, contravenes the relevant state constitutional provision pertaining to unalienable rights. The remedy lies in state court, but if the decision of the highest state court is found wanting, an appeal to the United States Supreme Court on the question of jurisdiction under Article IV would first have to be resolved and from what has been previously considered, the United States Supreme Court ought to deny the appeal on the basis that the Constitution's Article IV provides it with no jurisdiction to reach the merits.[14]

Federal courts are not otherwise free to roam among the archives of history or the laws of nature in order to enforce their own notions of unalienable or natural rights. Moreover, while republican principles pertain to adoption of a form of government suitable to secure unalienable rights, they do not define the unalienable rights themselves. Identification and articulation of unalienable rights is the business of the people and the states in the federal system. Moreover, the question of whether or not the state constitutional enumeration of rights by the people thereof are *bona fide* unalienable rights in that they are given by God to all human beings, is a political question not open to federal judicial review.[15]

The Privileges and Immunities Clause

With respect to option number 3) stated above, the Fourteenth Amendment, section 1, prohibits a state from making or enforcing any law "which shall abridge the privileges or immunities of citizens of the United States." It is self-evident that current judicial use of the due process or equal protection clause as a basis for federal courts to find, define and enumerate textually unspecified substantive rights is a fraudulent enterprise in the art of usurpation, and deserves no further comment except that which is reserved to the rule of expediency in construction.[16] Thus, the only other contender for consideration is the privileges and immunities clause which covers those persons born or naturalized in the United States and subject to its jurisdiction. Section 5 grants Congress power to enforce "by appropriate legislation, the provisions" of the amendment.

A. What are Privileges and Immunities?

Perhaps the first question in exploring this section and clause is what is meant by the terms "privileges or immunities of citizens?" Under the Fourteenth Amendment, no state can make or enforce any law which abridges the privileges and immunities of citizens of the United States--meaning those privileges which are extended by the United States to its citizens, and not any rights which are unalienable.

In *The Slaughter House Cases*,[17] Justice Miller, writing for the majority considered the notion set forth by Justice Washington in *Corfield v. Coryell*, that the privileges and immunities clause could include the liberty which belongs as a matter of right to the citizens of all governments exercisable subject only to such restraints "as the government may prescribe for the general good of the whole."[18] The Supreme Court, however, held that the "privileges and immunities" clause of the Fourteenth Amendment included only those civil rights which owe their existence to the federal government, its national character, its Constitution, or its laws, including the right to travel to the seat of its government to assert any claim a citizen may have upon it, transact any business with it, freely access its seaports and look to its protection when upon the high seas or subject to a foreign jurisdiction.[19]

In other words, the Court ruled that the privileges and immunities of an American citizen "are those which are incident to the citizenship of the United States, but do not include rights pertaining to state citizenship and derived solely from the relationship of the citizen and his state established by state law."[20] The dissent by Justice Field was of the opposite opinion, that the Fourteenth "amendment was intended to give practical effect to the declaration of 1776 of inalienable rights, rights which are the gift of the Creator, which the law does not confer, but only recognizes."[21]

In the context of education, parental rights and intellectual freedom it does not appear therefore that the Fourteenth Amendment's privileges and immunities clause was intended to secure by federal authority, unalienable rights. The right of parents and freedom of the mind are absolute; they are not given up as a precondition to enter into a state of society and they are not a function of or incident to citizenship of the United States. Such rights precede the existence of society and are a gift from God passing directly to their intended beneficiaries without first passing through the hands of either the state or federal government.

Given this understanding, Congress can pass no law, and no federal court could employ the privileges or immunities clause as a basis for the protection of the unalienable rights of parents or freedom of the mind. To conclude otherwise and include the educational rights sought herein to be vindicated, among the powers of the federal government, would be to confer upon Congress a vast and irresponsible power.

B. The Security of Unenumerated Education Related Unalienable Rights is not Granted To the Federal Government.

Did the Fourteenth Amendment's privileges or immunities clause confer such a vast power upon Congress? No, the amendment was not adopted in order to vest Congress with unbounded jurisdiction to find and define the unalienable rights of man, which have always been and still remain the province of the states' Bill of Rights, or under Article V. The Fourteenth Amendment was not meant to empower Congress to statutorily add to the federal Bill of Rights or statutorily supersede state constitutional provisions defining unalienable rights.

The security and protection of unalienable rights are not fit objects best protected by the people as one nation. The argument to the contrary may very well be compelling, but the principle that rights are a national object requiring uniformity dictated by the national government was only accepted in a limited way in Article I, sections 9 and 10, and subsequently in the Bill of Rights. These constitutional provisions, however, specifically spell out various rights in detail.

Consequently, the reference to the "privileges or immunities of citizens of the United States" is not a reference to unalienable rights. Justice Field's dissenting view that the words privileges and immunities mean "the declaration of 1776 of inalienable rights, rights which are the gift of the Creator, which the law does not confer, but only recognizes," is not correct. Thus, his conclusion that the amendment transferred enforcement of such rights to the federal government (either concurrently or exclusively) is contrary to the general notion of federalism and the limited and well defined exceptions to that theory. The Court's holding, therefore, in the *Slaughter-House Cases*[22] on the question of the limited scope of the privileges and immunities clause is correct.[23]

The amendment did not intend to completely overturn the state's exclusive power to define the bulk of unalienable rights by so fundamental and drastic a measure as to empower Congress with a virtually undefined power to find and articulate the unalienable rights of man. In close calls, express specificity is warranted for legal conclusions of such magnitude.

If all this sounds confusing, remember that generally speaking, the power to *define* unalienable right lies with the most immediate representatives of the people--the state legislatures. The power to *enforce* state enumerated unalienable rights lies with the state courts. This arrangement makes good sense because the people are free to define their liberties, rather than un-elected federal judges. As the situation now stands, repeal of compulsory education and financial support laws through the *state legislature* is the constitutional means of securing unalienable rights; a task well within the grasp of parents and common people of good will.

Notes

1. JAMES KENT, COMMENTARIES ON AMERICAN LAW (New York: O. Halsted, 1826; reprint ed., New York: Da Capo Press, 1971) 2:159 (citations omitted). "The wants and weaknesses of children render it necessary that some person maintain them, and the voice of nature has pointed out the parent as the most fit and proper person. The laws and customs of all nations have enforced this plain precept of universal law." *Id.* (citations omitted).

2. No matter how "politically noble" federal "reform" of education may appear, "the usurpation of powers not granted is criminal and odious." JAMES D. RICHARDSON, ED., COMPILATION OF THE MESSAGES AND PAPERS OF THE PRESIDENTS, 1789-1897 (Washington, D.C.: Government Printing Office, 1896) 2:311, First Annual Message of John Quincy Adams, December 6, 1825.

3. THE FEDERALIST NO. 48 (J. Madison).

4. The legal rule that the agent has no authority independent of the principal, has been long established. Thus, the agent has no primary or original right to teach children who are not his or her own, nor has the agent the right to teach that which is contrary to the directives of the student's parents.

5. No proper legislative principle can vindicate state interposition of the law in private contracts. Even Congress reiterated this principle, applying it to far more than contracts of indebtedness when it declared in The Northwest Territory Ordinance of 1787: "And, in the just preservation of rights and property, it is understood and declared, that no law ought ever to be made or have force in the said territory, that shall, in any manner whatever, interfere with or affect private contracts, or engagements, *bona fide*, and without

fraud previously formed." RICHARD PERRY, ED., SOURCES OF OUR LIBERTIES (American Bar Foundation: Chicago, Ill., 1978) 395.

6. Elementary and secondary public school expenditures (in constant 1987-88 dollars) are expected to increase from 161.5 billion in 1988-89 to 212.0 billion in 1999-2000. *See* National Center for Education Statistics, "Projections of Education Statistics to 2000," Office of Education Research and Improvement, U.S. Department of Labor (NCES 89-648) 1989.

7. The question of federal judicial remedies and their relationship to enforcement of Ninth and Tenth Amendment rights and powers is dealt with in Chapter 2.

8. A four-fold approach to disestablishment may include the following matters:

I. Preliminary Action
Local Level: 1. Run for election on the local school board; 2. Work to persuade the school board to adopt a liberal policy of accommodating parents who request that their child be exempt from participation in objectionable assignments or activities. Do not limit such a policy to a religious rationale.
State Level: 1. The state legislature should repeal laws that monitor or regulate home education and private schools; 2. The state legislature should repeal laws which require any home schooling parent or teacher to be state certified.
Federal Level: 1. Oppose Congressional voucher legislation.

II. Respecting Parental Rights
Local Level: 1. The school board should adopt a policy of accommodating the expressed wishes of a parent regarding the state education of his or her child; 2. Where accommodation of the express wishes of a parent regarding the state education of his or her child may cause a substantial disruption to the school's overall function and economy, the school board should excuse the child from attendance and permit the parent to bear the responsibility and cost.
State Level: 1. The state legislature should repeal laws which require compulsory attendance or penalize non-attendance at state elementary, secondary and high schools; 2. The state legislature should repeal its laws relating to accreditation of any educational institution or laws relating to granting diploma or degrees in its name; 3. The state legislature should enact general legislation securing the unalienable right of parents to direct the education and upbringing of their children free from state interference, regulation or control; 4. State constitutions should be amended to declare that the unalienable rights of parents are to be protected by the state and not subjected to balancing of interests.
Federal Level: 1. Congress should adopt measures to recognize and secure the unalienable right of parents who serve in the armed forces; 2. Congress should repeal legislation relating to education research and the collection of educational statistics.

III. Financial Freedom
Local Level: 1. Local governments should repeal laws that divert local tax revenues to educational objects of any type; 2. Local governments should either sell their state schools, rent them to private educational organizations or convert them to a legitimate governmental use.
State Level: 1. The state legislature should repeal laws (or the people should alter their constitution) to disestablish state elementary, secondary and high schools; 2. The state legislature should repeal state laws which divert tax revenues to state elementary, secondary and high school education, including teachers' and administrators' salaries.
Federal Level: 1. Congress should repeal legislation and related federal regulations (CFR) which divert federal tax revenues to state and local, elementary, secondary and high schools under any program, project, grant or special purpose fund.

IV. Freeing Higher Education

State Level: 1. The state legislature should disestablish its state supported institutions of higher learning, repeal laws that divert tax revenues thereto and sell its interests in such entities; 2. Community College property taxation districts should be abolished.

Federal Level: 1. Congress should repeal legislation establishing the Federal Department of Education and its unconstitutional functions; 2. Congress should repeal legislation and related federal regulations (CFR) which divert federal tax revenues to institutions of higher learning, including those located within the District of Columbia; 3. Congress should repeal legislation providing for federal student financial assistance.

9. This legislation is intended to operate in the spirit of the religious disestablishment law enacted in Virginia which declares:

> And though we know well that this assembly, elected by the people for the ordinary purposes of legislation only, have no power to restrain the acts of succeeding Assemblies, constituted with powers equal to our own, and that therefore to declare this act irrevocable would be of no effect in law; yet we are free to declare and do declare, that the rights hereby asserted are of the natural rights of mankind, and that if any act shall be hereafter passed to repeal the present or to narrow its operation, such act will be an infringement of natural right.

An Act for Religious Freedom, adopted by the Virginia General Assembly on January 16, 1786. VA. CODE ANN. § 57-1 (1950).

10. *See* Chapters 10-13.

11. The Fourteenth Amendment's due process clause is not a source of substantive rights, but was intended to curtail state power with respect to procedural due process. Though the Court has often looked to this provision and the equal protection clause, to judicially add their own notions of un-enumerated rights to the Constitution, the use of judicial power to do so is beyond the legitimate nature of judicial power as well as Article III. *See generally* ROBERT BORK, THE TEMPTING OF AMERICA (Free Press: New York, 1990) 30-32, 60, 83 and 129.

This, however, is not to say that the Constitution's Bill of Rights was not intended to enumerate unalienable rights. The submissions of the states to Congress suggesting the content of what would later become the Bill of Rights were generally prefaced with the statement that many of the proposed rights therein were unalienable. For instance, Virginia urged that a declaration of rights (*i.e.,* a Bill of Rights) should be added to the Constitution that would secure "from encroachment the essential and unalienable Rights of the People . . . ." DOCUMENTS ILLUSTRATIVE OF THE FORMATION OF THE UNION OF THE AMERICAN STATES, 69th Cong., 1st sess., House Document No. 398 (Washington, D.C.: Government Printing office, 1927) 1028, Ratification of the Constitution in Convention of the People of the Commonwealth of Virginia, June 26-27, 1788. North Carolina sought a "Declaration of Right, asserting and securing from encroachment the great Principles of civil and religious Liberty, and the unalienable Rights of the People." *Id.* at 1044, Conditions of Ratification of the Constitution in Convention of the People of the State of North Carolina, August 1, 1788, Ratified November 21, 1789. The point is that these petitions were properly made to the legislative branch (Congress), and not the judiciary (the Supreme Court).

12. *See* Chapter 3.

13. *See* Chapters 2 and 3 for a discussion on the importance of state legislative identification of unalienable rights.

14. Article IV is not a Constitutional mechanism empowering the United States to append *select* state constitutional provisions to the federal Bill of Rights.

15. The political question and doctrine of non-justiciability, preclude judicial review and are discussed in Luther v. Borden, 48 U.S. (7 How.) 1 (1849). These doctrines assert that Congress--the legislative branch--has jurisdiction to declare whether a specific form of government does or does not meet the requirements of a republican government. *Luther* and its progeny, therefore, prevent the judiciary under Article IV from declaring which rights are unalienable and which are not. *Id.* at 42.

16. *See* HERMINE H. MEYER, THE HISTORY AND MEANING OF THE FOURTEENTH AMENDMENT (New York, Vantage Press, 1977) 125-49.

17. 83 U.S. (16 Wall.) 36 (1872).

18. *Id.* at 75-76, quoting Corfield v. Coryell, 6 F. Cas. 546, 551-52 (C.C.E.D. Pa. 1823).

19. 83 U.S. (16 Wall.) 36, 79-80 (1872). Article IV, section 2 also refers to "privileges and immunities." It declares that "[t]he citizens of each State shall be entitled to all privileges and immunities of citizens in the several States." The privileges and immunities referred to by this Article include civil rights such as the right to make and enforce contracts, to sue and be a witness, to acquire, own and dispose of real estate and personal property, to engage in business, etc. They differ from those that the Fourteenth Amendment was intended to secure.

20. MEYER *supra* note 16 at 99. *See* Snowden v. Hughes, 321 U.S. 1, 6-7 (1944).

21. 83 U.S. (16 Wall.) at 105 (Field, J. dissenting). *See generally,* CLINT BOLICK, UNFINISHED BUSINESS: A CIVIL RIGHTS STRATEGY FOR AMERICA'S THIRD CENTURY (San Francisco, California: Pacific Research Institute for Public Policy, 1990) 60-68. The author indicates that the clause incorporates the unalienable rights recognized by the laws of nature and of nature's God. *See also* BORK *supra* note 11 at 180-82. Bork suggests that the clause does not incorporate unalienable rights and moreover that the clause did not vest federal judges with power to find and define these rights.

22. 16 Wall. (83 U.S.) 36, 71, 77-79 (1873).

23. *See also* MEYER *supra* note 16 at 90-111.

Chapter 16

Concerns and Objections

Exposure to something [in the classroom] does not constitute teaching, indoctrination, opposition or promotion of the things exposed.[1]

The school is designed to, and inevitably will, inculcate ways of thought and outlooks.[2]

Concerns and Objections

Disestablishment of the magnitude discussed herein will naturally result in many concerns and objections. Parents may not be sure how everything would work out if education were disestablished. Teachers may be concerned with how such actions would affect their jobs. Politicians may be concerned for the poor or for children who will not be educated by their parents just as they are now concerned about children who are not being educated by the state after 12 years of forced attendance.

It will also be helpful to remember another point illustrated by the two contradictory passages at the beginning of this Chapter. The first passage states that: "[e]xposure to something [in the classroom] does not constitute teaching, indoctrination, opposition or promotion of the things exposed." The second states quite the opposite: "[t]he school is designed to, and inevitably will, inculcate ways of thought and outlooks." These excerpts illustrate that the present approach to education is on a collision course with itself. It denies and admits in the same breath that forced exposure to ideas is truly what is at issue. The state denies that compulsory exposure promotes its ideas. Then it claims it has a right to engage in coercive exposure to its ideas and that this exposure will inculcate ways of thinking. With this background in mind, consider the following.

Concern 1.

What about the education of poor children?

Considerations in responding to Concern 1.

Simply because a parent is poor does not mean he or she is incapable of discharging parental rights. It does not mean that he or she is precluded from hiring or making charitable arrangements with others to educate their children if they so choose. Being poor, however, does mean that financial priorities will have to be scrutinized closely. It also means that local, state and federal taxes which are presently extracted from poor and rich alike to bolster the education monopoly, must be eliminated. It means that more of our money will go to people and places where we voluntarily choose to spend it, and less will go to prop up a monopolistic system of governmental controlled education.

In fact, true compassion for helping poor children receive the benefits of an education and rise above their circumstances must first begin with helping parents to see the nature of their rights and duties and then second, helping those parents who desire it, to obtain private aid and resources available to them in their local community.

With respect to the first, every parent rich or poor, has the right and duty to direct the education of his children. This right is to be exercised commensurate with the financial means available to a parent and with an appreciation of the child's abilities. Financial abundance or financial need does not alter or modify this right. Simply because parents are poor, suffer from adverse social attitudes, or suffer from the vestiges of past discrimination, does not diminish their unalienable right.

As previously noted, Francis Wayland has helped parents whether rich or poor, disadvantaged or advantaged, to understand their relative duties and rights. He says of a father for instance, that:

1.   He is bound to inform himself of the peculiar habits, and reflect upon the probable future situation, of his child, and deliberately to consider what sort of education will most conduce to his future happiness and usefulness.

2.   He is bound to select such instructors as will best accomplish the results which he believes will be most beneficial.

3.   He is bound to devote such time and attention to the subject, as will enable him to ascertain whether the instructor of his child discharges his duty with faithfulness.

4.   To encourage his child, by manifesting such interest in his studies as shall give to diligence and assiduity all the assistance and benefit of parental authority and friendship.

5.   And, if a parent be under obligation to do this, he is, of course, under obligation to take time to do it, and so to construct the arrangements of his family and business, that it may be done. He has no right to say

that he has no time for these duties. If God ha[s] required them of him, as is the fact, he has time exactly for them; and the truth is, he has not time for those other occupations which interfere with them. If he neglect[s] them, he does it to the injury of his children, and, as he will ascertain when it shall be too late, to his own disappointment and misery.[3]

In other words parents rich and poor, must review their lifestyles and priorities. If a father, for instance, examines his family's financial picture and determines to put the education of his children in proper perspective, but still finds that he has neither the time or the money to educate, he should again consider whether "the truth is, he has not time for those other occupations which interfere with them." Single parents must also examine their household finances in the same way.

Parents must be able to turn to family, neighbors, private philanthropy or religious benevolence for help. They should approach such organizations and seek to work out temporary arrangements by which their parental obligations can be financially met. Such organizations also have a need to be good stewards of their finances and are entitled to review the financial habits of applicants in making a determination of their need. This is an opportunity for family, friends and local religious organizations to help each other, and not for the government to usurp control of education or try to make parents dependent upon itself. Moreover, the opportunity for schools created, staffed and operated by Unions, to offer parents what they need will be abundant and will serve as the true test of Unionized devotion to education absent the club of a state operated monopoly.

Concern 2.

What parent has time to educate their children?

Considerations in responding to Concern 2.

Perhaps the real question is: "What parents can afford to risk the education of their children with the state?" When either the state or the parent neglects that child's education, it will always be to the ultimate injury of the parent. Parents understand this better than the state and consequently will take steps to ensure that their children are educated according to their own individual standards. The objection to parental rights based on parental prioritization of their own time, however, is really a spin-off of Concern 1 just discussed. In other words, the additional concerns and amusements of life must line up behind the education of children. Remember,

if a parent be under obligation to do this, he is, of course, under obligation *to take time to do it*, and so to construct the arrangements of his family and business, that *it may be done.* He has no right to say that *he has no time for these duties.* If God have required them of him, as is the fact, *he has time exactly for them;* and the truth is, he has not time for those other occupations which interfere with them.

<u>Concern 3.</u>
What about parents who fail to educate their child?
<u>Considerations in responding to Concern 3.</u>
It has been repeatedly observed that the failure of a parent to provide any education for their own children whatsoever, is not evidence to be considered in regards to the parent's unfitness. Such evidence *standing alone* is under the laws of nature (and ought to be under the laws of the states) insufficient to establish parental unfitness or neglect. Certainly mere failure to comply with compulsory attendance laws ought to constitute no basis for unfitness. Nor ought such a failure be considered criminal or result in loss of custody or imprisonment. The failure of a parent to educate his or her child *standing alone* ought not warrant loss of custody or imprisonment. In fact, it is no more neglect or criminal to fail to teach one's child to read his ABC's, than it is neglect or criminal to fail to teach one's child to read his catechism or religious doctrines. If those who allege unfitness were committed to ferreting out unfitness, then let it be recalled that the civil government is unfit whenever it construes the Constitution in an expedient manner, or abridges the natural rights of parents. Expediency and abridgment are by definition, unfitness.

Moreover, what about teachers in state schools who fail to educate the children? What civil punishment presently exists against the teacher for failure to educate our children? What civil remedy presently exists for the child who has been compulsorily instructed by the state, but can neither read nor write? Are all such children subjected to indifferent educators or negligent instruction at the hands of publicly paid professional educators? Is the failure of a child to learn an irrebuttable presumption of an educator's negligence? Does this make educators all child abusers?

The fact of the matter is that state school teachers are not jailed when their students fail to learn. In certain states, however, the parents of students who are home schooled are subject to being jailed if they continue to educate their children after failure to pass a state-approved standardized test. If punishment of parents for indifference were valid, then how much greater should the punishment be for those public servants who enjoy the backing of the state and assume control over education, and yet who discharge their teaching responsibilities in a negligent manner? State school teachers would be first in line for civil prosecution if legal remedies are to be applied to failed obligations.

Parents, who refuse to love their children do so at their own peril. Parents who refuse to educate their children do so to their own future grief. Parents who refuse to teach their children about God do so to their own jeopardy and future sadness. Such parents, however, break no rule which the civil government is empowered to punish. It is true that parents break the law of God which requires them to educate their own children, but it is also true that such law does not empower the state to judge what level of instruction constitutes a valid education.

Every state in the Union made a decision not to require parents to teach their children about God and religion when they disestablished their state churches. The states retained no penalty against parents who failed to educate their children about such matters. The civil government left to the parents themselves the exercise and consequences of failure to exercise their natural duty. If such disregard of parental duty is not punished by the state, how much more does the state lack authority to punish parents for failure to instruct in less significant matters than knowledge of the Creator and what he requires of human beings?

Is it not also obvious that the daily cares and exigencies of life, may in the judgment of parents, constitute a suitable education for their child? Do not forget the standard which Montgomery identified when he wrote:

> The law of nature and nature's God, which ordains that it is both the right and duty of parents to educate their children *"in such manner as they believe will be most for their future happiness"* is utterly disregarded and set at naught by the State, which ordains that it is neither the right nor the duty of parents, but of the State, to say when, where, by whom, and in what manner our children shall be educated.[4]

The law should not hinder parents, it should aid parents. The law should provide parents with a legal cause of action and legal remedy against those, who by public or private means, or under color of state law, interfere with the exercise of their unalienable rights. The civil government should not aid others in impairing the means, content or degree of instruction which parents consider suitable to their unique circumstances and their children's abilities. The law may provide no remedy for the child who, because of the indifference of the parent, fails to receive instruction. A legal remedy must be based on more than the failure of a parental duty to educate.

Concern 4.

What about parents who require their child to work for them at their home or business instead of teaching them about academic subjects?

Considerations in responding to Concern 4.

In other words, "May parents prefer suitable child labor over formal education?" The answer to that question depends on the answer to this; "Is the state qualified to declare that which is and is not educational?" "Is an apprentice program or labor, even for a child, appropriate instruction?" "Is the civil government instituted in order to secure the unalienable rights of its citizens, or instituted to certify and regulate the ideas and methods of instruction which its citizens employ?"

Remember that a parent, not the civil government "is bound to inform himself of the peculiar habits, and reflect upon the probable future situation, of his child." A parent is bound to deliberately "consider what sort of education" will most likely result in the "future happiness and usefulness" of his or her child. If a parent believes that the peculiar habits of his child warrant some form of appropriate labor, then the parent is entitled to direct the education of that child in that way.

Moreover if a parent reflects upon the probable future situation of his child and deems that the child will most likely succeed in a given vocational area, then the parent cannot be prosecuted for appropriate child labor relevant to that situation. The state is possessed of no inherent insight or knowledge not available to others which empowers it to decide what is best for the child. When the parent who knows the child best, has chosen a lawful occupation for his child to learn, the state is out of its league in declaring what the child shall learn and by whom the child shall be instructed.

Thomas Jefferson pointed out the vanity in the state's claim to know what is best for the child when he said:

> [T]he impious presumption of legislators and rulers, civil as well as ecclesiastical, who, being themselves but fallible and uninspired men, have assumed dominion over the faith of others, setting up their own opinions and modes of thinking as the only true and infallible, and as such endeavoring to impose them on others, hath established and maintained false religions over the greatest part of the world and through all time.[5]

If his analysis were applied to our educational system, the "impious presumption of legislators" and educators would be clear. Such officials including school board members, local superintendents and government lawmakers, have set up their own opinions regarding the only permissible means and degree of education. They have said that *family* child labor is impermissible or unacceptable, but *mandatory state* child labor, *i.e.*, "community volunteer work," is a necessary element of education. This is belligerent hypocrisy.

Concern 5.

Won't abolition of our public schools be discriminatory against African-Americans and other "protected groups?"

Considerations in responding to Concern 5.

Until 1954 public schools discriminated with legal impunity against African-Americans. Even today, many school districts are still under court supervision with respect to the implementation of a non-discriminatory desegregation plan. Indeed, that the public schools are no friend of "protected groups" is evidenced by a Gallup poll of the public's attitude toward the public schools indicating that 72 percent of non-whites polled supported some type of school choice option.[6]

It may be objected as discriminatory that white parents will send their children to all white schools and that black parents will have no choice but to send their kinds to all black schools. This objection would ring true under a state established system of education where the number of schools and choices were artificially limited by the state's education monopoly. But under a system of free schools, black parents would not be limited to the "left over" educational "choices" allowed them by the state monopoly.

The current problem, however, is that all parents are obstructed by the state in obtaining the education that they want their own children to receive. Some parent will object to his child being taught an Afrocentric curriculum and another will object to western history. Two-hundred years ago some parents objected to their child being taught an Anglican curriculum and another objected to Presbyterian doctrine. Not much changes when the state puts its power behind or against ideas.

Under the present system, parents who desire to have their child taught about their ethnic culture or heritage, or taught in their native tongue or instructed according to their religious values, are deterred from doing so. The schools are designed to assimilate, not liberate. Whether the state system seeks to expose a child to contrary ideas, assimilate the child into the dominate culture or completely prohibit transmission of parental values, the parents lose control no matter what their color or how economically disadvantaged they may be.

Abolition of state schools, however, will empower each parent to give his or her child exactly what each parent desires. Such an approach cannot be discriminatory unless we accept the absurd notion that parents will discriminate against their own children.

Under a disestablished system of free schools all of these objections, allegations and problems become irrelevant. These schools would be depoliticized. Parents would be free to direct the education of their own children however they wished. Parents would not be forced to subsidize education they did not agree with or simply did not wish to support. Such an approach to education, which recognizes the equal legal rights of parents, is not racially discriminatory anymore than disestablishment of religion was not religiously discriminatory.

It is true that some parents have no experience in educating their children themselves. Parents have grown so accustomed to the state exercising their rights for them that they may not know how to approach education. If these parents lack the confidence or experience to educate their own children, however, a system of parent directed education is still broad enough to recognize the right of these parents to make the choice to obtain instruction elsewhere.

It is absurd and offensive, however, to believe that African American, Hispanic American, Asian American or Native American parents for instance, are incapable of making educational choices for their children. Virtually all parents are able and competent to educate or provide for the education of their own children. With respect to those parents not so oriented, they are to be found scattered among all nations and are not unique to certain colors or peoples alone.

Many times the claim of racial discrimination in education involves the assertion that members of "protected groups" are not receiving the full opportunity to which they are entitled. In a system where the rights of parents are respected, the opportunity a child is entitled to is a function of what their parents choose to provide. The burden of education falls equally on all parents. The benefit falls on all children according to their parents' wishes, irrespective of their color or national origin.

Some may also object on the basis of economics. They point to statistics indicating that some parents are economically disadvantaged out of proportion to other parents. It is argued that such a financial impediment will result in a disproportionate impact on members of "protected groups," causing them to fall behind as a group. This argument has already been dealt with under Concern 1. It was observed that, every parent rich or poor, has the right and duty to direct the education of his children. This right is to be exercised commensurate with the financial means available to a parent and with an appreciation of the child's abilities. Simply because parents are poor or suffer from adverse social attitudes or the vestiges of past discrimination does not diminish their unalienable right to direct the education of their children free from state interference, regulation or control.

This argument has also been advanced in order to equalize tax revenues for state educational purposes across school district lines. The net effect of this approach will inevitably produce a government controlled system of education in which every state and district is required to spend an equal amount on every child. If this approach and argument are carried to their ultimate conclusion, it is only a matter of time before every state is compelled by the federal government to require those who live in more affluent districts *or states* to subsidize through judicially ordered taxation (or by legislative means), the education of children who live in less affluent districts or states. Indeed, this result has already been mandated within New Jersey as a requirement of the state constitution.[7]

Concern 6.

Won't vouchers and tuition tax credits give parents choice over their child's education?

Considerations in responding to Concern 6.

Vouchers and tuition tax credits will only "give" parents choice among state established, controlled or regulated schools. "Giving" parents choice of state approved schools, is contrary to recognition of their "right" to direct their child's education.

Examining the issue in more detail requires some definitions. What is an educational voucher? Educational vouchers are government payments to a parent who may use that payment at any educational institution as long as that institution is approved by the government. In other words, the government will only pay the educational institution which parents designate as long as it is government approved.[8]

A tax credit is different. A tax credit is a dollar for dollar allowance on a tax which is due and owing. Generally where a taxpayer owes the government taxes, but the government elects to reduce the tax because it wants to encourage a given activity, the government grants a tax credit. The taxpayer's tax bill is reduced one dollar for every one dollar which the taxpayer has spent on the encouraged activity. There is, however, almost always a limit or cap on the credit.

In the context of education, a tax credit up to a fixed dollar amount may be allowed where the activity sought to be encouraged by the government is education. Some state governments have allowed a tax credit on part of the tuition a parent has spent on private education.[9] A parent, however, may not enjoy the tax credit against tuition if the school to which the tuition was paid is not approved by the government. Of course, a parent which has no income tax due and owing is not entitled to a credit.

It should be obvious that vouchers and tuition tax credits do not give parents control of their child's education. They do not recognize the unalienable right of parents to educate their children nor do they acknowledge that no person should be forced to support ideas and curriculums which they do not support. As a matter of fact, both vouchers and tax credits are based on the contrary premise: that the civil government has the right to force taxpayers to support government approved educational curriculums, teachers and institutions. Indeed, if a parent wants to take a tuition tax credit, he must still subsidize the state system. Neither does a voucher or credit free the mind of children from government oversight and regulation of ideas.

Choice plans only give parents choice of government-approved schools, not choice in education.[10] Moreover these government programs more strongly entrench governmental control. The government increases its control by economically forcing private schools to either lower their rates in order to remain competitive with subsidized schools, or submit to government regulation in order to be eligible for the voucher or subsidy. Parents who "choose" to send their children to an unqualified private school will have to pay more out of their own pocket since they have no voucher or subsidy to set-off against tuition.

A voucher is not real choice, it is economic blackmail. It will result in more private schools either going out of business or becoming a "qualified recipient." A "qualified recipient" is a school which is government approved even more than private schools are presently state regulated! Parents also lose control since they are ineligible to redeem the voucher directly. A school loses control because it must now further conform to the government's educational perspective and qualifications in order to become eligible for redemption.

This situation presents no more a choice for parents than voting for an incumbent when the election rules only permit the incumbent's votes to be counted. To the extent parents are "allowed" to participate in the state's system of compulsory exposure to government approved ideas, a voucher or tuition tax credit is simply another name for abuse of parental and taxpayers' rights. Parents are co-opted into participating in a government-controlled system in which their choices are pre-determined by the government. This is not real freedom or real choice.

The offer of choice which involves parents in the state's system of compulsion is a false approach. Such an approach assumes that the state may coerce exposure to state approved ideas and implies that parents and taxpayers will be required to subsidize all schools, not just those in their district.

Though many types of choice proposals have nothing to do with unalienable rights, many parents, foundations and religious organizations have cast their support for vouchers and tax credits. They say "choice" is a good first step in light of the present political climate. In actuality, however, this "choice" tramples on God-given parental rights. In some cases, these rights are crushed in the name of religious liberty and freedom! But a bribe will always dull the mind and cloud judgment.

A true "choice" measure will not fail the essential test. It will recognize the unalienable right of parents to direct the education of their children free from state interference, regulation or control. We should not be satisfied with government-approved choices and government-authorized freedom when real choice and real freedom are available.

A final word on vouchers. Today's voucher movement is the educational equivalent of Virginia's 1785 *Bill Establishing A Provision For Teachers of the Christian Religion*. This bill was an attempt to bring all the differing Christian faiths under the jurisdiction of the civil government. It provided for the government to collect tithes (taxes) and to distribute them to the religious sect that each person designated, as long as the sect was statutorily approved and recognized. It was a wrong approach then and it is a wrong approach now in the present context of education. The voucher movement is an attempt to bring all the differing schools under the direct and complete jurisdiction of the civil government. It would permit the government to distribute taxes to the school that each person designated, as long as the school was approved and recognized. Governmental approval and recognition is just another way of saying that the government has offered a bribe called a voucher, and the recipient has accepted the bribe by conforming its standards to the government's will.

Like vouchers today, the Virginia bill was supported by the religious majority of that day. It was only when the "natural rights of man" (as Jefferson and the Commonwealth of Virginia referred to them) were recognized, that the religious leaders moved toward disestablishment. The same is true today. Not until religious leaders and organizations concerned with education and parental rights understand and believe that the natural and unalienable rights of parents may not be trifled away through political compromise, will the education of the next generation be placed on solid legal footing.

Concern 7.

I have strong religious objections to the civil government's controlling where, what, when and how I school my child. Should I claim that the government has violated my First Amendment right to the free exercise of religion?

Considerations in responding to Concern 7.

The unalienable right of a parent to educate his or her children free from the interference, regulation or control of the civil government applies to *all* parents. Every parent has this right irrespective of religious beliefs or lack of religious belief. Moreover, to claim that your religious beliefs entitle you to be exempt from a valid civil law would contradict the principle of equality. If a civil law does not violate the law of God or the law of the Land, then it is only right that the law fall equally upon everyone.

Compulsory attendance laws, laws that require instruction in state-approved curriculums, laws which require parents to obtain state certification or approval in order to engage in home instruction and laws which compel support of these activities (as discussed in previous Chapters), however, violate the rights of parents and contravene intellectual liberty. Consequently, their application to non-religious parents is as repugnant as when applied to religious parents. This is so because these educational laws violate the rights of all parents equally.

To assert, therefore, that religious parents alone should be exempt on the basis of their particular belief, would place the unalienable right on a subjective basis. It would set the unalienable right on relative ground--the relative ground of one's belief. But the Declaration asserts that all human beings have certain unalienable rights. It does not say they are endowed with a right because they believe they have that right. By way of example, every one has the right to speak freely, not simply those who posses a sincerely held belief to that effect. Viewed in this context, belief is not even germane to the existence of the right.

If we were to establish the validity of an unalienable right upon what a person believed, the whole repository of unalienable rights would be thrown into subjective turmoil. Such an approach would take that which God gave to all parents, and apply it only to those parents who have certain religious points of view. Such a tactic would do justice neither to unalienable parental rights or to the rule of equality.[11] If the state government has a parent up against the wall and is ready to jail the parent for a child's truancy, then by all means plead the First Amendment, plead that the ordinance or statute is void for vagueness, or plead that it is overbroad. But this does not mean that such pleading even if successful, makes a good legislative strategy.

Concern 8.

Governmental control of education has become a part of the American way of life. Wouldn't it disrupt too much to change things now?

Considerations in responding to Concern 8.

Governmental control of education has disrupted too much not to be changed. The need to disrupt the way things have become is great, because the problem at its root has been ignored for such a long time. Respect for the rights of parents to educate our children was disrupted at one point early in our history to our loss. Respect for the right of religious freedom at one point early in our history disrupted the state established and controlled church to our great advantage. If the way things are is the way things should always be, then we should not have abolished the state church. Just as the rights of the people to freely worship cried out for the first American disestablishment, so also the rights of parents to freely educate their children cry out for a second American disestablishment.

Concern 9.

I read that Afrocentric education was academically insupportable. Shouldn't the state keep such ideas from being taught?

Considerations in responding to Concern 9.

In closing his discussion on the subject of intellectual freedom, Thomas Jefferson declared:

> And finally, that truth is great and will prevail if left to herself; that she is the proper and sufficient antagonist to error, and has nothing to fear from the conflict unless by human interposition disarmed of her natural weapons, free argument and debate; errors ceasing to be dangerous when it is permitted freely to contradict them.

Truth is disarmed of her natural weapons--free argument and debate--when the civil government controls the curriculum or enforces politically correct thought. Jefferson is saying that as long as the civil government does not prevent free argument and debate on ideas, then the truth will be able to overcome that which is false.

The state lacks jurisdiction to say which ideas are true and which are false, which ideas are academically meritorious and which are not. If parents teach their children ideas that are not true, that is none of the state's concern. If parents teach their children that which is criminal, then the state may become involved, but this is not what is being discussed here. If a college teaches false ideas, then free argument and debate unencumbered by politically correct constraint, will confront the false ideas. To assume that the civil government has a monopoly on the truth or on true ideas, however, is a "dangerous fallacy" that destroys all liberty.

Concern 10.

I object to public schools because they promote anti-Christian values like evolution and teach liberal views on morals and sex education. If we just got the public schools to teach creationism or got prayer back in the schools, wouldn't that solve most of the problems?

Considerations in responding to Concern 10.

No. If the public schools taught creationism or put prayer back in the classroom, then we would have to assume wrongly that the majority of a community has the right to dictate what all shall learn. Recall that Attorney Zach Montgomery articulated the pertinent standard. He said that:

> [t]he teacher of a child is simply a person who, for the time being, acts as a substitute for its parents. But if a majority [of a community] has no right to select the principal, what right has it to select the substitute?

In other words, parents and not the wider community have the right to select their child's teacher, and by parity of reason their child's curriculum. If a parent wants a teacher to teach anti-Christian values, that decision lies between God, the parent, the teacher and the child. It is not community or state business. If a parent wants a teacher to teach Christian values, that decision lies between God, the parent, the teacher and the child. It is not the concern of the community or state.

This is not to say that evolution and sexual promiscuity are morally equivalent to creationism and fidelity. It is only to say that when it comes to teaching ideas, "truth is great and will prevail if left to herself." This is not to say that the state lacks jurisdiction, however, to intervene when ideas break out into overt action against the public safety or rights of others, but that is quite a separate issue.

Concern 11.

The framers and founders only objected to federal control of education, not state control. They thought state government had a legitimate interest in education as a means to perpetuate the Republic. Why are you saying that the framers are against all governmental control of education?

Considerations in responding to Concern 11.

I am not saying that the framers were against state involvement in education. It is inaccurate, however, to characterize the framers as ardent devotees of a *system* of coercive public education as we know it today. When the Declaration was agreed upon and the Constitution ratified, state systems of public education were non-existent. This situation lasted for fifty to seventy-five years.

Moreover, the argument put forward in this book is that the legal principles which the framers articulated in America's legal documents necessarily result in the conclusion that governmental control of education at either the state or federal level is contrary to the laws of nature and of nature's God, reason and the Bible. Moreover, federal intervention into education is also contrary to the Constitution.

Whatever the actual practices of the framers or founders on the subject of education, it is the principle, not their practice which ultimately controls the outcome. John Quincy Adams reminds us that the framer's or founder's practices were not always consistent with the principles they expressed. He observed for instance that there was "no congeniality of principle between the Declaration of Independence and the Articles of Confederation." These documents;

> were the productions of different minds and of adverse passions--one, ascending for the foundation of human government to the laws of nature and of God, written upon the heart of man--the other, resting upon the basis of human institutions, and prescriptive law and colonial charters.

In other words the framers declared that the principles of the Declaration would be their guide, and then proceeded to ignore those principles and establish a confederated form of government. The Declaration advocated a civil government founded upon the consent of the people, yet the confederation abandoned this principle in favor of the right of (state/colonial) governments to form a (federal) government. This departure from principle was not corrected until the Constitution was adopted and ratified by the people in convention. Reverend Martin Luther King, Jr. once wrote:

> When the architects of our republic wrote the magnificent words of the Constitution and the Declaration of Independence, they were signing a promissory note to which every American was to fall heir. This note was a promise that all men--black men as well as white men--would be guaranteed the unalienable rights of life, liberty, and the pursuit of happiness.
>
> [He added] I still have a dream. It is a dream deeply rooted in the American dream. I have a dream that one day this Nation will rise up and live out the true meaning of its creeds--we hold these truths to be self evident that all men are created equal.[12]

King recognized that the principle that "all men are created equal" was the controlling standard, not the racial practices of the framer's generation. Consequently King advocated that America should fulfill the promissory note to which every American would fall heir. Likewise it is not the educational practices of the framers, founders or succeeding generations which are an infallible guide. It is the timeless principles of unalienable rights which bind our course and the course of our children. It is the promissory note of unalienable rights to which every American parent has fallen heir and which now stands ready for redemption.

Let us now move from these concerns to some objections of various degrees of intensity and equally intense responses.

Objection 1.

Abolition of governmental control of education would result in uneducated children.

Responding to Objection 1.

In essence, this objection implies that children unofficially taught by their parents or their private or church school, are ignorant. It intimates that unless the civil government teaches children, that they cannot be educated.[13] This objection is not only an insult to parents and private schools, it is factually insupportable.

It is governmental control of education that has resulted in uneducated children. The federal education of Indian children and District of Columbia children are perfect examples. If governmental control were abolished, children would receive an education relative to their individual habits. Children could not be squeezed into a state-approved mold. All children would be free to learn at their own rate. It is true that some children would remain without a suitable education relatively speaking, but the situation under the present system is much worse and more expensive.

Furthermore the objection does not speak well of *parents educated in state schools!* It suggests that parents so educated are not able or willing to teach their own children or provide for their instruction. This is a poor testimony for state instruction. It says little for the products of American state education. It sits well for those who wish to use the system of state instruction to render the people perpetually dependant upon the state through a program of education for ignorance.

The objection is also egotistical, or as Jefferson says, it reflects an "impious presumption" that governmental control of the mind is for our benefit. But this is the least of its flaws. Those who seriously voice this objection should be asked: "What about the child who has been compulsorily instructed and graduated by the state, but can neither read nor write?" It has been estimated that over 700,000 children simply drop out of state controlled schools and another 700,000 *graduate* without the reading skills needed for an average job.[14] The objection that the abolition of governmental control of schools would result in socially unenlightened children seems fatuous when considered alongside the more plausible argument that non-government education has already resulted in a better educated student. It also illustrates that the real issue in education is *control.*

Objection 2.

Disestablishment of state controlled education will throw good teachers out of work and does not recognize that most teachers do their job well.

Responding to Objection 2.

This objection is only half right. Disestablishment will throw good teachers out of working in *state-controlled* schools. As a matter of practicality, however, abolishing state controlled schools will put good teachers into the employ of private schools and individualized tutorials. The number of students will not change, and the demand for teachers will probably increase slightly. Disestablishment will also give teacher Unions the opportunity to open and establish their own private schools devoted to their own academic propensities without necessitating that they consider the state's agenda. They would be free to offer parents exactly what they think parents want their children to learn in the way of an education.

The political, religious and ideological divisiveness present at school board meetings would be eliminated since those of like mind would tend to attend the same institution. The good teachers will be in demand, while the poor teachers will be pursuing another vocation or profession, thus improving the overall quality of education.

It is true that some teachers will be thrown out of work. But this is true of any profession. No one is guaranteed lifelong employment. If a teacher is not hired by the private sector because of poor past performance, that is as it should be. If the promotional literature of some teacher unions is true, however, virtually all of their members will find highly compensated teaching positions for life.

Objection 3.

No college can survive without federal funding.

Responding to Objection 3.

No college should survive unless it can do so without federal funding. If a College cannot obtain the voluntary support of its alumni and benefactors, then its continued existence is not desirable or necessary. If a college does not have the voluntary financial support of those who attend it, why should it have the coerced support of *those who do not?* President James Buchanan understood this when he said:

> I presume the general proposition is undeniable that Congress does not possess the power to appropriate money in the Treasury, raised by taxes on the people of the United States, for the purpose of educating the people of the respective States. It will not be pretended that any such power is to be found among the specific powers granted to Congress nor that "it is necessary and proper for carrying into execution" any one of these powers.[15]

The President added: "It cannot be pretended that an agricultural college in New York or Virginia would aid the settlement or facilitate the sale of public lands in Minnesota or California."[16] The Constitution simply does not empower

Congress to fund education from the federal treasury or compel the people of one state to pay for the education of those in another state.

Objection 4.
    Parents lack the educational background and expertise to educate their own children in today's culture.
Responding to Objection 4.
    No they don't. This objection is actually arguing that parents lack the state certifiable minimum educational background or expertise to educate their own children. Parents, however, don't need the state authorized educational minimum background or expertise to educate their own children. Parents do not need to meet the state's minimum standards because the state is not authorized to establish any minimum standards whatsoever for the mind. Parents posses their unalienable right to teach because God gave it to them. The state has a legal duty to protect the exercise of that right and not preclude its exercise through certification or regulation.
    [This argument was also used to keep the state established church in existence far longer than it should have. The State argued that parents lacked adequate knowledge of the Bible to teach their children (and themselves) properly about God.]
    Lack of official certification by the government has nothing to do with a parent's right to teach. The only legal qualification a parent needs in order to teach his own child is that he or she be a parent of that child. If parents, however, lack the educational background or expertise to educate their own children, they may choose whether they will educate their own children directly, or obtain another to undertake in part, that duty for them.
    The state should respect a parent's freedom of choice. It should respect their right to hire a teacher who, in the parent's judgment, will educate their children as the parents see fit. If parents lack the financial wherewithal to hire an instructor, let them consider the advice of Francis Wayland discussed in Concerns 1 and 2 or let them approach a Union-operated school for assistance as proposed in Objection 2. Let them approach private philanthropy for assistance. Let them join a church and seek its assistance. Let them approach those political parties who advocate compassion for the financially poor and seek to convert those representations into voluntary assistance.

Objection 5.
    The government must regulate education in order to ensure high standards are maintained.
Responding to Objection 5.
    The real objection is that the government must regulate education in order to ensure that *its* standards are maintained. Of course the government's standards are not high standards, they are *minimum* standards. The civil government's

jurisdiction, however, does not extend to regulation of education. It does not extend to certification of standards of thought, whether minimum or high standards.

Civil government has been entrusted by the people with the legal task of securing their unalienable rights. It was not entrusted by the people to standardize children at some minimum level. When the standards to be regulated are standards of thought, standards of ideas, or standards relating to the mind, is it not evident that the government is standardizing the people themselves? Is it not evident that the government is conforming the people to its own ideas?

High standards are not set by government. Government sets minimum standards of its own choosing and in our day and age those standards are very low. When 700,000 high school students *graduate* without the reading skills needed for an average job, the argument that government must regulate education to ensure high standards is outlandish. Moreover, the emphasis on college graduation of minority students in proportion to their enrollment as actively sought by various state Governors speaks poorly of maintenance of academic standards.[17]

Objection 6.

The civil government must control education in order to overcome parental and cultural bias and ensure that students are socially well adjusted and culturally diverse.

Responding to Objection 6.

Was it Justice Blackmun, John Dewey or Adolf Hitler who advanced this argument? Actually, all of the above. But, quite the opposite danger is to be avoided. The civil government uses the school to assimilate students to accept its bias, intolerance, and "clarified values." The civil government uses education to socialize students according to its own political and sometimes immoral agenda. It is the civil government that operates schools which are "designed to, and inevitably will, inculcate" its own way of thought and outlook. Everything inconsistent with that outlook is rejected; everything compatible is accepted.

Moreover, the increasing bias of public higher educational institutions *against diversity of thought* is a classic case of civil government enforcing its own brand of intolerance. This trend toward "politically correct" thought is essentially the logical extreme of the idea that the state has jurisdiction to declare and approve only those ideas which it considers valid and worthy of expression. The modern advent of thought police on campus is essentially the revival of the spirit of prosecutions for ideas as perpetrated under the Espionage Act of 1918 or more recently under state enforced McCarthyism. Such prosecutions employ the bias and intolerance of government against those who think and act differently.[18]

The alleged concern for overcoming parental or cultural bias, is indicative of a dangerous attitude--that government, and not parents or adult students should determine the intellectual climate and culture in which we live. This may appear only to be of concern to those who hold *unorthodox* views. Practically speaking, however, politically correct thought and its ilk spells danger for any person who simply holds *different or additional* views. This point should not be forgotten by parents, especially those who have the most to lose (relatively speaking) through assimilation of their religious and the ethnic culture.

Those who argue Objection 6 are unfortunately quite comfortable with trying to assimilate parental and cultural *differences* by construing those differences as parental and cultural bias, while falsely characterizing state-controlled intellectual thought as tolerant, objective and even accommodating. It has been said that pride in knowledge puffs up a man's head beyond its usual dimensions. When the government claims it must control education in order to overcome parental or cultural shortcomings, it puffs its own impious assessment of its knowledge and declares that the *standardized* American mind is the norm.

Objection 7.
    The state has a compelling interest in teaching children fundamental values in order to prepare them for citizenship in the Republic and for the preservation of our political system.
Responding to Objection 7.
    If the state has a compelling interest in teaching children fundamental values, prepare children for citizenship in the Republic, and for the maintenance of our political system, then why are state educated children and their state educated parents so ignorant of these things? An even better question is this: How can preparation of children for citizenship in the Republic and for the maintenance of our political system, be promoted by denial of the very thing taught?

The Declaration of Independence contains important principles of citizenship and participation. It refers to the purpose of civil government, how it is instituted, organized and abolished. That is fairly basic. The Declaration says that the people have certain unalienable rights from God. That is basic. The right of intellectual freedom is basic. The right of a parent to teach their children is basic. A parent has the unalienable right to teach his or her child, free from the oversight, or if you prefer, *free from any interest the state may have, compelling or otherwise which is asserted to counterbalance that right.*

That is what the Declaration of Independence teaches, but is that what the state teaches? No, of course not. The state says in effect, that the principles of intellectual freedom and unalienable rights are not valuable to learn. The state denies that parents have the intellectual freedom to consider only those ideas which they choose. The state denies that parents have an unalienable right to educate children according to parental desires and perspectives.

Moreover, the Constitution, which is the central organizational document of our political and legal system should also be taught. What does it say about Congressional entanglement in educational matters? What does it say about the

Department of Education and federal funding of education in the states? An honest observance of the Constitution prohibits these things. It prohibits them all. But despite what the Constitution states, the federal government continues to subsidize education in the states and the states continue teaching that the Constitution is something to be honored and venerated. The message the children are getting, however, is that observance in the breach is preferable to observance in the rule.

In *Board of Education v. Pico*, Justice Blackmun summed up the government's thinking by saying that "the Constitution presupposes the existence of an informed citizenry prepared to participate in governmental affairs, and these democratic principles obviously are constitutionally incorporated into the structure of our government."[19] One would expect that the Justice would examine the propositions founded in the Declaration of Independence in order to glean what the "Constitution presupposes" or what is "incorporated into the structure of our government." If he had undertaken such an analysis, he would have seen the principles of intellectual freedom and the unalienable rights of parents to educate their children. He did not do this. Perhaps his education did not prepare him to do this? Instead, he concluded that "[i]t therefore seems entirely appropriate that the State use 'public schools [to] . . . inculcat[e] fundamental values necessary to the maintenance of a democratic political system.'"[20] So much for observance of the Constitution.

It should also be pointed out that his entire quotation is no comfort to those who refuse to believe that the Constitution incorporates principles which went before it. If it is too great a leap of faith (which it is not at all) to believe that the Constitution simply cannot presuppose the laws of nature and nature's God, a standard which is expressly articulated in the Declaration, it must be an ever greater leap of blind faith to presuppose, *as the Court has already done*, that state schools are a viable means to perpetuate our "democratic political system." I say greater, because the systems of colonial education that pre-dated the Constitution were systematically controlled by parents and religious authorities and not the government. Justice Blackmun's conclusion is contrary to the weight of such evidence.

Consider another point. Doesn't it simply stand to reason from the perspective of political philosophy, that extending to the civil government the power to define and propagate "democratic principles" will eventually be employed as a pretext to enslave the people *and* ensure the perpetual existence of the regime?[21]

The lesson to be learned is that when the power of the state is brought to control that which is essential to the maintenance of the regime, its self-interest alone necessitates that it take whatever means are necessary to continue its existence. The state's object then becomes not education or true ideas, but maintaining control. Under our system of government, the people--not the government--are their own best guardians of liberty. The state has no compelling interest in teaching fundamental values in order to prepare children for citizenship in the Republic or for the maintenance of our political systems. Parents and their true agents have this responsibility and duty.

A free citizenry presumes an educated citizenry. But an educated citizenry itself presumes freedom from governmental control of education. No man is free to think when he has been told that he is free, but his mind is conditioned to ask only government approved questions and answer with government approved ideas. Surely if no man is free, how then can his nation preserve freedom? Such a freedom is horrible illusion. Indeed, if a man knowing only slavery is told his condition is freedom, will this new knowledge make him a free man?

<u>Objection 8.</u>
Private education costs too much.
<u>Responding to Objection 8.</u>
Then let parents discharge their duty directly. Moreover, if parents are freed from local, state and federal taxes which go to support and maintain state schools, then that money will be put back in their pocket and they will have it to pay for private education.

<u>Objection 9.</u>
Opposition to state control of education is contrary to public opinion.
<u>Responding to Objection 9.</u>
This is false, but so what?

<u>Objection 10.</u>
Only the federal government can save our children and public schools by establishing a national system of standards and testing.
<u>Responding to Objection 10.</u>
Federal education efforts have destroyed students, not saved them. The history of federal education of American Indian students admits of no other conclusion. It "has been one of coercive assimilation" and resulted in "disastrous effects on the education of Indian children." Moreover, federal oversight of the District of Columbia has resulted in a dropout rate which is 48 percent, the absolute worst in the nation. In SAT scores the District is third from the bottom.

It should be evident by now that parent directed education will produce more diverse students and eventually a diverse workforce. This is a far different result than exists under the present state system of education. A national solution will only magnify state uniformity and problems to a national level. If the federal government subjects children to uniformity of instruction and a standardized curriculum, this will only produce the same uniformity of thought presently found at the state level. The freedom of educational choice under a system of parental control is far superior to the uniformity of ideas which result from national testing of students.

National testing is, nevertheless endorsed by the Clinton Administration. National testing is one step away from a national standard curriculum. Recall that former HEW Secretary Califano warned that national control of curriculum is national control of ideas. It is only a question of time before national testing becomes a national curriculum. Indeed, this scenario has already been played out in the states. What originally began as state schools open to poor children has grown into state control of curriculum. Now state control of curriculum is state control of ideas. To blindly maintain that the federal government, therefore, will never use its power to further standardize the minds of children, evidences the profound power which federal bribes have already effected on the American mind.

Notes

1. Mozert v. Hawkins County Board of Ed. 827 F.2d 1058 (6th Cir. 1987) *cert. denied* 484 U.S. 1066 (1989).

2. Board of Ed. v. Pico, 457 U.S. 853, 879 (1982)(Blackmun, J., concurring in part).

3. FRANCIS WAYLAND, THE ELEMENTS OF MORAL SCIENCE, 4TH ED. (Boston: Gould, Kendall and Lincoln, 1841) 318-19.

4. ZACH MONTGOMERY, COMP., THE SCHOOL QUESTION FROM A PARENTAL AND NON-SECTARIAN STAND POINT, 4TH ED. (Washington: Gibson Bros., 1889; reprint ed.; New York: Arno Press, 1972) 52.

5. An Act for Religious Freedom, adopted by the Virginia General Assembly on January 16, 1786. VA. CODE ANN. § 57-1 (1950). *See also* ROBERT L. CORD, SEPARATION OF CHURCH AND STATE (New York: Lambeth Press, 1982) 249-50, quoting Thomas Jefferson's *A Bill for Establishing Religious Freedom.*

6. Minorities Overwhelmingly Favor Public School Choice, *The Washington Times,* Aug. 24, 1990, p. A-3 citing the 22nd Annual Phi Delta Kappa/Gallup Poll on Public Attitudes toward Public Schools. "Roscoe R. Nix, president of the Montgomery County Chapter of the National Association for the Advancement of Colored People, said black parents' growing interest in choice represents disillusionment with the job the public schools are doing and a growing awareness of options."

7. The New Jersey Supreme Court has held that the state must guarantee that funding in its 28 poorest districts be adjusted to funding in an equal or greater amount than the state's affluent districts. Texas and Kentucky have also passed legislation addressing this issue by raising taxes throughout their respective states. *See* Plugging the School Gap, *U.S. News & World Report,* June 25, 1990, p. 58-59. *See also* New Jersey Court seen as leader on Rights, *The New York Times,* July 18, 1990, p. B-1.

8. *See* MYRON LIBERMAN, PRIVATIZATION AND EDUCATIONAL CHOICE, (New York: Saint Martins Press, 1989) 7-9.

9. This arrangement has been upheld as Constitutional where the state provided for a limited tuition tax credit against state income taxes. *See* Mueller v. Allen, 463 U.S. 388 (1983). Mueller involved a Minnesota law which provided taxpayers an income tax deduction on their state tax return for expenses incurred in providing "tuition, textbooks and transportation" for their children attending elementary or secondary schools. Since the law permitted deductions by all parents, those whose children attended parochial schools were also equally entitled to the deduction. A group of taxpayers objected to equal application of the law to the parochial school parents arguing that the deduction constituted an establishment of religion in violation of the First Amendment. The Court

rejected this claim and sustained the law on Constitutional grounds.

10. A great deal of attention is being given to parental choice and restructuring of schools to improve education:

> The principled argument for public school choice asserts that a free and democratic society has a transcendent public interest in maintaining a public school system, but there is no similar interest in requiring children to go to one public school rather than another. Parents therefore should be allowed to choose which public school their children attend . . . .

Bella Rosenberg, Public School Choice: Can We Find the Right Balance?, *American Educator, The Professional Journal of the American Federation of Teachers* (Volume 13, No. 2, Summer 1989) 11.

11. *See* Matthew 23:2-4. Many religious groups assert that their religious belief entitles them to be exempt from otherwise applicable laws. See Employment Division, Department of Human Resources of Oregon v. Smith, 494 U.S. 872 (1990) and The Religious Freedom Restoration Act of 1993 (RFRA), 42 U.S.C. 2000bb *et seq.* The Act attempted to restore as a matter of federal law, the compelling state interest test to claims under the First Amendment's Free Exercise clause. The Act, which applied to the states and local governments pursuant to 42 U.S.C. 2000bb-2(1), provided, in pertinent part, as follows:

> (a) In general. Government shall not substantially burden a person's exercise of religion even if the burden results from a rule of general applicability, except as provided in subsection (b) of this section.
> (b) Exception. Government may substantially burden a person's exercise of religion only if it demonstrates that application of the burden to the person—
> > (1) is in furtherance of a compelling governmental interest; and
> > (2) is the least restrictive means of furthering that compelling governmental interest. [42 U.S.C. 2000bb-1.]

The Act, however, was held unconstitutional in City of Boerne v. Flores, ___U.S.___, No. 95-2074, June 25, 1997. The Court found that the Act exceeded the remedial or enforcement power of Congress under the Fourteenth Amendment, Section 5.

12. HOUSTON PETERSON, ED., A TREASURY OF THE WORLD'S GREATEST SPEECHES, (New York: Simon and Schuster, 1965) pp. 835-40.

13. "In spite of one of the Highest levels of spending (per capita) in the industrialized world, the American public school system is generating students who rank 13th out of 13 advanced nations in science and math and 11th out of 13 in social studies and languages." Warren Brookes, Public Education and the Global Failure of Socialism, IMPRIMIS (Volume 19, Number 4, April 1990) Hillsdale College, Hillsdale, Michigan.

14. Rep. Dick Armey, Let's Get moving with School Choice, *USA Today*, May 22, 1991, p. A-8.

15. JAMES D. RICHARDSON, ED., COMPILATION OF THE MESSAGES AND PAPERS OF THE PRESIDENTS, 1789-1897, (Washington, D.C.: Government Printing Office, 1896) 5:547, Veto Messages of President Buchanan, February 24, 1859. "Should Congress exercise such a power, this would be to break down the barriers which have been so carefully constructed in the Constitution to separate Federal from State authority." *Id.*

16. *Id.* at 5:550.

17. *See* Minority Graduation equity Sought, *The Washington Times*, Dec. 7, 1990, p. A-6, quoting a report of the task force of the Education Commission of the States.

18. *See generally* Taking Offense: Is this the New Enlightenment on campus or the new McCarthyism?, *Newsweek*, Dec. 24, 1990, pp. 48-57.

19. 457 U.S. 853, 876 (1982).

20. *Id.* at 876, quoting Ambach v. Norwick, 441 U.S. 68, 77 (1979).

21. Consider a European analogy. During the reign of King Henry VIII, the English government prohibited the printing of Bibles in the native language of the English people. The Latin text was considered sacred by the established clergy. They argued that to give the Bible to the common people in language they could read would result in a perversion of the very heart of the one true faith. In other words they sought to keep the people from teaching themselves and their children "false doctrine." The clergy used the force of the Crown (and the fear of damnation) to keep the people dependent upon themselves. They used knowledge to control the people. William Tyndale, among others, opposed this arrangement. He was persuaded that the people could understand the Scripture if allowed to read it in their native tongue. Due to his persistence, English Bibles were finally made available to the people and the people who immigrated to America eventually freed themselves from domination by state controlled religious authorities.

Bibliography

"An Act to Create a Department of Education." 14 Stat. L. 434, March 2, 1867.

"An Act donating Public Lands to the Several States and Territories which may provide Colleges for the Benefit of Agriculture and the Mechanical Arts." 12 Stat. L. 503 (1862).

"The Annals of the Congress of the United States." In The Debates and Proceedings of the Congress of the United States. 42 vols. Joseph Gales, Comp. Washington: Gales and Seaton, 1834).

"The Annapolis Convention." The U.S. Army Bicentennial Series, 1986.

Adams, John. Novanglus and Massachusettensis. New York: Russell and Russell, 1968.

Adams, John Quincy. "The Jubilee of the Constitution, a Discourse delivered at the request of the New York Historical Society, on Tuesday, the 30th of April, 1839." In J. of Christian Juris. 6 (1986).

Adams, Samuel. "The Rights of the Colonists (1772)." In The Annals of America. 18 vols. Ed. Mortimer J. Adler, Chicago: Encyclopedia Britannica, 1968.

Agthe, Dale R. "Validity of State Regulation of Curriculum and Instruction in Private and Parochial Schools." In 18 American Law Reports 4th, 649 (1982 and 1994 Supp.)

Alexander, Lamar. "Kansas Governor's Educational Summit, Wichita, Kansas, November 1-2, 1989." In 61 Education Reporter Feb. 1991.

Allison, Andrew M. The Real Thomas Jefferson. The American Classic Series, Washington, D.C.: National Center for Constitutional Studies, 1983.

Amos, Gary T. Defending The Declaration. Brentwood, Tennessee: Wolgemuth & Hyatt, Publishers Inc., 1989.

Angle, Paul M., ed. Created Equal? The Complete Lincoln-Douglas Debates of 1858. Chicago: The University of Chicago Press, 1958.

Aquinas, St. Thomas. Summa Theologica. 5 vols. Circa 1254-1271. Reprint. Westminster, Maryland: Christian Classics, 1981.

Arrowood, Charles F. Thomas Jefferson and Education in a Republic. New York: McGraw-Hill Book Co., Inc., 1930.

Bancroft, George. History of the Formation of the Constitution of the United States of America. New York: Appleton & Co. 1885.

Barnett, Randy, ed. The Rights Retained By The People. George Mason University Press, 1989.

Berger. "The Ninth Amendment." 66 Cornell L. Rev. 1 (1981).

Black, Henry Campbell. Black's Law Dictionary: Definitions of the Terms and Phrases of American and English Jurisprudence, Ancient and Modern. Rev. 4th. ed. St. Paul, MN: West Publishing Co., 1968.

Blackford, Daniel R. "The Extent of Civil Authority over Opinions and Ideas." Masters Thesis, Regent University, 1986.

Blackstone, Sir William. Commentaries on the Law of England. 4 vols. 1765. Reprint. Birmingham, AL: The Legal Classics Library, 1983.

Bolick, Clint. Unfinished Business: A Civil Rights Strategy for America's Third Century. San Francisco, California: Pacific Research Institute for Public Policy, 1990.

Bork, Robert H. The Tempting of America: The Political Seduction of the Law. New York: The Free Press, 1990.

Bourne, Edward G. The History of the Surplus Revenue of 1837. New York: G. P. Putnam's Sons, 1885.

Bracton, H. de. A Treatise on the Laws and Customs of England. 2 vols. Reprint. Cambridge, MA: Belknap Press, 1968.

Brookes, Warren. "Public Education and the Global Failure of Socialism." Imprimis. Hillsdale, MI: April 1990.

Brooks, Charles. Some Reasons for the Immediate Establishment of a National System of Education for the United States. 2d ed. Boston: John Wilson & Sons, 1869.

Brutus, Stephen Junius [Philippe du Plessis-Mornay]. "Vindiciae Contra Tyrannos [A Defense of Liberty Against Tyrants]". In Great Political Thinkers. 4th. ed. Ed. W. Ebenstein. Hinsdale, Illinois: Dryden Press, 1969.

Bureau of Census. "Projections of The Population of the United States, by Age, Sex, and Race: 1988 to 2080." In Current Population Reports - Population Estimates and Projections. U.S. Department of Commerce (Series P-25, No. 1018) Jan. 1989.

Bureau of Labor Statistics. "Projections 2000." U.S. Department of Labor (Bulletin 2302) March 1988.

Bureau of Labor Statistics. "Outlook 2000." U.S. Department of Labor (Bulletin 2352) April 1990.

Burlamaqui, Jean Jacques. The Principles of Natural and Politic Law. 1748. Reprint. New York: Legal Classics Library, 1995.

Butler, Stuart M., ed. Mandate for Leadership II. Washington, D.C.: The Heritage Foundation, 1984.

Califano, Joseph A. Jr. Governing America. New York: Simon & Schuster, 1981.

Caplan. "The History and Meaning of The Ninth Amendment." 69 Va. L. Rev. 223 (1983).

Chalcedon Report. Vallecito, CA: August 1990.

Chubb, John E. and Terry Moe. Politics, Markets and America's Schools. Washington, D.C.: The Brookings Institution, 1990.

Clark, Gordon H. A Christian Philosophy of Education. 2d rev. ed. Jefferson, MD: Trinity Foundation, 1988.

Conant, James B. Thomas Jefferson and the Development of American Public Education. Berkeley: University of California Press, 1962.

Cooper, Thomas. Two Essays: On the Foundation of Civil Government and On the Constitution of the United States. 1826. Reprint. New York: Da Capo Press, 1970.

Cord, Robert L. Separation of Church and State. New York: Lambeth Press, 1982.

Cornelison, Isaac A. The Relation of Religion to Civil Government in the United States of America. 1895. Reprint. New York: Da Capo Press, 1970.

Corpus Juris. Vol. 12. New York: The American Law Book Company, 1917.

Corpus Juris Secundum. Vol. 78A §§ 697-725 and §§ 734-743. St. Paul, MN: West Publishing Co., 1995.

Cubberley, Ellwood P. Public Education in the United States. New York: Houghton Mifflin Co., 1919.

Cubberley, Ellwood P. Public Education in the United States. 2d ed. New York: Houghton Mifflin Co., 1934.

Dewey, John. Democracy and Education, an Introduction to the Philosophy of Education. New York: The MacMillan Company, 1916.

Documents Illustrative of the Formation of the Union of the American States. 69th Cong., 1st sess., House Document No. 398. Washington, D.C.: Government Printing Office, 1927.

Dumbauld, Edward. The Declaration of Independence and What it Means Today. Norman, OK: University of Oklahoma Press, 1950.

Eastman, John C. "On the Perpetuation of Our Institutions: Thoughts on Public Education at the American Founding." Ph.D. diss., The Claremont Graduate School, 1993.

Elliot, Jonathan, Comp. The Debates in the Several State Conventions on the Adoption of the Constitution. 5 vols. Philadelphia: J.B. Lippincott Co., 1891.

Employment Standards Administration. "Opportunity 2000: Creative Affirmative Action Strategies for a Changing Workforce." U.S. Department of Labor, September 1988.

Force, Peter, comp. Tracts and Other Papers Relating Principally to the Origin, Settlement, and Progress of the Colonies in North America. 4 vols. 1836-1847. Reprint. Gloucester, MA: Peter Smith, 1963.

Fritz, Marshall. No More "Public School Reform." Fresno, CA: Separation of School and State Alliance, 1996.

Garrison, Albert L. "Legislative Basis for State Support of Public Elementary and Secondary Education in Virginia since 1810." Masters Thesis, Duke University, 1932.

Gatto, John T. Dumbing us Down: The Hidden Curriculum of Compulsory Schooling. Philadelphia: New Society Publishers, 1992.

Germann, George B. National Legislation Concerning Education. New York: Columbia University, 1899.

Grotius, Hugo. De Jure Belli Ac Pacis Libri Tres, [The Law of War and Peace]. 1646. Reprint. Oxford: Clarendon Press, 1925.

Hafen. "The Constitutional Status of Marriage, Kinship, and Sexual Privacy-Balancing the Individual and Social Interests." 81 Mich. L. R. 463 (1983).

Harmer, David. School Choice: Why you need it-How you get it. Washington, D.C.: CATO Institute, 1994.

Herbert, Auberon. The Right and Wrong of Compulsion by the State. Indianapolis: Liberty Classics, 1978.

Hinsdale, B. A. President Garfield and Education. Boston: Osgood & Co., 1882.

Hinsdale, B. A., Comp. Documents Illustrative of American Educational History. U.S. Office of Education. Washington, D.C.: Government Printing Office, 1895.

Holmes, Oliver W. Jr. The Common Law & Other Writings. 1881. Reprint. Birmingham, AL: The Legal Classics Library, 1982.

Huenefeld, Richard A. "The Challenge to Secure Unalienable Property Rights in the United States." Masters Thesis, Regent University, 1989.

Hunt, Gaillard, ed. The Journal of the Debates in the Convention which Framed the Constitution of the United States as Recorded by James Madison. 2 vols. New York: G.P. Putnam's Sons, 1908.

Hyneman, Charles S. & Donald S. Lutz. American Political Writing During the Founding Era 1760-1805. Indianapolis: Liberty Press, 1983.

James, Charles F. Documentary History of the Struggle for Religious Liberty in Virginia. 1900. Reprint. New York: Da Capo Press, 1971.

Jefferson, Thomas. Thomas Jefferson, Writings. New York: The Library of America, 1984.

Johnson, Clifton. Old-Time Schools and School-Books. Toronto: Dover Publications, 1963.

Kent, James. Commentaries on American Law. 1826. Reprint. New York: Da Capo Press, 1971.

Keppel, Francis. The Necessary Revolution in American Education. New York: Harper & Row, 1966.

Korpela, Allan E. "What Constitutes a Private, Parochial, or Denominational School Within Statute Making Attendance at Such School in Compliance with Compulsory School Attendance Law." 65 American Law Reports 3rd 1222 (1975 and 1994 Supp.).

Kursh, Harry. The United States Office of Education. Philadelphia: Chilton Company, 1965.

Liberman, Myron. Privatization and Educational Choice. New York: Saint Martins Press, 1989.

Lincoln, Abraham. "Speech at Springfield, 1857." In Living Ideas in America. Ed. Henry S. Commanger. New York: Harper and Row, 1964.

Lincoln, Abraham. "Gettysburg Address." In A Documentary History of the American People. Eds. A. Craven, W. Johnson and F. R. Dunn. Boston: Ginn & Co., 1951.

Lumsden, Scott. "The Ninth Amendment in Light of The Declaration of Independence." Masters Thesis, Regent University, 1990.

Machen, J. Gresham. Education, Christianity, and the State. Jefferson, Maryland: The Trinity Foundation, 1987.

Madison, James. Notes of Debates in the Federal Convention of 1787. Athens: Ohio University Press, 1966.

Mather, Cotton. Magnalia Christi Americana [The Great Works of Christ in America]. Carlisle, PA: Banner of Truth Trust, 1979.

Mayhew, Jonathan. "Concerning Unlimited Submission and Non-Resistance to the Higher Powers (1750)." In Pamphlets of the American Revolution 1750-1776. Ed. B. Bailyn. Cambridge, MA: The Belknap Press, 1965.

McCarthy, Rockne M., James W. Skillen, & William A. Harper, eds. Disestablishment a Second Time: Genuine Pluralism for American Schools. Grand Rapids, MI: Christian University Press, 1982.

McInerney, Virginia M. "Repeal of the Seventeenth Amendment: A Step toward the Restoration of Federalism in America." Masters Thesis, Regent University, 1987.

McNeill, J.T., ed. John Calvin, Institutes of the Christian Religion. 2 vols. 1536. Reprint. Philadelphia: Westminster Press, 1977.

Meyer, Hermine H. The History and Meaning of the Fourteenth Amendment. New York: Vantage Press, 1977.

Miles, Rufus E. Jr. The Department of Health, Education and Welfare. New York: Praeger, 1974.

Monroe, Paul, ed. A Cyclopedia of Education. 5 vols. New York: The Macmillan Press, 1919.

Montesquieu, Baron de. The Spirit of Laws. 1751. Reprint. Birmingham, AL: Legal Classics Library, 1984.

Montgomery, Zachariah, comp. The School Question from a Parental and Non-Sectarian Stand Point. 4th ed., 1889. Reprint. New York: Arno Press, 1972.

Morgan, Kerry L. "The Unalienable Right of Government by Consent and The Independent Federal Agency." 8 J. Christian Juris. 33 (1990).

Morrill, Justin. "An Address in Behalf of the University of Vermont and State Agricultural College, at Montpelier, October 10, 1888." Montpelier: Argus and Patriot Printing House, 1888.

National Center for Education Statistics. Digest of Education Statistics. Department of Education, 1988.

National Center for Education Statistics. "Projections of Education Statistics to 2000." Office of Education Research and Improvement, U.S. Department of Labor (NCES 89-648) 1989.

Note. "On Reading and Using the Tenth Amendment." 93 Yale L. J. 723 (1984).

Office of the United States Chief of Counsel for Prosecution of Axis Criminality. Nazi Conspiracy and Aggression. United States Government Printing Office: Washington, 1946.

Pangle, Lorraine S. and Thomas L. Pangle. The Learning of Liberty: The Educational Ideas of the American Founders. University of Kansas Press, 1993.

Perry, Richard L., ed. Sources of our Liberties Chicago, IL: American Bar Foundation, 1978.

Peterson, Houston, ed. A Treasury of the World's Greatest Speeches. New York: Simon and Schuster, 1965.

Prucha, Francis P., ed. Americanizing The American Indians, Supplemental Report on Indian Education. Cambridge, MA: Harvard University Press, 1973.

Prucha, Francis P. American Indian Policy in Crisis. Norman, OK: University of Oklahoma Press, 1976.

Randall, Henry S. The Life of Thomas Jefferson. 3 vols. New York: Derby & Jackson, 1858.

Randolph, J. W. Early History of the University of Virginia, as contained in the Letters of Thomas Jefferson and Joseph C. Cabell. Richmond, Virginia: C. H. Wynne, Printer, 1856.

Reed, Alan P. "State Education Laws and the Irrebuttable Presumption of Vlandis v. Kline." Masters Thesis, Regent University, 1989.

Richardson, James D., ed. Compilation of the Messages and Papers of the Presidents, 1789-1897. Washington, D.C.: Government Printing Office, 1896.

Richman, Sheldon. Separating School and State: How to Liberate America's Families. Fairfax, Virginia: The Future of Freedom Foundation, 1994.

Robe, Scott M. "The Objects, Authority and Limits of an Article V Constitutional Convention." Masters Thesis, Regent University, 1986.

Rosenberg, Bella. "Public School Choice: Can We Find the Right Balance?" In 13 American Educator. Summer 1989.

Rubin, David & Steven Greenhouse. The Rights of Teachers: The Basic ACLU Guide to a Teacher's Constitutional Rights. New York: Bantam, 1984.

Rutherford, Rev. Samuel. Lex, Rex. 1644. Reprint. Harrisonburg, Virginia: Sprinkle Publications 1980.

Sandoz, Ellis. Political Sermons of the American Founding Era, 1730-1805. Indianapolis, IL: Liberty Press, 1991.

Shakespeare, Sir William. Henry V. Part 2, Scene 2, lines 170-177.

Smith, Theodore C. The Life and Letters of James Abram Garfield. 2 vols. New Haven, CT: Yale Univ. Press, 1925.

Smith, Wilson, ed. Theories of Education in Early America 1655-1819. Indianapolis: Bobbs-Merrill Co., 1973.

Solzhenitsyn, Aleksandr. A World Split Apart. New York: Harper & Row, 1978.

Story, Joseph. Commentaries on Equity Jurisprudence. 1884. Reprint. Birmingham, AL: Legal Classics Library, 1988.

Tarcov, Nathan. Locke's Education for Liberty. Chicago, IL: University of Chicago Press, 1984.

Taylor, John T. [of Caroline]. New Views of the Constitution of the United States. 1823. Reprint. New York: Da Capo Press, 1971.

The Laws and Liberties of Massachusetts of 1648. Reprint. Birmingham, AL: The Legal Classics Library, 1982.

The Federalist Papers. 1788. Reprint. Birmingham, AL: The Legal Classics Library, 1983.

Thompson, Ernest T. Presbyterians in the South, 1607-1861. 3 vols. Richmond, Virginia: John Knox Press, 1963.

Thornton, John Wingate. The Pulpit and the American Revolution. 1860. Reprint. New York: Da Capo Press, 1970.

U.S. Congress, House, 39th Cong., 2d sess., 5 June 1866, The Congressional Globe.

U.S. Department of Education, Office of Civil Rights. "Sexual Harassment Guidance: Harassment of Students by School Employees, Other Students, or Third Parties." 62 Fed. Reg. 12033, March 13, 1997.

U.S. Department of Education. "America 2000: An Education Strategy." April 18, 1991.

U.S. Senate. "1969 Report of the Committee on Labor and Public Welfare, Special Sub-committee on Indian Education." Sen. Res. 80, 91st Cong., 1st Sess. Washington, D.C., 1969.

U.S. Senate, Committee on Governmental Affairs. "Legislative History of Public Law, 96-98, Department of Education Organization Act." pts. 1-2, 96th Cong., 2d sess. Washington, D.C.: Government Printing Office, 1980.

Unger, Steven, ed. The Destruction of American Indian Families. New York: Association of American Indian Affairs, 1977.

Vattel, Emerich de. The Law of Nations or The Principles of Natural Law. 1758. Reprint. New York: The Legal Classics Library, 1993.

Von Leyden, W., ed. <u>John Locke, Essays on the Law of Nature</u>. 1676. Reprint. Oxford: Clarendon Press, 1965.

Walsh, James J. <u>Education of the Founding Fathers of the Republic: Scholasticism in the Colonial Colleges</u>. New York: Fordham University Press, 1935.

Wayland, Francis. <u>The Elements of Moral Science</u>. 4th ed. Boston: Gould, Kendall and Lincoln, 1841.

Whitehead, John W. <u>Parents' Rights</u>. Westchester, Illinois: Crossway Books, 1986.

Williams, Roger. "The Bloudy Tenet, Of Persecution, for the Cause of Conscience." In <u>English Historical Documents, American Colonial Documents to 1776</u>. Ed. M. Jensen. New York: Oxford University Press, 1969.

Winthrop, John. <u>The History of New England from 1630 to 1649</u>. 2 vols. Boston: Little Brown and Company, 1853.

Wood, William C., Jr. "The General Welfare: A Constitutional Framework." Masters Thesis, Regent University, 1986.

Case Index

Subject Index

☞   About the Author . . . .

Kerry L. Morgan is an attorney, presently "Of Counsel" with the Southeastern Michigan law firm of Pentiuk, Couvreur & Kobiljak, P.C. His chief area of practice involves civil rights, discrimination and labor law. He also specializes in natural law and Constitutional theory. Prior to this affiliation, he served as an Attorney-Advisor with the United States Commission on Civil Rights in Washington, D.C. He came to the Commission in 1988 from Regent University where he was Director of the United States Constitution Bicentennial Project. Prior to that time he practiced law in Detroit, Michigan. He is admitted to the Michigan, Virginia and District of Columbia bars, various federal district courts and the United States Supreme Court.

Mr. Morgan has written thought provoking articles in the areas of natural law and unalienable rights. Published essays include *The Unalienable Right of Government by Consent and The Independent Agency,* and *The Declaration of Independence and American Education.* He is presently completing an extensive legal review of religious liberty principles and Supreme Court cases titled, *Unalienable Rights, Equality and The Free Exercise of Religion.*

An honors graduate of Michigan State University in Criminal Justice and Political Science, Mr. Morgan then entered The Detroit College of Law where he served on the College's Law Review as Managing Editor. After graduation and practice of law, he entered the Charter Class in Public Policy at Regent University and went on to receive his Masters of Arts, magna cum laude. He has also served the University as an Adjunct Professor. He is presently seeking a Ph.D. in Higher Education at the University of Michigan.

Kerry L. Morgan was born in Detroit, Michigan in 1955. He is married to Elizabeth A. Morgan, Ph.D. Her dissertation on "'To Fix the People on the Soyle': Family, Land and Settlement in Colonial Henrico County, Virginia, 1611-1675" is a landmark historical study of the colonial family's contribution to establishing stable and orderly civil government at the English founding of America. They have two sons, and make their home in Redford, Michigan, a suburb of Detroit.